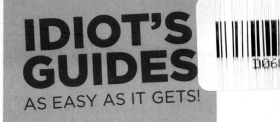

IDIOT'S GUIDES

AS EASY AS IT GETS!

D0689582

The U.S. Constitution

Second Edition

by Timothy Harper

WITHDRAWN

ALPHA

A member of Penguin Random House LLC

Publisher: Mike Sanders
Associate Publisher: Billy Fields
Acquisitions Editor: Jan Lynn
Development Editor: Christy Wagner
Cover Designer: Lindsay Dobbs
Book Designer: William Thomas
Compositor: Ayanna Lacey
Proofreader: Lisa Starnes
Indexer: Tonya Heard

*For my parents, Bud and Eleanor Harper, who taught me the rules
and how to challenge them.*

Second American Edition, 2016
Published in the United States by DK Publishing
6081 E. 82nd Street, Indianapolis, Indiana 46250

Copyright © 2016 Dorling Kindersley Limited
A Penguin Random House Company
16 17 18 19   10 9 8 7 6 5 4 3 2 1
002-295787-SEPTEMBER2016

ISBN: 9781465454362
Library of Congress Catalog Card Number: 2016930606

Note: This publication contains the opinions and ideas of its author(s). It is intended to provide helpful and informative material on the subject matter covered. It is sold with the understanding that the author(s) and publisher are not engaged in rendering professional services in the book. If the reader requires personal assistance or advice, a competent professional should be consulted. The author(s) and publisher specifically disclaim any responsibility for any liability, loss, or risk, personal or otherwise, which is incurred as a consequence, directly or indirectly, of the use and application of any of the contents of this book.

Trademarks: All terms mentioned in this book that are known to be or are suspected of being trademarks or service marks have been appropriately capitalized. Alpha Books, DK, and Penguin Random House LLC cannot attest to the accuracy of this information. Use of a term in this book should not be regarded as affecting the validity of any trademark or service mark.

DK books are available at special discounts when purchased in bulk for sales promotions, premiums, fund-raising, or educational use. For details, contact: DK Publishing Special Markets, 345 Hudson Street, New York, New York 10014 or SpecialSales@dk.com.

Printed and bound in the United States of America

idiotsguides.com

Contents

Appendixes

Introduction

It's fair to say there would not be a United States of America without the U.S. Constitution—the written foundation for the principles upon which the nation was founded and continues to operate. The Constitution is an agreement among the states—originally 13, now 50—to variously support and, when necessary, submit to a federal government that represents the union of the states as a single political entity.

The Constitution is a master document, the paramount or overriding set of laws that lays out the foundation of American democracy and the rule of law. The Constitution does not grant us rights, but rather gives our government the power to protect those rights that are natural to all citizens.

The Constitution establishes the three branches of the national government and the system of checks and balances that keeps any one branch from dominating. The Constitution also creates the framework for electing federal officials and limits their power. Finally, the Constitution lists individual rights that are the heart of our democracy.

The Constitution is a remarkable document, in some ways remarkably complicated and in some ways deceptively simple. It is the supreme law of the land, but it is not carved in stone. It is flexible and can be changed. Even if the actual words of the Constitution are not amended, court interpretations of what they mean can dramatically change the way we live, work, and play. The Constitution was forged from high principles—and hypocrisy. The authors were men dedicated to high-minded ideals for all people—and their own selfish interests. The Constitution uses seemingly straightforward language, yet many of the most basic passages are endlessly debated, interpreted, and reinterpreted. Neighbors can read the same passages of the Constitution and come to complete opposite conclusions.

The Constitution is something most Americans know a little about, but not as much as they think. This book presents an opportunity to learn more about the Constitution—how to approach it, how to begin understanding it, and how to think about it for yourself and form your own opinions. Yes, opinions about the Constitution do matter, whether the opinion is that of a Supreme Court justice, a political activist, or a tenth-grader being marched through American history.

This book begins at the beginning, with the American Revolutionary War and the founding of a new nation in a new way. It also offers the opportunity to browse, or dip in and out of particular aspects of the Constitution, from the founding fathers to the hotly controversial issues dividing us today.

Many Americans believe the Constitution has never been more important for the future of the country—no matter what kind of future they would like to see. Given the significance of the Constitution on today's political landscape, it makes sense that we are in the midst of a national discussion about the rule of law and constitutional rights as they relate to the future of America's national culture and character. The goal of this book is to present history and today's perspective in an even-handed, fact-based manner that both informs you and helps you do your own analysis of the day's headlines. Rather than the classic case-and-argument style of law books, this guide is written in a colloquial, conversational style aimed at being accessible for a broad range of readers. Lawyers will use it as a refresher on some of the finer points of the law of the land, and eighth-grade students will use it to figure out how to write term papers on the Constitution. The emphasis in this book is on telling stories—the stories of what happened and of the people who were involved.

This guide is informative, thoughtful, and thought-provoking. It does not aspire to be comprehensive, and it is by no means the last word in understanding or appreciating the Constitution. Rather, it is more of an overview and an introduction, providing the basics of what you need to know to be an informed citizen who understands the principles that underpin our legal system and our society. There is much more to be learned, and considered, about any and every aspect of the Constitution put forth here. If this is your first step in learning about the Constitution, I hope you have a long and rich journey.

How This Book Is Organized

This book is divided into four parts:

In **Part 1, Constitutional Basics,** we begin with a breezy history lesson that looks at both the development of our American legal principles, mostly from English common law, and the development of our American society, beginning in the colonies. The first chapter takes us through the American Revolution—the colonists regarded themselves as freedom fighters and patriots, while the British rulers regarded them as rebels—and the Declaration of Independence into the first tentative steps of a new nation. We review the foundations of the Constitution—the people give the government rights, not the other way around—and the historic convention that produced this remarkable set of ideas in Philadelphia during the sultry summer of 1789.

In **Part 2, Balancing the Branches,** we examine Articles I, II, and III of the Constitution, which laid out the framework for history's boldest experiment in democracy. We explore the reasons behind the separation of powers between three equal branches of government—executive, legislative, judicial—and the elaborate system of checks and balances the framers of the Constitution designed to keep any one branch of government from assuming too much power.

The remaining parts of the original Constitution, Articles IV, V, VI, and VII, look at the blue-print for how the new federal system is supposed to work, including the relationship between the individual states and the national government. This section also considers the wisdom of the framers of the Constitution who, in recognizing that a society must move forward and change and adapt to succeed, prescribed a way to amend the Constitution.

Part 3, Your Basic Rights, is devoted to the Bill of Rights—the first 10 amendments to the Constitution, the amendments that define so many of the individual rights that have become so important to Americans and are synonymous with the American ideal. We examine all 10 amendments in the Bill of Rights but focus primarily on the most significant, including the First Amendment, the so-called "great" amendment guaranteeing freedom of speech, religion, and the press; the Second Amendment and its controversial "right to bear arms" wording; the Fourth Amendment, which protects us against unlawful searches and seizures by authorities; the Fifth Amendment, which gives us the right against self-incrimination and Miranda warnings; the Sixth, Seventh, and Eighth amendments, which guarantee fair trials and punishment; and the Ninth Amendment's personal privacy protections.

Moving on, the book discusses each of the subsequent amendments individually but concentrates more on those that had a major impact on society or that continue to have implications for today, including the amendments that ended slavery and granted civil rights, at least in theory, to African Americans. We examine the far-reaching U.S. Supreme Court interpretations and applications of the Fourteenth Amendment and its Equal Protection Clause. There are some good stories—and some grumbling that continues today—behind the Sixteenth Amendment, which led to the national income tax, and the Seventeenth Amendment, which let Americans vote directly for their senators for the first time.

The early twentieth century was a time of striking change in America as we became the world's dominant nation, but it is unlikely that the framers of the Constitution ever saw their amendment process being used to outlaw alcohol or give women the vote—the results of the Eighteenth and Nineteenth Amendments.

In **Part 4, Modifying the Government,** we look at how Prohibition backfired and led to repeal in the Twenty-First Amendment and at the women's suffrage movement. Besides the other amendments passed in the last century, including one to limit presidents to two terms and another that gave the vote to 18-year-olds, we review some of the amendments that came close to ratification but failed, notably the Equal Rights Amendment.

The text closes with some thoughts on the future of the Constitution, including shifts in the balance of power among the three branches of government, and some speculation about future proposed amendments. Specifically, we'll look at possible attempts to amend the Constitution, and the constitutional questions raised by the February 2016 death of Justice Antonin Scalia and the vow by Republican senators not to consider confirmation of a successor until the winner of the 2016 presidential election is sworn into office in 2017.

Finally, in the back of the book, a glossary defines many of the terms commonly used in discussions of constitutional law, a list of references offers ideas for further reading, a third appendix explains how you can petition the government, and the end of the book is home to the full text of the Constitution.

Extras

As you go through the book, you'll notice a number of sidebars, small asides aimed at adding to your knowledge and illustrating the main points. There are four types of sidebars:

 **CASES**

Summaries of landmark cases that have changed the course of American history are detailed here.

 **DEFINITION**

In these sidebars, definitions of common legal terms and concepts are presented.

 WE THE PEOPLE

Brief profiles of those who played pivotal roles in constitutional cases, along with pithy quotes from many of those people, are shared in these sidebars.

WHAT IT MEANS TO YOU

These sidebars hold pointed commentary explaining the main points of constitutional law in simple terms.

Acknowledgments

My professors at the University of Wisconsin Law School, especially noted Supreme Court and constitutional scholar Mark Tushnet, now at Harvard Law School, deserve appreciation for putting up with a journalist who came back to law school not to become a lawyer but to become a better journalist. Law school would not have been as productive, nor nearly as much fun, without the support and friendship of too many classmates to mention here, but especially Ed Manydeeds, Jeff Mohr, Jim Grau, and Alan Olson—good lawyers and good guys.

Special thanks for considerable help, both in the original edition of this book and again now in the second edition, goes to Jim Tosone, the noted amateur constitutional scholar who offered many cogent insights on a number of key points. As a corporate consultant who often relies on his improvisational comedy background in career and management training seminars, Jim can always point out the irony and humor in the Constitution and its development over the years. Jim's background briefings were helpful on a number of issues and were especially useful in analyzing recent Second Amendment cases. His draft language on gun rights in America in effect became Chapter 7.

William Mathis, an outstanding young journalist, provided important research assistance. Anybody who can employ Will, short-term or long-term, as a researcher or reporter, will be pleased with the results.

Thanks to my agent, Bob Diforio, for bringing this project to me, and to the staff at Alpha Books who oversaw the editorial, design, and production process, especially Jan Lynn. Christy Wagner, who edited the book, did a great job in making it a smoother read.

Also, thanks to my colleagues at the CUNY Graduate School of Journalism, particularly Dean Sarah Bartlett and Associate Dean Andrew Mendelson, for encouraging this visiting professor and other faculty and staff to use our skills and experience for professional projects in the public interest.

Finally, my love and appreciation to my family, including my late parents, Maynard "Bud" Harper and Eleanor Eberle Harper, who taught me the rules, and when and how to break them, and especially my wife, Nancy Bobrowitz, and our now-adult kids, Lizzie and Jon. Together, we've learned a lot over the years about the value of rights, responsibilities, and flexibility— whether in a national constitution or in a family.

Constitutional Basics

Part 1's chapters look back at the historical and theoretical underpinnings of the Constitution, including the development of political thought on the way government can and should work.

We also meet some of the men, often called the founding fathers, who led the American Revolution in seeking liberty for the 13 colonies from England and King George III. In addition, we follow the framers, the men who went on to create the Constitution and change the world with a new form of government. We also explore how and why they created the Constitution, their mission and motives, and the many obstacles they had to overcome through compromise.

CHAPTER 1

The Founding Fathers and a New Form of Government

The creation of the U.S. Constitution is a remarkable story, and it's a remarkable tribute, not only to the intellect but also to the determination of the founding fathers and the citizens they represented, who wanted a new way of living and a new form of government.

The early Americans' first attempt at a shared government following the Revolutionary War was the Articles of Confederation, a loose confederation. It was designed to avoid the sort of powerful central government, with its oppression and disdain for individual rights, that sparked the American Revolution and, ultimately, independence and the opportunity to create a new nation.

In This Chapter

- The American Revolution
- The Declaration of Independence
- The founding fathers
- The Articles of Confederation

The American Revolution

Like many colonies throughout history, the Americans of the first half of the 1700s had a love-hate relationship with their mother country. They were proud to be British, but they resented the way their distant rulers seemed to take advantage of them.

The British, meanwhile, were at the height of their imperial power and haughtiness. Great Britain prized its American colonies for their vast natural resources and for the way the developing American middle class of shopkeepers and farmers was becoming an important market for trade. But to the British, Americans weren't even second-class citizens because they weren't citizens. Besides, India was the real jewel in the crown of the empire.

Taxation Without Representation

The British had handed a number of laws across the Atlantic that weren't well received in America, largely because many Americans saw numerous crown-imposed laws as economically unfair.

For example, the British put strict limits on the colonial iron industry in order to protect sales of British iron products in America. If Americans were allowed to operate their own forges and produce their own iron tools, they wouldn't buy them from Britain—and pay import taxes to the British, too. Similar laws restricted American production; forced Americans to buy only from Britain; and imposed high taxes on everyday items such as newspapers, playing cards, textiles, wine, beer, coffee, and tea.

> **WE THE PEOPLE**
>
> Wealthy Boston merchant and patriot John Hancock, best known today for that big signature on the Declaration of Independence, was a committed smuggler who defied British tax laws. When he finally got caught, his sloop *Liberty* and all its cargo were seized, and a judge—the British wouldn't allow a jury to hear the case—fined him £9,000, three times the value of the cargo.

Resentment toward British rule began to peak after 1760, when King George III assumed the throne. Parliament began taxing the colonies directly to help pay for "Mad" King George's wars against France and Spain and for the British troops he sent to America to keep order against an increasingly rebellious colonial population. What's more, new "quartering" laws required colonists to open their homes and kitchens to shelter and feed British troops.

The Americans organized boycotts, became enthusiastic smugglers, gave rousing speeches, and printed treasonous anti-British pamphlets. Some called themselves patriots, organized into rebel groups such as the Sons of Liberty, and launched violent attacks on the crown's property and agents. In today's language, we would call them freedom fighters; the British would call them terrorists.

As the British imposed more taxes, the colonists protested more. The British sent more troops to America to maintain order and then imposed more taxes to pay for the additional troops. New taxes on paper, glass, paint, and tea fueled more protests, and American juries began finding accused smugglers innocent even when they were caught red-handed. Then the British stopped allowing jury trials. In 1773, a group of patriots clownishly dressed like Mohawk Indians boarded three ships in Boston Harbor and threw the cargo of tea overboard rather than submit to new rules that said only agents of the crown could sell tea.

As Parliament moved to take away the colonies' limited self-rule authority, the first Continental Congress convened in Philadelphia. The representatives of 12 colonies (Georgia did not attend) declared their opposition to rule by Parliament and vowed to go home and promote the forming of local militia. In 1775, the first shots were fired at Lexington and Concord, Massachusetts, and the colonial Minutemen (so named because they could grab their flintlock rifles and be out the door in a minute) sent the British Redcoats (so named for their crimson uniforms) fleeing back to Boston.

As full-fledged war broke out, George Washington, who had been one of the leaders of the British-Colonial military forces that defeated the French in the French and Indian War a few years earlier, assumed command of the Continental Army.

The Declaration of Independence

In June 1776, the Continental Congress appointed a Committee of Five to draft a statement that would explain to the British, and the rest of the world, why the Americans wanted and deserved independence. The other four members of the committee asked Thomas Jefferson to take it on and get back to them. Jefferson penned a draft in a mere 17 days. He showed what he had to two other members of the committee, Benjamin Franklin and John Adams, who made a few suggestions. The full Committee of Five made a few more, and the document went before the Continental Congress on July 2. The Congress tinkered and debated that day, all the next, and into the late morning of the following day.

When the people of Philadelphia heard all the city's church bells pealing at once on July 4, they were exhilarated and terrified. Independence had been declared. It was war.

The Continental Congress signed the Declaration of Independence, which, for all practical purposes, changed little from Jefferson's original draft. It opened like this:

> "When in the Course of human events, it becomes necessary for one people to dissolve the political bands which have connected them with another, and to assume among the powers of the earth, the separate and equal station to which the Laws of Nature and of Nature's God entitle them, a decent respect to the opinions of mankind requires that they should declare the causes which impel them to the separation."

And then came the second paragraph, the words we all remember for their simple power:

> "We hold these truths to be self-evident, that all men are created equal, that they are endowed by their Creator with certain unalienable Rights, that among these are Life, Liberty and the pursuit of Happiness."

Simply and directly, the Declaration set out the rights claimed by the colonists—rights anybody who read them would agree were natural rights that should be afforded all people.

The foundation of the Declaration of Independence, and subsequently the Constitution, was straightforward and powerful: individual rights are inalienable, natural, and cannot be granted or taken away by governments.

The Declaration went on to cite a list of wrongs by the British crown—violations of those rights. As soon as the 56 signatures on the declaration were dry—maybe before they were dry—runners carried the document to printers for copies to be made and sent to the other colonies and to the commanders of the Continental Army. Within 5 days, all 13 colonies had approved the Declaration of Independence.

 WE THE PEOPLE

"In America the law is king. For as in absolute governments the king is law, so in free countries, the law ought to be king ...."

—Thomas Paine, "Common Sense"

The Revolutionary War was long and difficult, marked by numerous defeats, retreats, mass desertions, and a handful of mutinies for the Continental Army. The odds were against the Americans, but their cause was helped immeasurably by the shrewd generalship of Washington. In addition, the British were fighting far from home, while the Americans were literally defending their homes.

Most historians mark the end of the actual fighting with Lord Charles Cornwallis's ignominious surrender at Yorktown, Virginia, in 1781. The following year, the British Parliament voted to cease hostilities with America and urged King George III to negotiate for peace. The British troops began returning from the former colonies, and the Treaty of Paris, in which Britain recognized the United States of America, was signed in 1783.

The Founding Fathers

The men who attended what eventually became known as the Constitutional Convention of 1787 are commonly regarded as founding fathers of the United States of America. Others we consider founding fathers include the men who signed the Declaration of Independence 11 years earlier and those who played major roles in the Revolutionary War and the eventual political, economic, and cultural separation from England—the soldiers, politicians, statesmen, merchants, bankers, teachers, farmers, artisans, physicians, and others.

The seven men generally acknowledged as the key founding fathers were John Adams, Benjamin Franklin, Alexander Hamilton, John Jay, Thomas Jefferson, James Madison, and the undisputed leader of the founders, George Washington, sometimes called "the Father of His Country." The framers of the Constitution were all men, all white, mostly Protestant, all well educated, and all well-to-do. (Although few of them, including Washington, were downright rich.) Most were born in the 13 colonies.

Only six men, including Franklin, signed both the Declaration of Independence and the draft Constitution. Two signed those documents plus the Articles of Confederation. Only one man, Roger Sherman of Connecticut, signed all four key documents in the founding era: the charter for the Continental Association, the Declaration of Independence, the Articles of Confederation, and the Constitution.

Influential Women

In recent years, amid criticism that the term *founding fathers* diminishes the role of many women of the era, historians have pointed out how a number of women played influential but relatively quiet roles, from the first daring days of rebellion, through the bitter and bloody war, and into the early years of a weak and infant nation that had big dreams but little else. Many women provided ideas; inspiration; material support; behind-the-scenes services in kitchens and hospitals; and sometimes, the moral support to keep fighting, whether against the British or for a new democratic republic or both.

Some of those women included Abigail Adams, Dolley Madison, Elizabeth Schuyler Hamilton, and Deborah Read Franklin, all wives of founding fathers who supported the rise of the new national intellectually or materially or both; Mercy Otis Warren, an influential essayist whose writings promoted independence; Deborah Sampson, who dressed like a man to enlist and fight the Redcoats; Phillis Wheatley, a slave whose widely published poetry argued passionately for independence; Molly Pitcher, who may or may not have been a real person but represents the many women volunteers who provided food, water, clothing, and medical care to Continental soldiers; and Betsy Ross, a patriotic entrepreneur who ran an upholstery business and is credited with sewing the first American flag for George Washington (which is probably more legend than fact).

WE THE PEOPLE

"The great aim of the struggle for liberty has been equality before the law."

–Constitutional scholar Friedrich A. Hayek

A New Framework

The American founders began thinking about a framework for their government even before the Declaration of Independence. And the Continental Congress, which was formed in 1775 as war was breaking out, began working on a framework for a new government only days after the Declaration of Independence was signed. Throughout the Revolutionary War, even when things looked darkest for the American insurgents, various influential patriots continued to think and talk about what a new United States of America might look like and how it might function.

The outcome of the war was in doubt for years. Victory and independence did not appear to be a sure thing until several years into the war, when it became clear that England—the king, Parliament, the English economy, the English military, and the English people—were being worn down by the costs, in both blood and treasure, of this faraway war.

As the war wound down, the questions in the Continental Congress became more urgent. How would the relationships among the 13 former colonies change? Would independence mean 13 new sovereign nations? Or one nation with 13 states? Would there be a king? As it became clear that the patriots were going to win the war, the theoretical "what if" discussions became more real … and more heated.

Many Americans hated the idea of a king and regarded George III as a tyrant. But more than a few believed the new country needed a king, largely because they knew of no secure, successful nation that did not have a king or queen in charge. How else would a government work? All the major nations of Europe had a monarchy.

"Taxation without representation" had been a battle cry for the Revolution, and many Americans hated the idea of any government imposing taxes on them. But without taxes, how would America expand, or provide infrastructure and services to improve the quality of life for its citizens?

The Articles of Confederation

In 1777, the Second Continental Congress approved the Articles of Confederation, a pre-Constitution agreement that was more like an alliance among 13 sovereign nations than a charter for a new nation. The Articles were not fully ratified by the states until March 1, 1781, several months before the British surrendered on October 19, 1781. The Treaty of Paris in 1783 formalized independence with England and gave the United States formal recognition with the other major nations of Europe.

The Articles of Confederation created the Confederation Congress. Each state could send between two and seven delegates to Congress, but no matter how many delegates, each state had just one single vote.

The Articles of Confederation were never meant to be a constitution overseeing a single nation. The 13 states weren't ready for that. The Articles defined the new political entity as the "United States of America" but specifically said each state retained its "sovereignty, freedom, and independence."

Instead, the Articles created "a firm league of friendship" that was in effect a treaty among 13 states, concerned primarily with mutual defense and foreign affairs. In many ways, the United States under the Articles of Confederation in the 1780s was more like the European Union of the twenty-first century than the United States of today.

The Articles of Confederation were in effect from 1781 until 1789, and some good things happened during those years. Congress set a standard system of weights and measures. The first bank was chartered, and the forerunner to the U.S. Mint was created. Trade with China was opened.

After the Continental Army was disbanded (the patriots were distrustful of standing armies, including their own), the Articles of Confederation required every state to maintain its own militia, although the militias were banned from waging foreign wars. The Confederation

Congress soon laid the foundation of the modern U.S. Army by establishing a standing force of several hundred men to guard West Point and a handful of outposts on the western frontier.

One very big question was the future of the huge mass of land that made up the rest of North America. Some states wanted to be able to establish colonies of their own in what is now the Midwest, South, and West. Instead, the Confederation Congress passed the Land Ordinance of 1785 and the Northwest Ordinance of 1787, establishing the procedures for Western Territories to become states equal in every way to the original 13 states. (An interesting historical wrinkle: Article XI made provisions for Canada to be accepted as a state if Canada was interested.)

> **WE THE PEOPLE**
>
> "Yes, we did produce a near-perfect republic. But will they keep it? Or will they, in the employment of plenty, lose the memory of freedom? Material abundance without character is the path of destruction."
>
> —Thomas Jefferson

Insufficient Powers

Despite the positive steps, the Articles of Confederation proved insufficient in a number of ways. One of the biggest problems was that Congress had little power to settle disagreements between states. This was especially important in commerce; states were imposing taxes and tariffs on each other and trying to limit other states' use of rivers that created shared boundaries. One state would see its taxes and tariffs as economic protection; other states would see those taxes and tariffs as economic interference. Whatever the rationale, such disputes hindered economic growth.

Congress also had little power to levy taxes on the states. Congressional leaders often pleaded with state officials to provide money to expand the military, especially to counter Indian attacks or keep pirates from plundering American merchant ships. Under this largely voluntary tax system, the states often ignored Congress's requests for contributions or offered only token sums.

Even when raising money for the central government was not an issue, it was difficult to get things done. Major Confederation rules and policies had to be approved by 9 of the 13 states, and it took a unanimous vote—all 13 states—to amend the Articles of Confederation. That meant every state had a veto.

The ineffective government contributed to widespread fear and uncertainty, along with an economic downturn. Citizens complained that the taxes imposed by the states were too high. Many people were hurt by the difficulty of getting credit and the shortage of currency following the collapse of the Continental dollar. Farmers were especially hard hit. Agriculture dominated the American economy at that time; the typical farm family included eight children; crop prices were depressed. Farmers claimed they were victims of policies that led to inequality as their income dropped and they were unable to repay their debts on time. They clamored for debt relief, for easier credit, and for a better system of paper money. The difficult economy, in the face of lagging debt repayments, led many creditors to go to court seeking foreclosures on homes and farms and forcing bankruptcies on the people who owed them money.

Historians see Shays' Rebellion as a pivotal point. In 1786 and 1787, a Revolutionary War veteran named Daniel Shays led or inspired a series of raids, including the attempted shutdown of courts, mostly in Massachusetts, where tax and debt cases were being heard. A number of people were injured or killed in skirmishes between protestors and private militia funded by merchants, and the rebellion was eventually cut down after an attempt to take over the federal arsenal in Springfield, Massachusetts. But Shays and his followers showed the need for broader cooperation and uniform rules across the states—both in economic policy and in military readiness.

George Washington had all but removed himself from public life in the first years after the war, but he emerged from retirement to bemoan the Shays' Rebellion and the conditions that caused it. He noted that undisciplined internal insurrections such as Shays' Rebellion were exactly what critics in England and elsewhere in Europe had predicted for the United States without the firm hand of an established monarchy.

WE THE PEOPLE

George Washington himself called the new nation, and its new form of government, "an experiment": "The preservation of the sacred fire of liberty, and the destiny of the republican model of government, are justly considered deeply, and perhaps as finally, staked on the experiment entrusted to the hands of the American people."

Washington and other influential figures, notably James Madison of Virginia and Alexander Hamilton of New York, who were both able politicians and respected public intellectuals, joined in widespread agreement: changes were needed to the Articles of Confederation. The weak central government was holding back the new nation, which needed broader regulations to build a smoothly operating economy across all 13 states.

The Federalists

In 1786, Madison and Hamilton participated in a meeting in Maryland for representatives of five northeastern states. Called the Annapolis Convention, the gathering's original goal was to try to find a way for states to lower some of their economic barriers for each other. The delegates, led by Madison and Hamilton, came away from Annapolis intent on revising the Articles of Confederation—or scrapping the Articles completely and coming up with an entirely new constitution.

Madison and Hamilton were the political liberals of their day—in the sense that liberals wanted more change than conservatives, who were happier with the status quo or less change. These Federalists, as they were called, wanted a unified nation, a democratic republic of states rather than a looser alliance of sovereign states. Madison believed a pure democracy, ruled by the direct votes of the people, would work in a small geographic area with a relatively small, homogenous population. A republic of separate states under a strong central government, Madison thought, was much better suited to a sprawling, growing nation with a diverse population. The Federalists foresaw a single nation that allowed the states to retain many powers while following the rules and laws laid down by the national government.

But not everyone wanted a new constitution or a stronger central government. Many members of the Confederation Congress agreed that change was needed, but not too much. Madison, Hamilton, and other Federalists were seen as big-city people, concerned primarily with business, commerce, and trade. The larger states—Virginia was largest with about 400,000 residents, followed closely by Pennsylvania and Massachusetts—typically had more sentiment for a strong central government (although that could not be said for New York's small delegation to the Constitutional Convention). The smaller states typically had more anti-Federalist sentiment. They were more likely to be concerned with the welfare of plantation owners and farmers and issues such as credit and a viable paper currency.

Lurking underneath the immediate political concerns was a larger and more ultimately wrenching economic and moral issue—slavery.

In February 1787, the Confederation Congress agreed that a convention would be held in Philadelphia, starting in May, "for the sole and express purpose of revising the Articles of Confederation."

The Least You Need to Know

- The founding fathers were determined to create a government based on individual liberty, free of the tyranny they experienced under English rule.
- The Articles of Confederation created more of an alliance among the states than an actual new nation.

- The Articles proved inadequate; states quickly fell into conflict with each other, and the weak central government was ineffective.

- A convention, ostensibly to improve the Articles of Confederation not create a new Constitution, was called for Philadelphia in 1787.

The Birth of the Constitution

The convention in Philadelphia contemplated not only a totally new document, but also a totally new form of government. The delegates, mostly well educated and prosperous, were well versed in political thought and theory, and they knew their history.

From the beginning of the convention, the men were confronted with deal-breaker issues. But through sheer determination, they came up with acceptable compromises, although often grudgingly and rarely unanimously.

In This Chapter

- The Constitutional Convention of 1787
- Historical and theoretical influences
- Controversy and compromise
- The Preamble

The Constitutional Convention

It was already warm in Philadelphia in May 1787, and it promised to be a long, hot summer—not the best circumstances for bringing together several dozen strong-minded men, each with his own priorities and problems, in an often-sweltering debating hall. Their task was to try to save their new nation. The former colonies had won the War of Independence, the American Revolution, and they had won their freedom from England and the rule of King George III.

But after winning the war, America was losing the peace. The new United States of America was being held together—barely—by the Articles of Confederation. If the Articles had worked, we probably would not have our present Constitution—or our present form of government. But in 1787, the Articles weren't working.

Philadelphia, 1787

As the delegates gathered for the Constitutional Convention, Philadelphia, the City of Brotherly Love, was the largest city in America, with a population of about 40,000. (New York was second, at about 30,000, and Boston third, at about 18,000.) The convention was set to begin on May 14 at the Pennsylvania State House, where the Declaration of Independence had been signed. The building, now Independence Hall, the centerpiece of Independence National Historical Park, had been the seat of the revolutionary American government, home at times to the Second Continental Congress and then the Confederation Congress.

James Madison, from Orange County, Virginia, was one of the first to arrive. But the convention did not actually begin until 11 days later, on May 25, when enough delegates had arrived to declare a quorum. As frequently happened, the bad roads, deeply rutted and in places washed out, made for slow travel on horseback or via horse-drawn coaches.

A number of prominent founding fathers did not attend. John Adams was serving as the American minister to England, and Thomas Jefferson was the minister to France, but both were known supporters of a stronger central government. Among the founding fathers who did not attend because they opposed changes to the Articles of Confederation was Patrick "Give me liberty or give men death" Henry, who stayed home in Virginia, where he was a frequent critic of the convention in general and Madison in particular.

Twelve states sent delegations. Rhode Island, the smallest state but one of the most aggressive at trying to tax other states, did not send a delegation out of fear that its tariffs would be outlawed by the other states. Pennsylvania had the largest delegation, with eight men. New York and Connecticut sent only three delegates each, and New Hampshire's two delegates did not arrive until late July.

The Delegates

Of the 74 delegates who had been designated to attend, only 55 ever appeared at the convention through the summer. Some delegates, such as Madison, attended regularly; others rarely attended. Of the 55, 29 had fought in the Revolutionary War. Most had served in the Continental Congress, the Confederation Congress, or state and local government.

Benjamin Franklin, the oldest delegate at age 81, attended convention sessions infrequently, sometimes being carried by men in a sedan chair from his home. His contributions during floor debates were infrequent, and his remarks were sometimes read by a younger delegate with a heartier voice. But Franklin was a revered figure, and his opinions and observations were still highly regarded. He played a considerable role behind the scenes, in the many conversations among delegates informally in the evenings, often over dinner.

> **WE THE PEOPLE**
>
> Benjamin Franklin was an octogenarian, frail in body but not mind, in 1787. But his written notes and comments were influential. He swayed other delegates before the final vote by saying the Constitution wasn't perfect, but it was good enough. One of his regrets in life is that he felt in serving the cause of independence and nation-building, he neglected his wife, Deborah Read Franklin. She was reported to have agreed.

The delegates were acutely aware of the issues that led to the War of Independence, and particularly the dangers of a strong executive in the form of a monarchy. As they gathered in Philadelphia, they were resolved to live by the *rule of law,* not the rule of a king, although Washington was held in such high regard there was talk of making him king.

> **DEFINITION**
>
> The **rule of law** is the principle that everyone in society, including top officials, are equally subject to the law.

More than half the delegates in Philadelphia were lawyers. Others were bankers, farmers, physicians, shippers, land speculators, and manufacturers. Many of the delegates were familiar with the process of creating a constitution because they had been involved in drafting and debating their state constitutions.

The delegates also were well versed in political and legal theory, including "natural" law holding that people are born with natural rights such as life, liberty, and the pursuit of happiness, as expressed in the Declaration of Independence. (The idea was that instead of the government granting rights to the people, the people were born with inalienable rights, and the people granted the government the right to govern them.) With their vast knowledge, the delegates could discuss the advantages and disadvantages of various types of models of government, going back to early Greece and the Roman Empire.

Political Thought and Government Theory

America's grand experiment in democracy is based on a relatively new and radical idea: a government by and for all citizens. Various forms of participatory and representative government have been tried throughout history; however, until the United States was formed, democracy was a largely failed theory.

We have made it work, more or less, thanks to our Constitution, the document upon which we base our rule of law. It's important for us to remember, though, that the words of the Constitution—what it says—are not as significant as the fact that we, as a society, have agreed to live by the spirit of the rules laid down in the Constitution.

Society's Agreement

Ever since our ancestors began to gather in tribes and villages, humankind has been looking for the best way to live together and create civilization. Chieftains and kings handed down laws and enforced them, often according to their own whims. But even when the leader was kind and just, people wanted to know the rules. And they wanted assurances that the rules would be applied fairly and equally for everyone. In other words, they wanted the rule of law—a government of laws rather than men.

A constitution, whether for a powerful nation or for a local garden club, is a set of charter rules, a supreme or paramount law that outlines how the organization will operate. In terms of a nation, the constitution sets forth political principles, establishes power and authority, and defines rights and responsibilities. The constitution outlines the general principles for what a government can and cannot do. Specific laws enacted by the government, also called statutory law, spell out the details. For example, the U.S. Constitution gives the government the authority to collect taxes but leaves it to the government to decide who and what will be taxed and how much.

WE THE PEOPLE

"The rule of law is a solution to a problem, and as the classical liberal tradition has always recognized, the problem is tyranny."

—Political scientist Noel B. Reynolds

The U.S. Constitution establishes a federal system of state governments that operate with a certain amount of self-rule under a single national government. There is a constant balancing of interests to preserve the rule of law and prohibit any person or group of people from dominating the government. There are balances among the three branches of government, between the states and the federal government, and among individual states.

Not all constitutions are codified. Israel, New Zealand, and the United Kingdom have constitutional governments, but instead of a single written document, their constitutional laws derive from a number of different documents and unwritten principles that are sometimes called *common law*.

DEFINITION

Common law is the body of law, largely unwritten, that evolved in England through prevailing customs, widely accepted principles, and decisions by courts rather than through administrative rule or legislative action.

Written or not, it's important to remember that a constitution is so much more than its actual words. The former Soviet Union had a beautifully written constitution, full of the same sort of high-minded language the U.S. Constitution uses to guarantee liberty. But the Soviet constitution was little more than lip service; instead of the rule of law, the Soviet Union was ruled by a single political party that imposed what many Soviet citizens thought was a particularly harsh brand of communism.

Back to the Magna Carta

The earliest written laws date to ancient Babylon (now Iraq) and King Hammurabi, who had his Hammurabi Code carved into stone and put on public display in the eighteenth century B.C.E.

In the seventh century B.C.E., Draco became the first law scribe in ancient Greece, although the laws he codified were extraordinarily harsh by today's standards and often carried the death penalty for even minor crimes (hence the modern word *draconian*). Another Greek lawgiver, Solon, put forth the idea that laws should be equal for rich and poor. Whether or not people lived in a democracy, he believed they should be able to rely on the rules being applied fairly and equally to everyone. Aristotle advanced the notion of a constitutional form of government based on a set of master laws. In Rome, Cicero promoted the idea that rather than taking away individual freedom, laws *promote* freedom when everyone agrees to live by the rules.

The Germanic tribes who dominated Europe in the Dark and Middle Ages had various sets of laws, sometimes written and sometimes not, but the precedents for our Constitution were not confined to Europe. Japan had an early constitution based on Buddhist lessons on morality. Mohammed drafted the Constitution of Medina. And the Iroquois nation had a constitution that was said to inspire the early American settlers.

For the American colonists, however, perhaps the most important legal document in history was the Magna Carta, signed reluctantly by King John of England in 1215. The king was waging foreign wars against Muslims, and members of the nobility were upset at the cost in taxes and men. England's barons objected to the way the king used his authority, and they threatened him with rebellion unless he signed.

It's worth remembering that the Magna Carta actually did little or nothing for common citizens; it was strictly for the benefit of the feudal lords who supported the king. But for the first time, the king was *subject* to the law instead of *making* the law, and the Magna Carta became the foundation for our rule of law. The Magna Carta put some limits on the king's ability to levy taxes, but its most important provision was the right of habeas corpus, which said that the king could not imprison or execute anyone without *due process*. Article 39 of the Magna Carta said, "No free man shall be arrested, or imprisoned, or deprived of his property, or outlawed, or exiled, or in any way destroyed, nor shall we go against him or send against him, unless by legal judgment of his peers, or by the law of the land."

DEFINITION

> **Due process** is the catch-all term for procedures that guarantee a person's legal rights are all recognized and considered properly and fairly under the law.

The Magna Carta was short-lived (so was King John), but the principles became a cornerstone over the following centuries into the so-called Age of Enlightenment. English common law increasingly recognized the rights of individuals, particularly when kings abused their power by granting economic favors to their friends, such as monopolies over certain aspects of trade and industry. Public dissatisfaction with both crown and cronies, particularly in the way the courts came to be controlled by politicians, helped inspire the English Civil War (also called the Glorious Revolution) in 1688.

While the American colonists were carving out their own brand of rugged individualism on the other side of the Atlantic, thinkers such as John Locke helped England embrace the idea of more individual rights and less government authoritarianism. Locke stressed that a government's role was to protect the property of its citizens. Locke and others also stressed that certain rights are natural to humankind and cannot be given or taken away by kings or governments. Those ideas were embraced on our side of the Atlantic.

 WE THE PEOPLE

"The end of the law is, not to abolish or restrain, but to preserve and enlarge freedom. For in all the states of created beings capable of laws, where there is no law there is no freedom."

—John Locke

The delegates to the Constitutional Convention of 1787 knew it was important to remember that a constitution, whether written or not, is so much more than its actual words. Their goal was a constitution based on what can be described as a free-market premise: society should be a marketplace of ideas, and people should be able to use their knowledge and their energy to make better lives for themselves. The rationale is that no government can know what's best for all its citizens; instead, people know what's best for themselves.

At the same time, it is important to recognize that democracy does not necessarily mean individual liberty. Democracy can mean tyranny by the majority if individual rights are not protected. Instead, our form of democracy, as outlined in the Constitution, strives to preserve and protect individual rights: I have the right to do whatever I want as long as it's not prohibited by law and it doesn't violate anyone else's individual rights.

Washington's Return

George Washington was the pivotal figure in the American Revolution, the biggest hero, the Father of His Country. But Washington initially was reluctant to attend the convention in Philadelphia. When the war ended and he resigned his commission as commander in chief of the Continental Army, he looked forward to a quiet life back home at Mount Vernon in Virginia. He had been one of the richest men in America, but he had neglected his estate to pursue the war. He and his wife, Martha, were intent on reviving Mount Vernon and restoring their fortune. (Martha had not wanted her husband to go to the convention. She also later objected to him becoming the first president of the United States and did not attend his inauguration in New York in 1789.)

But Washington, heeding the pleas of other founding fathers, decided he had to go to Philadelphia. He had seen how the colonies nearly lost the Revolutionary War because of the weak central government's difficulty in raising and supporting his army. Also, Shays' Rebellion had alarmed him and made him question whether the states, under the Articles of Confederation, could withstand threats, either from other countries or from within. And as a farmer and businessman, he wanted a fluidly operating continental marketplace. Washington finally agreed to participate. The chances of success, he acknowledged, would be greater if he lent his reputation and gravitas to the proceedings.

When the convention finally opened on May 25, the first action was to elect George Washington as presiding officer. Washington made few substantive contributions over the 4 months of the convention, but he kept proceedings moving in an orderly fashion. And although it might seem ironic today, given the significance of open government and freedom of the press as constitutional issues, the delegates agreed to keep the proceedings secret. It was going to be difficult to reach agreement, the delegates reckoned, and it would be even harder if every proposal were dissected in newspapers and in coffee shops.

Another procedural wrinkle that helped the process was the convention's agreement to meet frequently as a committee of the whole instead of splitting off into separate committees that would report back with findings or recommendations to be debated. As a committee of the whole, all the delegates could participate in any debate on any issue and then vote immediately.

> ### WE THE PEOPLE
>
> Before being persuaded to attend and then lead the Constitutional Convention, George Washington doubted whether a democratic republic, a federation of states, could work. He thought a ruling class, a monarchy, might be the only answer. In a letter to John Jay in March 1787, Washington wrote: "Among men of reflection few will be found I believe, who are not *beginning* to think that our system is better in theory than practice—and that, notwithstanding the boasted virtue of America it is more than probable we shall exhibit the last melancholy proof that Mankind are not competent to their own government without the means of coercion in the Sovereign."

Contentious Issues

Madison knew he and other proponents of a new constitution were facing an uphill battle. The oldest son of a wealthy Virginia plantation family, Madison was one of the younger delegates, still in his thirties. He had a wide-ranging education, both formal and self-directed, heavy on the classics. After graduating in the early 1770s from the College of New Jersey (now Princeton University), he became involved in local Virginia politics and the independence cause, and

Thomas Jefferson soon became a mentor. Madison became a colonel in the Virginia militia, but his frail health kept him out of combat against the British. He served in the Continental Congress both before and after the war, and in the Confederation Congress.

In his first days in Philadelphia, while waiting for a quorum to traverse the rutted roads so the convention could begin, James Madison began drafting a plan for a new constitution. It could have been called the Madison Plan but instead was named the Virginia Plan. Madison consulted primarily with members of the Virginia and Pennsylvania delegations, who also favored a new constitution and a stronger central government.

Madison did not present the Virginia Plan himself, even though he was its chief architect. Only 5-foot-4, not even weighing 100 pounds, Madison was a slight, frail man, and not an imposing or powerful public speaker. Instead, the Virginia Plan was submitted by the more robust Edmund Randolph, the popular governor of Virginia and the leader of the state's delegation.

The Virginia Plan met immediate opposition, especially among delegates who were against a new constitution. When it became clear that the momentum at the convention was moving inexorably toward a new constitution, some delegates all but stopped attending sessions. Two of the three New York delegates packed up and went home, saying they would not have come if they had known the convention was going to do anything more than amend the Articles of Confederation. New York's remaining delegate, Alexander Hamilton, an ardent Madison ally and supporter of a strong central government, stayed in Philadelphia and took an active role in the convention.

A number of significant parts of Madison's Virginia Plan have become common precepts of democratic government the world over, such as the system of checks and balances among three different branches. Historically, England had two branches of government—the legislative branch in the form of a representative Parliament and the executive branch in the form of the monarch and the crown courts. Madison, concerned about limiting the executive branch, called for a separate third branch, the judiciary. The early judicial branch in the United States was relatively weak, however, and did not become a truly meaningful part of the checks and balances until the Supreme Court established itself through bold and popular decisions in the nineteenth century.

The Virginia Plan called for two legislative chambers, with members of each elected by popular vote—a sharp contrast to the unicameral Confederation Congress under the Articles of Confederation. The Virginia Plan called for congressional seats to be allocated to the states according to population, which would mean the larger states would have more votes—again, a sharp contrast to the Articles of Confederation, which gave each state one vote. Under the Articles of Confederation, Rhode Island's single vote counted the same as Virginia's single vote.

Also extremely controversial was the provision in the Virginia Plan for the national government to have the authority to veto state laws.

To counter the Virginia Plan, the smaller states came up with the New Jersey Plan. It would have kept the Articles of Confederation while adding some fine-tuning to facilitate smooth interstate commerce, raise revenues more reliably, and outline diplomatic channels for dealing with other countries. There would still be just one congressional house, and each state would still have just one vote. The real power would continue to lie with the sovereign states rather than a national government.

The convention quickly bogged down, falling into what looked like a fatal impasse. Franklin, the elder statesman, made a rare personal appearance on the convention floor, beseeching his fellow delegates to take a few days off to meet informally outside the hall. Instead of spending that time with friends and allies who shared their views, he urged delegates to seek out opponents and listen to other points of view. Franklin, too frail to stand and deliver a speech, had a fellow Pennsylvania delegate read his words to the convention, including, "We are sent here to consult, not to contend, with each other."

The Great Compromise

We don't know how much good it did for the delegates to converse with fellow delegates with opposing views during Franklin's suggested recess. We do know that Roger Sherman of Connecticut huddled with a committee of one delegate from each state at the convention, and the group came back to the convention with what quickly became known as the Connecticut Compromise and later the Great Compromise.

The compromise called for a new constitution with a bicameral legislature, the House and the Senate. The members of the House would be selected by popular vote, and seats would be apportioned to the states by population. Each state would have two seats in the Senate, no matter how large the state. Instead of a popular vote, the states themselves would choose their senators. It was an acceptable and elegant solution at the time, although in later years, the system of allowing state legislatures to select senators led to decades of corruption—candidates could in effect "buy" seats in the Senate—until the Seventeenth Amendment in 1913 required that senators be elected by popular vote, too.

The Connecticut Compromise also scrapped the Virginia Plan's provisions for the national government to veto state laws.

But a big question remained: how would population be counted for apportioning seats to the House of Representatives? It was widely accepted that only "free" men would vote—not women, and not slaves or Indians. But free women would count in the population totals that decided how many seats each state got in the House of Representatives and, eventually, in the Electoral College that would choose the president.

Would slaves be counted as part of the population? The Southern states, who had large numbers of slaves, wanted them counted in the population totals because that would give them more seats. The Northern states did not want slaves counted because that would give the Southern states more power. Another compromise was reached: all free people would be counted, with the exception of Indians who did not pay taxes, and "all other persons"—that is, slaves—in each of the states would be counted as three-fifths of their states' total population. In other words, 100 slaves would be counted as 60 people in a state's population total.

> ### WE THE PEOPLE
>
> "'We the People.' When the Founding Fathers used this phrase in 1787, they did not have in mind the majority of America's citizens ...."
>
> —Thurgood Marshall, the first African American justice on the U.S. Supreme Court

After the convention had worked out the basics of the legislative branch, Article I, the delegates' discussion turned to the executive branch, Article II. It's a popular belief that George Washington was asked to be king and demurred, but a monarchy was never really considered at the convention. Even the relatively few monarchists left in America (many of King George III's most loyal Loyalists had fled back to England, taking their riches with them) did not think King George Washington would be a good idea. According to some accounts, the reasoning was, at least in part, because he and Martha had never had children. When he died without an heir, presumably there would be a political upheaval in choosing his successor. It's true that Washington didn't want to be king, but he didn't want to be president, either.

The new nation wanted to get as far away from a monarchy as possible. A king or queen was not compatible with the democratic principles the founders of the United States had in mind. The delegates in Philadelphia agreed on a president who would serve a 4-year term and could run for reelection. Washington considered not running for a second term in 1792 because of his advanced age—he was 60 years old. But he did serve a second term and then retired, which gave rise to the popular conception that the founding fathers believed it unseemly for any president to serve more than two terms. Some other presidents did pursue a third term—notably Ulysses S. Grant—but none succeeded until Franklin D. Roosevelt was reelected to a third term in 1940, on the brink of World War II, and then reelected to a fourth term in 1944, months before his death in 1945. The Twenty-Second Amendment, ratified in 1951, formally limited presidents to two election victories plus 2 years of a 4-year term if they assumed the office as vice president or some other presidential succession role.

Despite the misgivings about having a king or any sort of strong executive, the Constitutional Convention offered the president more power over the United States than King George had over the colonies. The president would serve as commander in chief of the armed forces, could make treaties with other nations, had the power to veto congressional legislation, and could issue pardons. The president also had the duty to appoint ambassadors, Supreme Court justices, federal judges, and executive branch department heads—his Cabinet. He would be the chief law enforcement officer. The Constitution would be the law of the land, and the president would ensure the law of the land was upheld.

The founding fathers feared the power of a king, but they feared the power of the people, too. The people could be easily swayed by populist movements and led to vote for candidates who were charismatic but charted a destructive path. (In the extreme, think Hitler, although many Americans across the political spectrum might be forgiven for pointing toward recent presidential candidates—and perhaps recent presidents—who were charismatic but destructive.)

So instead of a direct popular vote for president, the convention created an Electoral College that gave the state legislatures the power to vote for presidents. The Electoral College remains in effect, although the process was changed with the election of Andrew Jackson to choose the president by popular vote (still through the Electoral College).

The convention eventually added a vice president to the executive branch, in Article II, to be available if the president could not serve. The vice president's chief official duty—then and now—was to serve as president pro tempore, the presiding officer, of the Senate.

After the legislative and executive debates, the convention handled the third branch of government—the judicial branch—relatively easily, in a much less contentious manner, in Article III. At that point, the judiciary was seen not so much as a third separate and equal leg of the checks and balances, but more as a brake to keep the legislative and executive branches from dominating each other. The convention, reflecting the delegates' relative lack of concern for the role and impact of the judiciary, ended up creating just one federal court—the Supreme Court. The convention specified that justices would receive lifetime appointments, and their salaries could not be cut while they were still on the bench. The details of setting up the Supreme Court, and the lower federal courts, were left to Congress.

Judicial review—the power of the federal courts to overturn laws passed by Congress or executive actions on the grounds that they violated the Constitution, the supreme law of the land—apparently was not contemplated by the convention on a practical basis. After the convention, James Madison and other federalists advocated strongly for the principle of judicial review but with little result until the Supreme Court itself, beginning with the 1803 case *Marbury* v. *Madison,* began to assert the court's right to declare federal laws and regulation unconstitutional.

It was much later that the federal courts asserted the right to void state and local laws as unconstitutional.

Once the separation of powers was established in the first three articles, the delegates turned to Articles IV, V, and VI to set forth the rules for states to work together. Article IV required that laws be applied equally across state borders. One state cannot nullify another state's laws, and "The United States shall guarantee to every State in this union a Republican Form of Government." That turned out to be an important constitutional provision during the Civil War.

The delegates in Philadelphia in 1787 wanted the Constitution to stand the test of time, but they were under no illusion that it could not be improved as the nation grew. Article V set forth the procedure for amending the Constitution, allowing either the states or Congress to propose amendments, and for a new constitutional convention to be called for amendments proposed by the states. The convention agreed that no matter where an amendment started, in Congress or with the states, it had to be ratified by three-fourths of the states to become effective.

The Constitution includes no specific mention of God, even though the majority of today's state constitutions refer to God, Almighty God, or a Supreme Being. However, Article VI insists, "No religious Test shall ever be required as a Qualification to any Office of public Trust under the United States."

Article VII, in a straightforward manner, outlined how the Constitution would be ratified, with approval from nine states.

WE THE PEOPLE

When the states were considering ratification, one of the big objections to the Constitution was that the federal judiciary would undermine the role of state courts and, therefore, weaken the states. In his Federal essays, Alexander Hamilton's memorable defense argued that the judiciary would be the branch of government "least dangerous to the political rights of the Constitution." He pointed out that the court system would not have any means of enforcement or coercion, unlike the executive branch with the military or Congress with the power to approve or withhold spending.

The Preamble

The Preamble, or introduction to the Constitution, is another example, like the opening of the Declaration of Independence, of stirring rhetoric that sums up the high ideals of the founding fathers and their hopes for the future:

"We the People of the United States, in Order to form a more perfect Union, establish Justice, insure domestic Tranquility, provide for the common defence, promote the general Welfare, and secure the Blessings of Liberty to ourselves and our Posterity, do ordain and establish this Constitution for the United States of America."

When the convention agreed on the general basics of a constitutional framework, a Committee of Detail was appointed to come back with a rough draft. When the rough draft was approved, the convention gave another committee, the Committee of Style, the task of polishing a final version. One of the committee's assignments was to write an introduction laying out the intentions of the United States and its Constitution.

In the Committee of Style, a New Jersey delegate, Gouverneur Morris, did much of the actual writing of the final draft. The previous draft of the Preamble began, "We the States …" and went on to list each of the 13 former colonies by name. Morris is credited with rewriting the first few lines to create the stirring, now classic, opening phrase of the Preamble: "We the people of the United States, in order to perform a more perfect union …." Those opening lines, eloquent as they are, created more opposition among some critics back in state legislatures during debates over ratification. For instance, Patrick Henry in Virginia objected that the new wording de-emphasized states' rights and showed that the framers' intent was a strong central government that would dominate the states.

WE THE PEOPLE

Gouverneur Morris was a true member of the small American aristocracy, but unlike many of the patrician class, he was also committed to independence and liberty. Serving as the primary writer of the Constitution was the highlight of his political career, which suffered on a number of occasions because of his penchant for sarcasm. For example, when discussing the role of the presidency at the convention, Morris announced that he "had no doubt that our Executive like most others would have too much patriotism to shrink from the burden of his office, and too much modesty not to be willing to decline the promotion."

When you think about it, those early American colonists participated in two revolutions—one military and one ideological. In many ways, the military war against England was easier. We're still fighting our other revolution, the one that for the first time established a government by and for the people, based on "popular sovereignty" rather than on the sovereignty of a king or any other form of government.

By our standards today, however, the framers of the Constitution were not especially enlightened. They were white guys, most of them old and rich, and their Constitution was written for themselves and the other old, rich, white guys who ran the states and the country. They did not envision women voting. Some of them may have envisioned black men being free some day, but many of them were themselves slave owners.

The Preamble sets a tone and lays out the goals of the Constitution, but it is worth noting that the Preamble itself, unlike the rest of the Constitution, is not regarded as part of the supreme law of the land. It is merely an introduction. You cannot sue based on the Preamble in the same way you can on the First Amendment if your rights to free speech are violated, for example, or on the Fourth Amendment if the police search your house illegally.

Nonetheless, the Preamble to the Constitution emphasizes the democratic nature of the new nation. The Articles of Confederation sought a "perpetual union," while the Preamble has the loftier goal "to form a more perfect union." The Preamble speaks of justice and liberty and offers aspirations of peace and prosperity. In seeking "to secure the blessings of liberty" for all who come after "our posterity," the founders obviously were thinking about their legacy. The Preamble sets the tone for a Constitution that was written to offer hope, both in 1787 and today.

The Least You Need to Know

- The United States is an ongoing experiment in democracy, and the Constitution is the blueprint for that experiment.
- The power of the U.S. Constitution comes not from the document itself, but rather from our society's agreement to live under the rule of law.
- The Constitution does not grant rights to the people; rather, it identifies the powers the people grant to the government.
- The government's role under the Constitution is to protect both the United States as a nation and individual rights.
- The Constitution is the supreme law of the land, dealing less in specifics than in the spirit of the law.

Ratification and the Bill of Rights

Ratification of the new Constitution by the states was not a slam dunk. Some states had objections to the omission of a Bill of Rights. And some states did not want a new Constitution at all.

Madison and his allies resorted to writing and publishing a series of articles called the Federalist Papers that served—and still serve—as some of the clearest explanations of the Constitution, and some of the best rationale for ratification.

The Constitution was ratified, of course, creating a new government with George Washington as the first president. The Bill of Rights was soon added in the form of the first 10 Amendments.

In This Chapter

- Beginning ratification
- Objections from the states
- Changing minds with the Federalist Papers
- The Bill of Rights
- What about slaves and Native Americans?

The Process of Ratification

On September 17, 1787, the convention put the Constitution to a vote. Among the original 55 delegates, 13 had gone home already, some because of political objections and some because of personal or professional obligations. Three delegates still at the convention refused to sign.

One of the continuing concerns throughout the long summer had been whether the Constitution should include provisions protecting individual liberty—a Bill of Rights. One of those who abstained, Roger Mason, who had drafted Virginia's Bill of Rights, said he could not endorse the Constitution without a national Bill of Rights. Back in Massachusetts, another founding father, Sam Adams, agreed that the convention should have included a Bill of Rights to protect individual freedoms such as speech and religion.

However, James Madison and other leaders at the convention argued that a Bill of Rights was not necessary because individual rights were protected in the bills of rights the states were including in their individual constitutions.

On the other hand, those calling for a federal Bill of Rights were afraid that a strong central government might someday restrict the individual rights of citizens, even if those rights were guaranteed by state laws.

Madison acknowledged those concerns, but he and other leaders were afraid that introducing something as large and potentially controversial as a Bill of Rights would risk further friction and delays at the convention that could imperil passage of the Constitution. The vast majority of the delegates agreed—no Bill of Rights would be debated, at least not then, in Philadelphia. The delegates wanted to get the job done and go home before the winter of 1787 settled on them.

The Constitution was, and still is, a model of brevity. The final draft of the original seven Articles and the Preamble, as approved by the delegates, was about 4,400 words, compared with the typical 26,000 words for a state constitution. (Although over the years, the 27 amendments swelled the count for today's U.S. Constitution to a still-succinct 7,500 words.)

Signing the Constitution

George Washington was the first to sign the new Constitution on September 17, followed by the delegates from the states, in order, from north to south. Alexander Hamilton signed, but because the other two members of the New York delegation had departed, New York did not have a quorum and its vote did not count. But 11 states approved, and only 9 were required under Article VII, so the Constitution was approved, sent to printers, and dispatched from the Constitutional Convention to the Confederation Congress and the 13 state legislatures for ratification.

During the long convention, delegates had often remarked on the Chippendale chair, decorated with a sun on the back, that had served as Washington's presiding seat throughout the proceedings. When Franklin rose and gave a final speech, he noted that he and other delegates had often wondered, through that long summer, whether the sun was rising or setting on their infant nation. Now, he said, with the signing of the Constitution, he knew: it was a rising sun.

 WE THE PEOPLE

"The makers of our constitution undertook to secure conditions favorable to the pursuit of happiness .... They sought to protect Americans in their beliefs, their thoughts, their emotions, and their sensations. They conferred, as against the government, the right to be let alone—the most comprehensive of the rights and the right most valued by civilized men, ..."

—Supreme Court Justice Louis Brandeis

The story may be apocryphal, but it has been widely reported over the years that a woman who knew Benjamin Franklin encountered him as he was leaving what is now Independence Hall after the signing ceremony. The framers had done an admirable job keeping their proceedings secret through all those months—there was still talk in the coffee shops and some newspapers of making Washington king, even though the delegates never seriously considered it—and now the public was eager for news. The woman reportedly asked, "Well, Doctor Franklin, what have we got? A republic or a monarchy?"

Franklin supposedly answered immediately. "A republic," he replied. "If you can keep it."

That evening, after the signing ceremony in Philadelphia, most of the delegates celebrated with a convivial supper at the City Tavern on Second Street. Within a day or two, many of them had packed up and headed home, knowing they would be called on to explain and defend the new Constitution to their states' citizens and legislatures.

The States Vote

When the delegates returned to their home states, they typically followed a common line: "This is a good Constitution, maybe a very good one, but it is not without flaws." Nobody liked everything in the Constitution, but it was good enough. It provided the framework for growth, ensured balanced state and federal power, and was flexible enough to be changed.

The Constitution was generally well received by the public. It meant a lot to have so many big names from the Revolution attached—Benjamin Franklin, James Madison, Alexander Hamilton, John Jay, and especially George Washington. But there was still stiff opposition from two different groups, the anti-Federalists who thought the Constitution went too far in limiting the rights of the states, and the liberal critics who thought it didn't go far enough in protecting individual rights, particularly in failing to have a Bill of Rights. Some people were in both camps with misgivings toward the Constitution.

The first wave of ratification came quickly. The Delaware Legislature was the first state to vote to ratify the Constitution on December 7, 1787. Pennsylvania followed on December 12, and New Jersey on December 18. Georgia ratified on January 2, 1788, followed by Connecticut on January 9. Massachusetts voted in favor of ratification on February 7, but it was close—187 for, 168 against. If 10 votes had gone the other way, Massachusetts would have rejected the Constitution. That was one of several very narrow votes to ratify. In Virginia and New Hampshire, the Constitution would have been rejected with a swing of 5 votes each, and in New York, only 2 votes would have had to change.

To build support, in the autumn of 1787, soon after the convention ended, James Madison, John Jay, and Alexander Hamilton began publishing a series of articles called the Federalist Papers, explaining and promoting the Constitution. These essays—eventually 85 in all—were published under the pseudonym *Publius.* (In those days, it was common for pamphlets and newspaper articles to be published anonymously because newspapers had relatively little straightforward news as we know it, especially local news. Periodicals were rife with opinion, and people were typically drawn to those that espoused their particular political slant, much like some television news networks today. Madison probably reckoned, correctly, that his arguments in favor of the Constitution would be considered more fairly if his name wasn't on them.)

To appease those demanding more protections for individual liberties, Madison and other leading Federalists agreed to push for a Bill of Rights after the Constitution was ratified and the new U.S. government was functioning. The promise apparently helped push other states to vote for ratification: Maryland in April, South Carolina in May, and New Hampshire and Virginia in June. The June 21 endorsement by New Hampshire was the ninth from the states and meant that the Constitution was ratified. Virginia followed 4 days later. On July 2, the Confederation Congress made the formal announcement: America had a new Constitution. New York, North Carolina, and Rhode Island were the remaining states holding out, but to no purpose. The Constitution would go into effect with or without their votes.

On July 23, 1788, thousands of professionals, artists, and craftsmen marched through the streets of New York City in support of the Constitution. Three days later, the New York State Legislature finally approved it by a vote of 30 to 27. Like a number of other states, New York's vote came with a call for amendments, including a Bill of Rights. North Carolina eventually voted for ratification in 1789, and Rhode Island in 1790.

Ratification!

With ratification, the Confederation Congress began closing itself down and transferring power to the new government. The new government would be based temporarily in New York, until the new Congress could acquire a site for a new federal government district—which turned out to be land donated by Maryland and Virginia along the Potomac River. (Washington, who had been a land surveyor as a young man, personally approved the proposed site that became the capital named after him.)

Today's critics of the modern federal government and its power might fondly note the period from November 1, 1788, to April 1, 1789, when the United States formally had no central government. The first presidential election was held on February 4, 1789, and George Washington defeated John Adams 69 to 34 in the Electoral College to become the first president. Adams, as the runner-up, became the first vice president.

The new Congress was supposed to open its first session on March 4, 1789—and thereby mark the beginning of the new federal government. But just as bad roads kept the Constitutional Convention from starting on time in Philadelphia 2 years earlier, it took until April 1 to gather a quorum in the House of Representatives and until April 6 in the Senate.

Adams was sworn in as vice president on April 21, and Washington, then 57 years old, was sworn in on April 30 on the balcony of Federal Hall. (The original hall was demolished long ago, but the site—26 Wall Street, then and now, the heart of the Financial District—became the Federal Hall National Memorial, part of the National Park Service.) Throngs watched Washington swear the oath of office, his hand on a Bible borrowed from a nearby Masonic lodge, and then ad lib the words, "So help me God," at the end of the oath. He was required, by an act of Congress, to attend a service afterward at nearby St. Paul's Church. An inaugural ball was held a week later.

In the autumn of 1789, Congress established the judiciary with the first federal courts—the Supreme Court, the federal district courts, and three regional circuit courts that became the U.S. Courts of Appeal. Congress also established the U.S. Army—a standing force of 1,000 men—along with the national census and the Thanksgiving holiday.

WE THE PEOPLE

After two terms in the House, Madison served as Thomas Jefferson's secretary of state from 1801 to 1809 and then was elected to succeed Jefferson. He served as the fourth U.S. president, from 1808 to 1816. His wife, Dolley Madison, is widely credited for defining the public role of First Lady. Madison was known as a benevolent slave owner, but he never freed Montpelier's slaves.

The Bill of Rights

The failure to offer a Bill of Rights at the Constitutional Convention was a rare miscalculation by James Madison. But he was able, through the Federalist Papers and his own assurances to critics, to achieve ratification of the Constitution and then soon add the Bill of Rights.

Madison, who had narrowly defeated another future president, James Monroe, for a seat in the first House of Representatives, proposed the amendments that became the Bill of Rights. The Bill of Rights was probably familiar, at least in concept, to many Americans, as an echo of the Bill of Rights that was part of their respective state constitutions. Freedom of speech, for example, was a given—that was sure to be in the federal Bill of Rights. So was freedom of assembly, freedom of religion, and the right to bear arms, along with the right to a free trial and guarantees against cruel and unusual punishment.

But Madison offered a few unexpected wrinkles. For instance, the states more often said they "ought not" violate the freedom of the press. Madison, in the First Amendment, wrote that the government "shall not" impinge upon freedom of the press. Most of the states did not require compensation to private citizens when the government took their property via eminent domain, but Madison included compensation in the federal Bill of Rights. Double jeopardy— the prohibition against being tried twice for the same offense—was another Madison effort to strengthen the Bill of Rights beyond the rights typically guaranteed by the states.

Once approved by Congress and ratified by the states, the Bill of Rights became part of the Constitution in 1791. The assurances in the Bill of Rights originally applied to the federal government only; those assurances were expanded to cover the states, too, beginning with the Fourteenth Amendment in 1868.

Considering Slaves and Native Americans

In retrospect, many believe a greater failing by Madison and the other framers was putting off resolution of the issues of slavery and treatment of Native Americans.

 WE THE PEOPLE

"It is much to be wished that slavery may be abolished. The honour of the States, as well as justice and humanity, in my opinion, loudly call upon them to emancipate these unhappy people. To contend for our own liberty, and to deny that blessing to others, involves an inconsistency not to be excused."

—John Jay, statesman, diplomat, politician, and the first Chief Justice of the Supreme Court

Yes, the United States was the first government built entirely from scratch, with an entirely new structure that became a model for many other governments around the world as they struggled out of monarchy, dictatorships, and colonialism. But it was hypocritical, at best, to declare a new nation based on the natural rights of human beings and the rule of law while at the same time ignoring or even violently abusing the rights of Native Americans and African Americans, who together represented a substantial part of the population. One in five Americans was a slave at the birth of the United States. Nobody knows how many Indians there were because they were not counted, and little thought was given to the future of Native Americans despite the inevitability of a huge westward population expansion.

Many of the convention delegates, including some of the Northerners, owned slaves or had owned them in the past. Many of the slave owners, even the Southerners, had misgivings about the morality of slavery. Yet the framers were constrained by the realities of eighteenth-century economics. Much of their personal wealth was tied up in land and slaves—and their land was worth much less without slaves to work the farms and plantations. The economy of the South— and maybe the entire continental economy—would have collapsed without slaves.

It was not unusual for prominent Americans, including some of the founding fathers, to own slaves, hate slavery, yet refuse to set their slaves free. Virginia's George Mason was one of the prominent slave owners at the Constitutional Convention who had qualms about the morality of owning another human being. During a debate on slavery, he warned, "By an inevitable chain of causes and effects, providence punishes national sins by national calamities." He did not list potential calamities, but certainly the Civil War would count.

Thomas Jefferson, himself a prominent slave owner, described the slavery issue as trying to hold "a wolf by the ears." In the Confederation Congress, he tried to ban slavery in any new states beyond the original 13. He also called for a ban on slavery after 1800. Both those proposals were defeated. The word *slavery* does not appear in the Constitution.

Beyond resolving the slave question in terms of population for voting purposes—were they property or were they people?—with the clumsy "three-fifths" compromise, the Constitutional Convention's only potential restraint on slavery was a prohibition against Congress banning slavery for at least 20 years, not before 1808. As it turned out, of course, slavery lasted much longer, until the Civil War.

Between the signing of the Declaration of Independence and the signing of the Emancipation Proclamation in 1863, the slave population of the United States grew from about 500,000 to an estimated 4 million.

The Least You Need to Know

- The Constitutional Convention wrapped up its 4 months of work in September 1787, when the delegates signed the new Constitution.
- Many Americans, including some delegates and other important founding fathers, opposed some or all of the Constitution.
- One of the most controversial omissions from the Constitution was a federal Bill of Rights to protect individual liberties.
- The Federalist Papers were influential in explaining and promoting the Constitution.
- The Bill of Rights was added soon after the new U.S government came to power.

Balancing the Branches

Part 2 examines the structure of the Constitution, with its system of checks and balances devised to limit government power and protect the rights of individual citizens. We examine the practical aspects of Articles I through III, which draw the lines among the three branches of government. We also consider Articles IV through VI, which outline the way federal agencies and executives work with each other as well as with state executives and agencies.

CHAPTER 4

Articles I Through III: Separation of Powers

The first three original Articles of the Constitution, also called the "Powers" section of the Constitution, defined the three branches of government: legislative, executive, and judicial. This part of the Constitution also set up the separation of powers, a sort of rock-paper-scissors arrangement aimed at keeping any one branch of government from amassing too much power.

The legislative branch can pass legislation for the president to sign into law, but the legislature has the authority to override a presidential veto. The president has broad powers to appoint government administrators and regulators, but many of the top appointees are subject to approval by the legislative branch. The president makes appointees to sit on the federal courts, but those also are subject to legislative approval. And federal and Supreme Court justices can overturn laws approved by the legislative branch and regulations enforced by the executive branch if they are ruled unconstitutional. It's all about maintaining balance.

In This Chapter

Article I: The Legislative Branch

Article I establishes the branch of government that includes the elected representatives of the people, where laws are proposed, debated, and voted up or down.

The framers of the Constitution had choices for how to set up the new nation's Congress. At first they considered a unicameral system—a single legislative body, like the old Continental Congress. But how to pick the representatives? Should each state have the same number of representatives? Or should representation be based on population?

Balancing and compromising, as they so often did, the framers ended up with a bicameral legislature with two houses: the House of Representatives, with members chosen according to population, and the Senate, which allowed two members for each state no matter what their population.

Note that when quoting from the text of the Constitution, here and elsewhere, I've preserved the quaint original capitalization, punctuation, grammar, and spelling, such as *chuse* for *choose*. In addition, the phrases in italic represent language that was not in the original articles but added later by amendments.

Section 1: Congress

"All legislative Powers herein granted shall be vested in a Congress of the United States, which shall consist of a Senate and House of Representatives."

The "vesting" language in effect prohibits direct voting by citizens and prohibits the other branches of government, the executive and the judicial, from enacting laws. Most states have a mechanism for referendum voting, allowing citizens to vote directly on proposed state legislation, but this clause prohibits national referendum voting.

Section 2: The House of Representatives

"The House of Representatives shall be composed of Members chosen every second Year by the People of the several States, and the Electors in each State shall have the Qualifications requisite for Electors of the most numerous Branch of the State Legislature.

"No Person shall be a Representative who shall not have attained to the age of twenty five Years, and been seven Years a Citizen of the United States, and who shall not, when elected, be an Inhabitant of that State in which he shall be chosen.

"Representatives and direct Taxes shall be apportioned among the several States which may be included within this Union, according to their respective Numbers, which shall be determined by adding to the whole Number of free Persons, including those bound to Service for a Term of Years, and excluding Indians not taxed, three fifths of all other Persons. The actual Enumeration shall be made within three Years after the first Meeting of the Congress of the United States, and within every subsequent Term of ten Years, in such Manner as they shall by Law direct. The Number of Representatives shall not exceed one for every thirty Thousand, but each State shall have at Least one Representative; and until such enumeration shall be made, the State of New Hampshire shall be entitled to chuse three, Massachusetts eight, Rhode-Island and Providence Plantations one, Connecticut five, New-York six, New Jersey four, Pennsylvania eight, Delaware one, Maryland six, Virginia ten, North Carolina five, South Carolina five, and Georgia three.

"When vacancies happen in the Representation from any State, the Executive Authority thereof shall issue Writs of Election to fill such Vacancies.

"The House of Representatives shall chuse their Speaker and other Officers; and shall have the sole Power of Impeachment."

Section 2 establishes the House of Representatives, the "people's house," and specifies that elections will be held every 2 years for all members of the House. When a vacancy occurs between regular elections, the governor of that state can call a special election. This section allowed the states to set the requirements for citizens to be eligible to vote for House candidates, but later amendments said states could not keep people from voting because of their race or their sex, if they are at least 18 years old, or if they did not pay a *poll tax*.

DEFINITION

A **poll tax** is a fee a voter must pay before being allowed to vote. Historically, poll taxes have been used to keep poor people from voting.

Interestingly, there is no requirement that members of the House of Representatives actually live in the district they represent, although they are supposed to be at least 25 years old and have been a citizen of the United States for at least 7 years.

Each state must have at least one representative, but otherwise House districts (there have been 435 since 1911) are spread proportionately across the nation by population. A sparsely populated state such as Wyoming might have only one representative, while Illinois might have several—densely populated Chicago might have five members, plus several from the outlying suburbs.

The Constitution called for a census every 10 years to reconfigure congressional districts in response to population shifts.

Note the language in the third paragraph of Section 2 that mentioned "three fifths of all other Persons," in determining population for the purposes of deciding how many representatives each state would send to Congress. In effect, the framers of the Constitution were counting a slave as "three fifths" of a person as a compromise designed to limit the power in Congress of slave-holding states. The Fourteenth Amendment, after slavery was abolished, removed the three-fifths clause, and today all inhabitants of a state are counted, whether they are citizens or not.

When a House seat becomes vacant, a new election is held. When a Senate seat becomes vacant, the governor of the state can appoint a replacement.

That same clause, beginning "Representatives and direct taxes shall be apportioned …," was aimed at ensuring each state's share of any taxes collected by the federal government would be proportionate to the state's population. The Sixteenth Amendment changed this so individual income taxes could be collected.

The Constitution borrows the British Parliament's procedure for impeaching a president; only the House can vote to impeach, and it is up to the Senate (Section 3) to put an impeached president on trial.

Finally, this section allows the House to choose its own Speaker. Nothing says the Speaker actually has to be a member of the House, but so far every one in American history has been.

Section 3: The Senate

"The Senate of the United States shall be composed of two Senators from each State, chosen by the Legislature thereof, for six Years; and each Senator shall have one Vote.

"Immediately after they shall be assembled in Consequence of the first Election, they shall be divided as equally as may be into three Classes. The Seats of the Senators of the first Class shall be vacated at the Expiration of the second Year, of the second Class at the Expiration of the fourth Year, and of the third Class at the Expiration of the sixth Year, so that one third may be chosen every second Year; *and if Vacancies happen by Resignation, or otherwise, during the Recess of the Legislature of any State, the Executive thereof may make temporary Appointments until the next Meeting of the Legislature, which shall then fill such Vacancies.*

"No Person shall be a Senator who shall not have attained to the Age of thirty Years, and been nine Years a Citizen of the United States, and who shall not, when elected, be an Inhabitant of that State for which he shall be chosen.

"The Vice president of the United States shall be president of the Senate but shall have no Vote, unless they be equally divided.

"The Senate shall chuse their other Officers, and also a president pro tempore, in the Absence of the Vice president, or when he shall exercise the Office of president of the United States.

"The Senate shall have the sole Power to try all Impeachments. When sitting for that Purpose, they shall be on Oath or Affirmation. When the president of the United States is tried the Chief Justice shall preside: And no Person shall be convicted without the Concurrence of two thirds of the Members present.

"Judgment in Cases of Impeachment shall not extend further than to removal from Office, and disqualification to hold and enjoy any Office of honor, Trust or Profit under the United States: but the Party convicted shall nevertheless be liable and subject to Indictment, Trial, Judgment and Punishment, according to Law."

Senators were originally chosen by state legislatures, but that was later changed so voters chose them directly for 6-year terms. Unlike House seats, which came up for reelection every 2 years, roughly one third of the Senate seats come open every 2 years. Senators need to be older than representatives—30 years old—and a citizen for 9 years. In addition, senators, like members of the House, must be residents of the states from which they are elected. The vice president was named president of the Senate but can vote only to break ties.

When the House votes to impeach a president, or any other federal official or judge, the Senate in effect acts as a jury, and a two-thirds majority is needed to convict. If a president has been impeached, the chief justice presides over the trial in the Senate. Someone who is convicted is tossed out of office, can be barred from holding any other office, and may still face criminal charges.

WE THE PEOPLE

The most recent president to be impeached was Bill Clinton, for perjury and obstruction of justice in connection with the dalliance he eventually admitted having with a White House intern. Only 45 senators voted to convict, far short of the 67 votes needed to remove Clinton from office.

Section 4: Elections and Sessions

"The Times, Places and Manner of holding Elections for Senators and Representatives, shall be prescribed in each State by the Legislature thereof; but the Congress may at any time by Law make or alter such Regulations, except as to the Places of chusing Senators.

"The Congress shall assemble at least once in every Year, and such Meeting shall be on *the first Monday in December,* unless they shall by Law appoint a different Day."

The states oversee federal elections, but this section allowed Congress to set a standard date for congressional elections. That turned out to be the Tuesday following the first Monday in November of even-numbered years. Congress could simply have specified the first Tuesday in November but didn't want to conflict with November 1, the religious holiday All Saints' Day, when it falls on a Tuesday.

In the second paragraph, the requirement to meet on the first Monday meant that because the new Congress originally was not sworn in until the following March, the gathering in December was a *lame duck* Congress. The Twentieth Amendment changed the rules so newly elected or reelected members of the House and Senate took office in early January.

> **DEFINITION**
>
> A **lame duck** is an elected official or body of officials whose terms in office are expiring.

Section 5: Housekeeping

"Each House shall be the Judge of the Elections, Returns and Qualifications of its own Members, and a Majority of each shall constitute a Quorum to do Business; but a smaller Number may adjourn from day to day, and may be authorized to compel the Attendance of absent Members, in such Manner, and under such Penalties as each House may provide.

"Each House may determine the Rules of its Proceedings, punish its Members for disorderly Behaviour, and, with the Concurrence of two thirds, expel a Member.

"Each House shall keep a Journal of its Proceedings, and from time to time publish the same, excepting such Parts as may in their Judgment require Secrecy; and the Yeas and Nays of the Members of either House on any question shall, at the Desire of one fifth of those Present, be entered on the Journal.

"Neither House, during the Session of Congress, shall, without the Consent of the other, adjourn for more than three days, nor to any other Place than that in which the two Houses shall be sitting."

This is a housekeeping section for Congress, allowing the Senate and House to make their own rules. For example, when a 29-year-old won election to the Senate, the Senate bent its rules to let the young senator-elect wait a few months until his thirtieth birthday to assume his seat. The quorum clause requires each chamber to have a majority present to do business, but this rule is widely ignored.

Each house can censure one of its own members by a simple majority vote, but it takes a two-thirds majority to expel a member.

Each chamber must keep a journal of what happens on the floor, but it can keep anything out of the journal or put things into the journal that didn't actually happen. For example, members of Congress sometimes have speeches entered in the *Congressional Record* without ever actually giving the speech.

Neither house can adjourn without the consent of the other for more than 3 days, but this simply means that the House and Senate frequently meet the constitutional requirement simply by calling themselves to order every 3 days—often for less than a minute—without actually doing any business.

Section 6: Pay and Privileges

"The Senators and Representatives shall receive a Compensation for their Services, to be ascertained by Law, and paid out of the Treasury of the United States. They shall in all Cases, except Treason, Felony and Breach of the Peace, be privileged from Arrest during their Attendance at the Session of their respective Houses, and in going to and returning from the same; and for any Speech or Debate in either House, they shall not be questioned in any other Place.

"No Senator or Representative shall, during the Time for which he was elected, be appointed to any civil Office under the Authority of the United States, which shall have been created, or the Emoluments whereof shall have been encreased during such time; and no Person holding any Office under the United States, shall be a Member of either House during his Continuance in Office."

Under this section of the Constitution, members of Congress are allowed to set their own pay, but they're prevented from starting to collect the raise until after the next election. To prevent harassment from the executive branch, special privileges granted to members of Congress include immunity from arrest for minor crimes—in effect, this barred "civil" arrests, which are rare these days—while they are in session or on their way to or from Congress. Members of Congress can be arrested on criminal charges, either misdemeanors or felonies; however, they can't be sued for slander for remarks on the floor.

In another move toward financial propriety, and to shore up the separation of powers, members of Congress must wait until their terms expire to take higher-paying jobs in government. They can't resign one day and start collecting the higher pay the next day.

Section 7: Legislation

"All Bills for raising Revenue shall originate in the House of Representatives; but the Senate may propose or concur with amendments as on other Bills.

"Every Bill which shall have passed the House of Representatives and the Senate, shall, before it become a law, be presented to the president of the United States: If he approves he shall sign it, but if not he shall return it, with his Objections to that House in which it shall have originated, who shall enter the Objections at large on their Journal, and proceed to reconsider it. If after such Reconsideration two thirds of that House shall agree to pass the Bill, it shall be sent, together with the Objections, to the other House, by which it shall likewise be reconsidered, and if approved by two thirds of that House, it shall become a Law. But in all such Cases the Votes of both Houses shall be determined by Yeas and Nays, and the Names of the Persons voting for and against the Bill shall be entered on the Journal of each House respectively. If any Bill shall not be returned by the president within ten Days (Sundays excepted) after it shall have been presented to him, the Same shall be a Law, in like Manner as if he had signed it, unless the Congress by their Adjournment prevent its Return, in which Case it shall not be a Law.

"Every Order, Resolution, or Vote to which the Concurrence of the Senate and House of Representatives may be necessary (except on a question of Adjournment) shall be presented to the president of the United States; and before the Same shall take Effect, shall be approved by him, or being disapproved by him, shall be repassed by two thirds of the Senate and House of Representatives, according to the Rules and Limitations prescribed in the Case of a Bill."

Senators or representatives can introduce bills, but all legislation raising revenue—tax bills, in other words—must originate in the House. The House also claims it must initiate appropriations bills—spending bills. The Senate historically has disagreed, but in practice, all appropriations bills do originate in the House. If the Senate initiates a spending bill and sends it to the House, the House simply returns it without any action.

The Presentment Clause sets forth the way a bill becomes law: when both chambers have approved a bill in exactly identical forms, it is sent to the president, who has 10 days (not counting Sundays) to sign it so it becomes law or veto it (send it back to the originating chamber with an explanation of his objections). The bill can still become law if both chambers, by two-thirds majorities instead of the usual simple majorities, override the president's veto. If the president does not return a Congress-approved bill within 10 days, it becomes law—unless Congress has adjourned in the meantime. If Congress has adjourned, this is called a pocket veto, and the bill dies because the president could not return it to the House or Senate.

This section of the Constitution also includes one of its most important provisions—the procedure for changing the Constitution itself. Two thirds of both houses of Congress can approve a proposed amendment and send it to the states for ratification. The president doesn't get a crack at a veto—a clear example of the framers' intentions to limit the power of the executive branch. The states then vote on ratification. This is usually done by each state's legislature, but an amendment can instead call for each state to hold a ratification convention. Either way, a simple majority is needed for ratification. When three fourths of the states have ratified an amendment, it becomes part of the Constitution.

CASES

***Clinton v. City of New York* (1998):** In 1996, Congress approved the Line Item Veto Act, which allowed the president, instead of vetoing or signing a bill, to veto certain spending provisions. President Clinton used the line-item veto to trim spending for health programs in New York City. The city sued, and the Supreme Court declared the act unconstitutional.

Section 8: Enumerated Powers

"The Congress shall have Power To lay and collect Taxes, Duties, Imposts and Excises, to pay the Debts and provide for the common Defence and general Welfare of the United States; but all Duties, Imposts and Excises shall be uniform throughout the United States;

"To borrow Money on the credit of the United States;

"To regulate Commerce with foreign Nations, and among the several States, and with the Indian Tribes;

"To establish an uniform Rule of Naturalization, and uniform Laws on the subject of Bankruptcies throughout the United States;

"To coin Money, regulate the Value thereof, and of foreign Coin, and fix the Standard of Weights and Measures;

"To provide for the Punishment of counterfeiting the Securities and current Coin of the United States;

"To establish Post Offices and post Roads;

"To promote the Progress of Science and useful Arts, by securing for limited Times to Authors and Inventors the exclusive Right to their respective Writings and Discoveries;

"To constitute Tribunals inferior to the supreme Court;

"To define and punish Piracies and Felonies committed on the high Seas, and Offences against the Law of Nations;

"To declare War, grant Letters of Marque and Reprisal, and make Rules concerning Captures on Land and Water;

"To raise and support Armies, but no Appropriation of Money to that Use shall be for a longer Term than two Years;

"To provide and maintain a Navy;

"To make Rules for the Government and Regulation of the land and naval Forces;

"To provide for calling forth the Militia to execute the Laws of the Union, suppress Insurrections and repel Invasions;

"To provide for organizing, arming, and disciplining, the Militia, and for governing such Part of them as may be employed in the Service of the United States, reserving to the States respectively, the Appointment of the Officers, and the Authority of training the Militia according to the discipline prescribed by Congress;

"To exercise exclusive Legislation in all Cases whatsoever, over such District (not exceeding ten Miles square) as may, by Cession of Particular States, and the Acceptance of Congress, become the Seat of the Government of the United States, and to exercise like Authority over all Places purchased by the Consent of the Legislature of the State in which the Same shall be, for the Erection of Forts, Magazines, Arsenals, dock-Yards and other needful Buildings;—And

"To make all Laws which shall be necessary and proper for carrying into Execution the foregoing Powers and all other Powers vested by this Constitution in the Government of the United States, or in any Department or Officer thereof."

The sweeping provisions of this part of the Constitution, known as the "enumerated powers," give Congress a laundry list of its authority. For example, 1 of the 17 powers specifically listed allows Congress to establish a national post office. But Congress, obviously, has also established a Social Security system, a Department of Education, and many other government agencies and functions that are not enumerated. How?

The opening clause of Section 8 is known as the General Welfare Clause, allowing Congress to provide for the common defense and general welfare, without defining either. Under a broad interpretation of this clause, Congress has been able to decide what's good for the country and then pass laws and spend money to make it happen. A narrow interpretation of the Constitution, particularly among those who are critical of the welfare state, maintains that a broad interpretation would in effect give Congress unlimited power—something the framers did not contemplate.

The third clause is the wide-ranging Commerce Clause, allowing Congress to regulate trade with foreign nations and among the states. It originally was intended to keep the 13 states from erecting trade barriers or tariffs that would prevent the free flow of goods and services within the new nation. It also gave federal laws and regulations precedence over conflicting states' rules.

In the twentieth century, as the government began regulating more aspects of everyday life and work, the clause provided Congress much of its authority to impose rules on companies that do business across state borders. Libertarians protest that Congress has assumed more regulatory power than the Constitution intended, including to some noncommercial activities conducted entirely within states. In several cases, the Supreme Court has ruled that Congress has gone too far, particularly in limiting New Deal programs in the 1930s. In a more recent case, however, the Supreme Court ruled that the Commerce Clause applied to a person growing marijuana for personal medical use, even though no profits or interstate commerce was involved.

 **CASES**

National Labor Relations Board v. Jones and Laughlin Steel Co. (1937): This case expanded Congress's authority under the Commerce Clause by approving the authority of the National Labor Relations Board to punish employers for "unfair labor practices," including firing workers for trying to unionize.

Other clauses in Article I, Section 8, of the Constitution give Congress the power to pass laws relating to a broad range of areas: bankruptcy, coining money, counterfeiting, the value of U.S. dollars on the foreign currency exchanges, the post office, standards for weights and measures, copyrights, and patents. It is up to the federal government, not the states, to determine who is and who is not a citizen.

The War Powers Clause says only Congress can declare war, although the specifics of how and when this can happen are left unsaid. Congress has declared war only five times in U.S. history, and always at the request of the president—most recently for World War II in 1941.

After presidents waged undeclared wars in Korea in the 1950s and Vietnam in the 1960s and 1970s, Congress passed the War Powers Resolution of 1973. In theory, this act was designed to have Congress and the president share the power to declare war, but in practice, it has given the president more authority—perhaps more than the Constitution intended, according to some critics—to wage war with or without the Congressional approval. The president has engaged in military conflicts several times since then with Congress's approval but without a formal declaration of war, including in Iraq in 1991, Afghanistan in 2001, and Iraq again in 2003.

Congress has the authority to establish and finance an army, but the framers' misgivings about standing armies led them to require that military funding not be for more than 2 years at a time—which is irrelevant today, because military budgets are routinely approved each year. Congress still has the superior authority over the executive branch in terms of rules and regulations for the land and naval military forces, although in practice, the executive branch, through the Pentagon, has much more to do with overseeing the military. The president has the authority to call out a state's militia, as when National Guard troops were used to enforce desegregation in the 1950s and quell urban unrest in the 1960s.

This section also gives Congress authority to oversee the District of Columbia's locally elected government, although many residents of the nation's capital believe they would be better off if their city had more autonomy.

The last clause of Section 8 is the Necessary-and-Proper Clause, which affords Congress broad authority to do whatever it needs to do to carry about the section's enumerated powers—including reorganizing the executive or judicial branches. A landmark case was *McCulloch* v. *Maryland* in 1819, when the Supreme Court endorsed the concept of a national bank despite strong opposition from those who feared that a federal banking system would weaken the states. Justice John Marshall said all the powers in the clause need not be enumerated and that the General Welfare and the Commerce Clauses gave Congress authority to decide a national bank was necessary and proper.

WE THE PEOPLE

Late in their lives—40 years after the Constitutional Convention—two of the most venerated founding fathers took opposite sides of the public debate over the national bank issue ultimately decided in *McCulloch* v. *Maryland*. Thomas Jefferson said a bank was not necessary and, therefore, unauthorized. Alexander Hamilton said a national bank was necessary to collect taxes, borrow money, and regulate trade. The Supreme Court agreed with Hamilton's position.

One of the most important U.S. Supreme Court cases in recent years was the 2012 decision that upheld, by a 5–4 margin, the legality of the Affordable Care Act (ACA), also known as Obamacare. The ACA, which aimed to make health care more easily available and affordable for millions of uninsured or underinsured Americans, was one of the most controversial social-engineering moves in modern American history. Conservatives, including many Republican members of Congress, saw the ACA as unconstitutional, and it was the subject of many legislative and judicial attacks. Opponents were unable to mount enough support in Congress to overcome a veto from President Obama, but the court cases eventually made their way to the Supreme Court.

Several state and federal cases were rolled into one case before the Supreme Court: *National Federation of Independent Business* v. *Sebelius*. (NFIB is an association of small businesses, and Kathleen Sebelius was President Obama's Secretary of Health and Human Services, the federal department that administered the ACA.) The case was seen as largely hinging on the Supreme Court's interpretation of Article I, written all those many years ago in Philadelphia by James Madison and other framers. The key portions of the ACA under attack were the individual mandate, which imposed a financial penalty on uninsured people who were eligible for health insurance coverage but refused to sign up for it, and the Medicare penalty, the government's threat to withhold all Medicare spending from any state that did not expand its Medicare program to facilitate wider use of the ACA.

The court ruled that the Commerce Clause did not authorize the individual mandate because Article I was aimed at commercial activity—not inactivity, the refusal to buy an ACA policy.

However, the majority decision—bitterly contested in dissents by the court's conservative wing— found that the individual mandate was authorized under Article I's Taxing and Spending Clause. The penalty on uninsured people who refused to buy ACA coverage was characterized by the court as a tax, not a fine.

WE THE PEOPLE

"The Framers knew the difference between doing something and doing nothing. They gave Congress the power to regulate commerce, not to compel it."

—U.S. Chief Justice John Roberts in his majority decision in *NFIB* v. *Sebelius*

Section 9: Restrictions on Congress

"The Migration or Importation of such Persons as any of the States now existing shall think proper to admit, shall not be prohibited by the Congress prior to the Year one thousand eight hundred and eight, but a Tax or duty may be imposed on such Importation, not exceeding ten dollars for each Person.

"The Privilege of the Writ of Habeas Corpus shall not be suspended, unless when in Cases of Rebellion or Invasion the public Safety may require it.

"No Bill of Attainder or ex post facto Law shall be passed.

"No Capitation, or other direct, Tax shall be laid, *unless in Proportion to the Census of Enumeration herein before directed to be taken.*

"No Tax or Duty shall be laid on Articles exported from any State.

"No Preference shall be given by any Regulation of Commerce or Revenue to the Ports of one State over those of another: nor shall Vessels bound to, or from, one State, be obliged to enter, clear or pay Duties in another.

"No Money shall be drawn from the Treasury, but in Consequence of Appropriations made by Law; and a regular Statement and Account of the Receipts and Expenditures of all public Money shall be published from time to time.

"No Title of Nobility shall be granted by the United States: And no Person holding any Office of Profit or Trust under them, shall, without the Consent of the Congress, accept of any present, Emolument, Office, or Title, of any kind whatever, from any King, Prince or foreign State."

This section is noted, or notorious, for the compromise that allowed the importing of slaves to continue until 1808. Most of the members of the Constitutional Convention in 1787 abhorred slavery—even the slave owners such as Ben Franklin said it was immoral—but they needed to keep the slave-owning states on board. They also allowed a tax of up to $10 per year per slave. On January 1, 1808, the first day it was possible to outlaw bringing new slaves into the country, Congress did so.

There's a bit of irony, perhaps, in one brief phrase in this section. The colonists cherished the right of habeas corpus under British rule, and in fact, it was one of the reasons for the American Revolution. This part of the Constitution prohibits suspending the *writ of habeas corpus* except in cases of rebellion or invasion. The Supreme Court later shored up this provision by holding that habeas corpus could not be suspended as long as the civil courts were operating. This section also bans *bills of attainder* and *ex post facto laws.*

DEFINITION

A **writ of habeas corpus,** from the Latin "you have the body," is a legal order, known as "the Great Writ," from a judge that orders a prisoner be brought in front of the court to determine whether he or she is being held legally. **Bills of attainder** are laws passed by a legislative body to single out one person or group of people for punishment without the usual protections of due process in the judicial system. **Ex post facto laws** are passed "after the fact" and punish people—or increase previous punishments—for actions taken before the laws were passed.

The provision against "direct" taxes led the Supreme Court to declare income taxes unconstitutional until they were expressly legalized by the Sixteenth Amendment.

This section also prohibits Congress from taxing exports from any state, prohibits Congress from granting any titles of nobility, and prevents any American government official from accepting any office or title—or any meaningful gift—from a foreign country. That's why a president can't keep all the loot collected on those grand foreign tours. It all belongs to the people of the United States and is turned over to the government.

Section 10: Restrictions on the States

"No State shall enter into any Treaty, Alliance, or Confederation; grant Letters of Marque and Reprisal; coin Money; emit Bills of Credit; make any Thing but gold and silver Coin a Tender in Payment of Debts; pass any Bill of Attainder, ex post facto Law, or Law impairing the Obligation of Contracts, or grant any Title of Nobility.

"No State shall, without the Consent of the Congress, lay any Imposts or Duties on Imports or Exports, except what may be absolutely necessary for executing its inspection Laws: and the net Produce of all Duties and Imposts, laid by any State on Imports or Exports, shall be for the Use of the Treasury of the United States; and all such Laws shall be subject to the Revision and Controul of the Congress.

"No State shall, without the Consent of Congress, lay any Duty of Tonnage, keep Troops, or Ships of War in time of Peace, enter into any Agreement or Compact with another State, or with a foreign Power, or engage in War, unless actually invaded, or in such imminent Danger as will not admit of delay."

This section aims to make it clear to states that some powers are solely the providence of Congress and the federal government. States are not allowed to enter into treaties or alliances, coin money, tax imports or exports, or have their own warships or standing armies. However, states were allowed to have local militia—today's National Guard—with federal oversight. States also may not declare war or grant titles of nobility. (Presumably a Kentucky colonel is not noble enough to violate the Constitution.)

The first paragraph contains the sometimes-controversial Contracts Clause, which bars states from interfering with contract law. In an 1810 case, *Fletcher* v. *Peck*, the Supreme Court ruled that the state of Georgia could not annul contracts made by corrupt members of the state legislature to sell off state lands, even if the deals were blatant with bribery.

Article II: The Executive Branch

Article II sets out the executive branch of government, including the president and vice president, and defines their authority.

Section 1: President and Vice President

"The executive Power shall be vested in a president of the United States of America. He shall hold his Office during the Term of four Years, and, together with the Vice president, chosen for the same Term, be elected, as follows:

"Each State shall appoint, in such Manner as the Legislature thereof may direct, a Number of Electors, equal to the whole Number of Senators and Representatives to which the State may be entitled in the Congress: but no Senator or Representative, or Person holding an Office of Trust or Profit under the United States, shall be appointed an Elector.

"*The Electors shall meet in their respective States, and vote by Ballot for two Persons, of whom one at least shall not be an Inhabitant of the same State with themselves. And they shall make a List of all the Persons voted for, and of the Number of Votes for each; which List they shall sign and certify, and transmit sealed to the Seat of the Government of the United States, directed to the president of the Senate. The president of the Senate shall, in the Presence of the Senate and House of Representatives, open all the Certificates, and the Votes shall then be counted. The Person having the greatest Number of Votes shall be the president, if such Number be a Majority of the whole Number of Electors appointed; and if there be more than one who have such Majority, and have an equal Number of Votes, then the House of Representatives shall immediately chuse by Ballot one of them for president; and if no Person have a Majority, then from the five highest on the List the said House shall in like Manner chuse the president. But in chusing the president, the Votes shall be taken by States, the Representatives from each State having one Vote; a quorum for this Purpose shall consist of a Member or Members from two thirds of the States, and a Majority of all the States shall be necessary to a Choice. In every Case, after the Choice of the president, the Person having the greatest Number of Votes of the Electors shall be the Vice president. But if there should remain two or more who have equal Votes, the Senate shall chuse from them by Ballot the Vice president.*

"The Congress may determine the Time of chusing the Electors, and the Day on which they shall give their Votes; which Day shall be the same throughout the United States.

"No Person except a natural born Citizen, or a Citizen of the United States, at the time of the Adoption of this Constitution, shall be eligible to the Office of president; neither shall any person be eligible to that Office who shall not have attained to the Age of thirty five Years, and been fourteen Years a Resident within the United States.

"In Case of the Removal of the president from Office, or of his Death, Resignation, or Inability to discharge the Powers and Duties of the said Office, the Same shall devolve on the Vice president, and the Congress may by Law provide for the Case of Removal, Death, Resignation or Inability, both of the president and Vice president, declaring what Officer shall then act as president, and such Officer shall act accordingly, until the Disability be removed, or a president shall be elected.

"The president shall, at stated Times, receive for his Services, a Compensation, which shall neither be encreased nor diminished during the Period for which he shall have been elected, and he shall not receive within that Period any other Emolument from the United States, or any of them.

"Before he enter on the Execution of his Office, he shall take the following Oath or Affirmation:—'I do solemnly swear (or affirm) that I will faithfully execute the Office of president of the United States, and will to the best of my Ability, preserve, protect and defend the Constitution of the United States.'"

The chief executive is called president. Both president and vice president are elected to 4-year terms. The Constitution originally set no limit on the number of terms a president could serve, and George Washington may well have been able to serve as many 4-year terms as he wanted. Washington thought no more than two terms were proper, and every president followed that tradition until Franklin Delano Roosevelt, who was elected four times. After his death, the Twenty-Second Amendment officially limited the president to two terms.

The president and vice president are not elected directly by the people but instead by electors chosen by the state legislatures. Each state has the same number of electors as it has members in Congress—representatives and senators combined. However, no representatives or senators can serve as electors.

Today, there are 538 electors in what came to be known as the Electoral College, representing 100 senators, 435 representatives, and 3 representatives from the District of Columbia. A presidential ticket (president and vice president) that wins a state is presumed to win all the electoral votes from that state. On election night, returns are counted unofficially, state by state, and a presidential candidate is declared the winner by amassing 270 or more electoral votes, a majority.

The original language, calling for each elector to vote for two candidates, one of them from a different state, proved cumbersome as the House struggled before declaring Thomas Jefferson the new president after a tie vote with Aaron Burr in 1800. Under changes implemented by the Twelfth Amendment, after a national election in November, electors officially cast their ballots in December for both president and vice president, and Congress formally counts those votes in January. If no candidate has a majority of the electoral votes, the House of Representatives chooses the next president and vice president.

In practice, the actual popular vote does not count, and there have been instances of a presidential candidate getting the most votes nationally but losing the election. That's what happened in 2000, when George W. Bush won more electoral votes even though more people across the nation voted for Al Gore.

Section 1 of Article II also requires that both the president and the vice president be "natural born" citizens who are at least 35 years and who have lived in the United States for at least 14 years. However, no courts have ruled on what "natural born" means, and whether it applies to citizens born in overseas territories or to parents who are citizens living in other countries. The eligibility requirements have ruled out presidential bids for a number of popular figures over the years. For example, it would take a Constitutional amendment to allow Austrian-born Arnold Schwarzenegger to become president. Two other prominent popular public figures who were considered presidential timber, at least in some circles, but were ineligible for being born abroad included statesman and lawyer Frederick Lehman, born in Prussia in 1853, and comedian Bob Hope, born in England in 1903.

The Twenty-Fifth Amendment superseded the section on succession, providing for the vice president to assume the presidency if the president is disabled or leaves office. This section also prohibits Congress from changing a president's salary ($400,000 a year as of the 4-year term expiring in 2008) during that term and prohibits the president from accepting any other pay while in office.

The familiar oath of office administered by the chief justice at the inauguration, beginning, "I do solemnly swear that I will faithfully execute the office of the president …," is also spelled out in this section.

WE THE PEOPLE

When George Washington took the oath of office, he ad libbed, "So help me God," at the end. Every president since then has added it, too.

Section 2: Presidential Powers

"The president shall be Commander in Chief of the Army and Navy of the United States, and of the Militia of the several States, when called into the actual Service of the United States; he may require the Opinion, in writing, of the principal Officer in each of the executive Departments, upon any Subject relating to the Duties of their respective Offices, and he shall have Power to Grant Reprieves and Pardons for Offences against the United States, except in Cases of Impeachment.

"He shall have Power, by and with the Advice and Consent of the Senate, to make Treaties, provided two thirds of the Senators present concur; and he shall nominate, and by and with the Advice and Consent of the Senate, shall appoint Ambassadors, other public Ministers and Consuls, Judges of the supreme Court, and all other Officers of the United States, whose Appointments are not herein otherwise provided for, and which shall be established by Law: but the Congress may by Law vest the Appointment of such inferior Officers, as they think proper, in the president alone, in the Courts of Law, or in the Heads of Departments.

"The president shall have Power to fill up all Vacancies that may happen during the Recess of the Senate, by granting Commissions which shall expire at the End of their next Session."

The president is commander in chief of the military, has the authority to grant pardons or reprieves, and may require "the principal officer" of executive departments—Cabinet officers, in other words—to offer written advice. The president can make treaties with the approval of the Senate and can appoint judges and ambassadors, also with the approval of the Senate.

This section specifically authorizes the "recess" appointments that have become controversial under recent presidents. Rather than risking a tough confirmation battle and possible rejection, presidents can appoint judges and other officials while the Senate is in recess and cannot confirm the nominations. The political thinking holds that it is more difficult for the Senate to reject a nominee who is already serving.

The president—this article specifies "he" but presumably applies if and when a woman is elected president—can fire many appointed officials but not federal judges, who are appointed for life to insulate them from political pressures.

Section 3: Executive Responsibility

"He shall from time to time give to the Congress Information on the State of the Union, and recommend to their Consideration such Measures as he shall judge necessary and expedient; he may, on extraordinary Occasions, convene both Houses, or either of them, and in Case of Disagreement between them, with Respect to the Time of Adjournment, he may adjourn them to such Time as he shall think proper; he shall receive Ambassadors and other public Ministers; he shall take Care that the Laws be faithfully executed, and shall Commission all the Officers of the United States."

This section lists a number of presidential responsibilities, including making an annual State of the Union speech to Congress, calling the House or Senate or both into special session, commissioning military and Foreign Service officers, receiving foreign ambassadors, and generally executing or enforcing the laws of the United States.

WE THE PEOPLE

Thomas Jefferson thought personally delivering a State of the Union speech was too much like a king making an address. Instead, he sent a written summary to Congress that was read by a clerk. Every subsequent president did the same until Woodrow Wilson returned to Congress and made the speech himself. That's what every president since Wilson has done.

The "missing clause" from this section covers executive privilege—a president's authority to withhold information from the courts, Congress, and the public. The Supreme Court has agreed that the president does have limited executive privilege but cannot withhold information simply by claiming that releasing it would harm the presidency or threaten national security. Richard Nixon, for example, tried to withhold the secret tapes from his office on the grounds of executive privilege, but the Supreme Court rejected his claim and ordered the tapes released, which led to Nixon's resignation in the face of possible impeachment.

Section 4: Impeachment

> "The president, Vice president and all Civil Officers of the United States, shall be removed from Office on Impeachment for and Conviction of, Treason, Bribery, or other high Crimes and Misdemeanors."

This section allows Congress to remove the president, vice president, and other members of the executive branch, as well as federal judges. The House votes for impeachment, and the Senate then sits as the jury at a trial. If convicted, the official is removed from office and may be barred from holding any other federal government post.

The contentious part of this section is what constitutes "high crimes and misdemeanors." In practical matters, the House decides what are or aren't high crimes and misdemeanors.

Article III: The Judicial Branch

This article sets forth the federal court system, including the Supreme Court. It outlines the rules for appointing judges and establishes the authority of the courts.

Section 1: Federal Courts

> "The judicial Power of the United States, shall be vested in one supreme Court, and in such inferior Courts as the Congress may from time to time ordain and establish. The Judges, both of the supreme and inferior Courts, shall hold their Offices during good Behaviour, and shall, at stated Times, receive for their Services, a Compensation, which shall not be diminished during their Continuance in Office."

This section makes it clear that there will be one, and only one, Supreme Court and leaves it to Congress to create the lesser federal courts. The main courts today are the District Courts, but there are also regional Circuit Courts of Appeal, an intermediate level where losers in the District Courts can appeal. The Supreme Court generally hears only cases that have been appealed from the Circuit Courts.

Federal judges are appointed by the president with the approval of the Senate and can be removed only through impeachment, which is so rare that it has happened only a handful of times in American history.

Section 2: Jurisdiction and Judicial Review

"The judicial Power shall extend to all Cases, in Law and Equity, arising under this Constitution, the Laws of the United States, and Treaties made, or which shall be made, under their Authority;—to all Cases affecting Ambassadors, other public ministers and Consuls;—to all Cases of admiralty and maritime Jurisdiction;— to Controversies to which the United States shall be a Party;—to Controversies between two or more States;—between a State and Citizens of another State;— between Citizens of different States;—between Citizens of the same State claiming Lands under Grants of different States, and between a State, or the Citizens thereof, and foreign States, Citizens or Subjects.

"In all Cases affecting Ambassadors, other public Ministers and Consuls, and those in which a State shall be Party, the supreme Court shall have original Jurisdiction. In all the other Cases before mentioned, the Supreme Court shall have appellate Jurisdiction, both as to Law and Fact, with such Exceptions, and under such Regulations as the Congress shall make.

"The Trial of all Crimes, except in Cases of Impeachment, shall be by Jury; and such Trial shall be held in the State where the said Crimes shall have been committed; but when not committed within any State, the Trial shall be at such Place or Places as the Congress may by Law have directed."

This section makes it clear that the federal courts have jurisdiction for all cases arising from the Constitution or from federal law and for all conflicts that cross state lines, such as disputes between different states or lawsuits between citizens of different states. However, the Eleventh Amendment prevents a state from being sued in federal court. Federal courts also have jurisdiction over all cases involving foreign governments and admiralty and maritime cases. This section also guarantees the right to trial by jury in criminal cases and lists certain cases that can be taken up directly by the Supreme Court without appeal from lower courts.

One of the biggest issues surrounding the federal judiciary, from the earliest days of the United States through today, is the authority of the courts to review, and overturn, laws and regulations enacted by other branches of the government. On one hand, the Constitution never specifically mentions judicial review; on the other, the system of checks and balances would not work nearly as effectively if it was up to Congress and the president to decide whether their actions were constitutional or not.

CASES

Marbury v. Madison **(1803):** Without the principle set forth in this landmark case, the system of checks and balances might not work as well, or at all. The decision by Chief Justice John Marshall established the concept of judicial review by declaring an act of Congress unconstitutional for the first time. Since then, the Supreme Court has reinforced its authority to overrule laws and regulations approved by the other branches of government in more than 120 other cases.

A court can overturn existing law—literally throw it out and wipe it off the books—by finding that the law is itself illegal. This is what happens, for example, when a law is declared unconstitutional. Besides nullifying legislation, a court also can declare administrative regulations and procedures illegal. Sometimes the courts offer suggestions or guidelines about how to correct the procedures. This is what has happened in a series of court rulings that shaped the way the death penalty is administered by states. A new set of rules or guidelines set forth by a court stands as the law unless and until superseded by legislative action or a higher-court ruling.

A court can overturn existing laws, regulations, and procedures by finding that they violate existing law, including the Constitution. Our judicial system follows precedent, which means courts also can overturn all or part of existing laws because of conflicts with previous court rulings. Courts are typically reluctant to overturn their own precedents, and the Supreme Court has been known to go through gymnastics of creative reasoning to reach a desired result without flatly overruling an earlier court decision.

In truth, however, courts can find many reasons for overturning existing law, including "public policy." Whatever the reason, critics often complain about judicial activism and criticize "activist judges" for overturning legislation approved by the public's elected representatives.

The debate continues today, in law schools, on blogs, in courtrooms, and within the chambers of the Supreme Court itself: when and how the courts can and should exert the authority to review legislation.

WE THE PEOPLE

Have there ever been two U.S. Supreme Court justices serving at the same time who were so different in legal philosophy, social views, and temperament? Justice Antonin Scalia, the fiery-tongued originalist who liked to cite the founding fathers' original intention, and Ruth Bader Ginsburg, the coolly calm, social-minded liberal, often sparred in their court decisions but were close friends off the bench and shared a love of opera.

Section 3: Treason

"Treason against the United States, shall consist only in levying War against them, or in adhering to their Enemies, giving them Aid and Comfort. No Person shall be convicted of Treason unless on the Testimony of two Witnesses to the same overt Act, or on Confession in open Court.

"The Congress shall have Power to declare the Punishment of Treason, but no Attainder of Treason shall work Corruption of Blood, or Forfeiture except during the Life of the Person attainted."

Treason, the only federal crime specified in the Constitution, is defined as an act of war against the United States, or lending "aid and comfort" to its enemies. Cases of treason have been rare in American history, although there are some notable instances. Former Vice President Aaron Burr, fleeing murder charges after killing Alexander Hamilton in a duel in 1804, was tried and acquitted of treason in 1807 after being accused of trying to muster an army to establish a rival nation, perhaps in Mexico, with himself as president.

Many wanted the so-called American Taliban, John Walker Lindh, to be charged with treason after being captured fighting American troops in Afghanistan in 2001, but Walker ended up accepting a 20-year sentence and agreeing to plead guilty to lesser charges.

The Least You Need to Know

- The three branches of government—executive, legislative, and judicial—operate in a system of checks and balances designed to keep any one branch from exerting too much power.

- The legislative branch is the bicameral Congress—made up of the House of Representatives, with 435 districts set by population, and the Senate, which includes two members from each state—and is empowered to approve federal laws.

- The president is the chief executive, whose power comes from the constitutional obligation to administer the government and execute and enforce its laws.

- The judiciary's ultimate power in the system of checks and balances comes from the principle of judicial review, which allows the federal courts to throw out laws and regulations for violating the Constitution.

CHAPTER 5

Articles IV Through VII: Making the Federal System Work

Articles IV, V, VI, and VII together establish a framework for relationships among the states and their relationships with the federal government, including provisions for admitting new states to the union and amending the Constitution.

Article IV: Full Faith and Credit

In many ways, the original 13 colonies viewed themselves, and each other, as more like independent mini-nations than as part of a single entity, and one colony did not necessarily have to respect the laws of another colony. The Articles of Confederation allowed the fledgling states to maintain much of that independence from each other. Article IV of the Constitution, however, redefined the relationships among the states, requiring them to recognize and honor each other's laws.

Section 1: Full Faith and Credit

"Full faith and credit shall be given in each state to the public acts, records, and judicial proceedings of every other state. And the Congress may by general laws prescribe the manner in which such acts, records, and proceedings shall be proved, and the effect thereof."

The Full Faith and Credit Clause is one of the most important in the Constitution. The clause requires the states to honor each other's laws, records (including licenses), and court decisions. If you win a legal case in one state, that same case cannot be reopened in another state.

One of the key factors back when the Constitution was being debated was that this provision would allow a plantation owner from a slave-holding state to travel with his slave to a nonslave state and the slave would not become free merely by setting foot in a free state. Without this provision today, your driver's license might not be recognized by the next state.

The Full Faith and Credit Clause has had a major significance on domestic law, including marriage and child custody issues. For example, it presents a major obstacle to a divorced parent who is unhappy with a court's child custody orders in one state and takes the kid to another state to seek a new custody order.

 CASES

"The primary purpose of this clause," the Supreme Court said of the Full Faith and Credit Clause in a 1948 case, "was to help fuse into one Nation a collection of independent sovereign States."

And without this section of the Constitution, your spur-of-the-moment marriage in Las Vegas might not be recognized back home. Hawaii sent ripples across the mainland's legal landscape in 1993, when the state courts recognized gay marriage. Three years later, Congress enacted the

Defense of Marriage Act, which defined marriage as between a man and a woman. The act also said that despite the Full Faith and Credit Clause, states could refuse to recognize same-sex marriages recognized as legal in other states.

That all changed, of course, with the subsequent Supreme Court rulings citing constitutional grounds beyond the Full Faith and Credit Act that struck down the Defense of Marriage Act and recognized same-sex marriage in all 50 states (see Chapter 13).

Section 2: Privileges and Immunities

"The citizens of each state shall be entitled to all privileges and immunities of citizens in the several states.

"A person charged in any state with treason, felony, or other crime, who shall flee from justice, and be found in another state, shall on demand of the executive authority of the state from which he fled, be delivered up, to be removed to the state having jurisdiction of the crime.

"No person held to service or labor in one state, under the laws thereof, escaping into another, shall, in consequence of any law or regulation there, be discharged from such service or labor, but shall be delivered up on claim of the party to whom such service or labor may be due."

The Privileges and Immunities Clause was a key part of the framers' desire to create a seamless nationwide economic union, where residents of one state could work and travel and do business in other states, too. This clause ensures that when you visit another state, you have the same rights and privileges as the residents of that state have, and states you are visiting cannot discriminate against you just because you are a nonresident. For example, a state cannot say you have to be a resident of that state to get a job there.

However, the courts have outlined some exceptions. For example, you cannot vote in another state without meeting that state's requirements, including residency.

WHAT IT MEANS TO YOU

Despite the Privileges and Immunities Clause, the courts have ruled that states can charge nonresidents higher fees for services or privileges that residents support with their taxes. For example, nonresidents can be required to pay more for their fishing licenses, and out-of-state tuition can be higher at state-funded colleges and universities for nonresidents.

The second part of this section provides for extradition—the return of an accused criminal to the state where the alleged crime occurred. If you commit a crime in one state and run away to another state, the police in that state can arrest you and hold you. The state where the offense allegedly occurred can then request extradition. You can fight it in court, but accused prisoners are usually routinely extradited.

CASES

Mahon v. Justice **(1888):** When an armed posse from Kentucky captured a suspected criminal in West Virginia and took him back to Kentucky for trial, the accused man appealed. The Supreme Court nonetheless ruled he could be tried and convicted in Kentucky.

The final part of this section, the Fugitive Slave Clause, allowed slave owners to pursue runaways into nonslave states and bring them back. It was overturned by the Thirteenth Amendment.

Section 3: The Equal Footing Clause

"New states may be admitted by the Congress into this union; but no new states shall be formed or erected within the jurisdiction of any other state; nor any state be formed by the junction of two or more states, or parts of states, without the consent of the legislatures of the states concerned as well as of the Congress.

"The Congress shall have power to dispose of and make all needful rules and regulations respecting the territory or other property belonging to the United States; and nothing in this Constitution shall be so construed as to prejudice any claims of the United States, or of any particular state."

The framers of the Constitution envisioned the United States growing. More states could be created as areas of the Western frontier—such as what is now Tennessee and Ohio—were settled. And perhaps the new nation would acquire more of the foreign-held land west of the Mississippi River. This section of the Constitution allows for Congress to admit new states to the union. But Congress has to give permission. The District of Columbia, for example, tried to become the fifty-first state but was turned down by Congress in 1993.

This section says no new state could include land that had been within another state, unless that state approved. In addition, a new state could not be formed by a merger of two states unless they both approved. No hostile takeovers, in other words. Out of the original 13 colonies, 5 additional states were created: Vermont was originally part of New York, Kentucky was part of Virginia, Tennessee was part of North Carolina, Maine was part of Massachusetts, and West Virginia was part of Virginia.

In the latter case, Virginia didn't actually approve of creating West Virginia. But when West Virginia declared independence and asked Congress for approval to become a state soon after the Civil War ended, the Reconstruction Congress said Virginia had forfeited its right to keep West Virginia by fighting on the Confederate side in the war.

This section doesn't specifically address the issue, but subsequent court cases have held that new states would have equal status to the other states. "Equality of constitutional right and power is the condition of all the States of the Union, old and new," the Supreme Court ruled in an 1883 case. Similarly, new states cannot have more powers than the other states. Texas was an independent nation before it joined the Union and, like most independent nations, claimed authority over waters up to 3 miles from its shore. When Texas became a state, however, it ceded that authority to the federal government, just like the other states did. The federal government also has control of all public lands within the states as well as authority over American-owned territories, including American Samoa, Guam, Puerto Rico, and the Virgin Islands.

There are no provisions in the Constitution for a state to withdraw or secede. So just as Northern California cannot secede from the rest of California and declare itself a state, it cannot secede and declare itself an independent nation. The courts have held that the Constitution stands for the "perpetuity and indissolubility of the Union"—and of course, the federal government launched the bloodiest war in American history when the Confederate states, using the same reasoning and even some of the same language as the Declaration of Independence, tried to declare themselves a new and separate nation.

Section 4: The Guarantee Clause

"The United States shall guarantee to every state in this union a republican form of government, and shall protect each of them against invasion; and on application of the legislature, or of the executive (when the legislature cannot be convened) against domestic violence."

The Guarantee Clause says that the federal government will ensure each and every state has a "republican" form of government, but the clause doesn't define *republican*. One theory is that it simply means there can never be a king of Nebraska. A more practical view is that every state must have a government of representatives elected by the people.

Luther v. Borden **(1849):** In this case from Rhode Island, the Supreme Court said it is up to Congress, not the courts—not even the Supreme Court—to decide whether a state has a "republican" form of government. In effect, if Congress admits a state's representatives and senators, it has a republican form of government.

Section 4 of Article IV also provides for the federal government to protect the states against invasion and domestic violence. The president's authority to call in troops even without a state's request was established in 1894. Railroad workers for the Pullman Palace Car Company went on strike in Chicago and severely disrupted the nation's commercial transportation system. President Grover Cleveland sent in 2,000 Army troops to end the strike on the grounds that it was interfering with the delivery of the U.S. mail.

A president also has the authority to call on a state militia—the National Guard—but this power took an odd turn in 1957 in Arkansas. A federal court had ordered the public schools in Little Rock to desegregate, but Governor Orval Faubus vowed to block any attempt to allow black children to integrate white-only schools. President Dwight Eisenhower nationalized the Arkansas National Guard, not to enforce the integration, but to temporarily remove the Guard from Faubus's control. Eisenhower then sent in regular Army troops to ensure the schools were integrated.

Ironically, this provision of the Constitution was originally approved in 1787 because of Southern states' fears of slave uprisings.

Article V: Amending the Constitution

"The Congress, whenever two thirds of both Houses shall deem it necessary, shall propose Amendments to this Constitution, or, on the Application of the Legislatures of two thirds of the several States, shall call a Convention for proposing Amendments, which, in either Case, shall be valid to all Intents and Purposes, as Part of this Constitution, when ratified by the Legislatures of three fourths of the several States, or by Conventions in three fourths thereof, as the one or the other Mode of Ratification may be proposed by the Congress; Provided that no Amendment which may be made prior to the Year One thousand eight hundred and eight shall in any Manner affect the first and fourth Clauses in the Ninth Section of the first Article; and that no State, without its Consent, shall be deprived of its equal Suffrage in the Senate."

The framers of the Constitution wanted to make it difficult to change the Supreme Law of the Land and established two methods of amending the Constitution. One has never been used: a new Constitutional Convention. Two thirds of the states (34 of 50) can petition Congress for a new convention, but there have long been misgivings that a convention might have the authority to go beyond the amendment on the table. The Constitution has always held such a sacrosanct place in American democracy that few people would want to open it up to a wholesale retinkering. If and when a full-blown Constitutional Convention would take place, three quarters of the states (38 of 50) would have to ratify an amendment for it to go into effect.

The more common and accepted manner of amending the Constitution calls for both houses of Congress to approve the proposed amendment by two-thirds majorities. The proposed amendment is then sent to the states for ratification. A proposed amendment is usually considered by the state legislature, and again, three quarters of the states must approve for ratification.

The Constitution sets no time limit on the ratification process, except to say it must be "reasonable." In practical terms, this means it is up to Congress. Ordinarily in recent times, Congress has said that a proposed amendment must be ratified within 7 years to take effect or else it expires. However, the Twenty-Seventh Amendment, limiting congressional pay raises, was originally proposed in 1789 but not approved until 1992, more than 200 years later.

Article VI: The Supreme Law of the Land

"All Debts contracted and Engagements entered into, before the Adoption of this Constitution, shall be as valid against the United States under this Constitution, as under the Confederation.

"This Constitution, and the Laws of the United States which shall be made in Pursuance thereof; and all Treaties made, or which shall be made, under the Authority of the United States, shall be the supreme Law of the Land; and the Judges in every State shall be bound thereby, any Thing in the Constitution or Laws of any state to the Contrary notwithstanding.

"The Senators and Representatives before mentioned, and the Members of the several State Legislatures, and all executive and judicial Officers, both of the United States and of the several States, shall be bound by Oath or Affirmation, to support this Constitution; but no religious Test shall ever be required as a Qualification to any Office or public Trust under the United States."

Article VI is an incongruous mix of a centuries-old bookkeeping footnote and a sweeping historical precedent called the "linchpin of the Constitution." The first part of the Article is straightforward bean counting: the new U.S. government will assume the debts of the old government that operated under the Articles of Confederation.

The second part, however, is the Supremacy Clause, the glue that holds together the whole crazy idea of a democracy wrapped in a republic wrapped in a federal system wrapped in a system of checks and balances. In effect, the clause says the Constitution, federal laws, and treaties take precedence over state laws, and all judges must follow that rule. In other words, any law in conflict with the Constitution is invalid. Without the Supremacy Clause, states could be mini-nations unto themselves, passing any laws of their own, refusing to acknowledge the laws of other states, and ignoring the federal laws of the United States.

The final section of Article VI buttresses the Supreme Clause by requiring all government officials, both state and federal, to give precedence to the U.S. Constitution over any state constitution or other laws.

The "religious test" phrasing prohibits any sort of religious requirement or restriction on holding any federal office. This requirement was extended to state officeholders under the Equal Protection Clause of the Fourteenth Amendment.

Article VII: Ratification

"The Ratification of the Conventions of nine States, shall be sufficient for the Establishment of this Constitution between the States so ratifying the same."

The article that specifies how the proposed new Constitution will be ratified offers another of those delicious little ironies and contradictions from 1787.

The Constitutional Convention was held under the Articles of Confederation, right? And the Articles of Confederation required the approval of all 13 states for any major changes, right? So why did the framers at the Constitutional Convention decide only 9 of 13 states needed to approve the new Constitution? And what gave them the authority to change the rules midstream?

The answers are pretty simple. The men who gathered in Philadelphia that hot summer were not confident all the states would vote for ratification. They didn't even want to take a chance by requiring 10 states—enough for the three-quarters majority they specified for approving any future amendments—to vote to ratify. They thought 9 had a decent chance, so they said 9. And their only authority to change the rule was that they went ahead and changed the rule. And like the Constitution itself, everybody agreed to go along.

The Least You Need to Know

- The Constitution prohibits any state you visit, whether for work or leisure, to discriminate against you simply because you are not a resident.
- States can charge more for some services, such as out-of-state tuition at state universities that are supported by residents' tax dollars.
- If Congress approves a constitutional amendment, three quarters of the states (38 of 50) must ratify before it changes the Constitution.
- The Constitution and federal laws take precedence over state laws.

Your Basic Rights

Many Americans think they know their rights, but most of us have at least a few misconceptions, if not downright misinterpretations. Part 3 concentrates on landmark court decisions telling us what the Constitution means and how that affects everyday Americans in everyday life.

We also examine the impact of the Bill of Rights on our lives, along with other amendments that affect individual liberties and civil rights.

CHAPTER 6

The First Amendment: Freedom of Expression

"Congress shall make no law respecting an establishment of religion, or prohibiting the free exercise thereof; or abridging the freedom of speech, or of the press; or the right of the people peaceably to assemble, and to petition the Government for a redress of grievances."

In This Chapter

- Freedom of religion
- Freedom of speech
- Freedom of the press
- Freedom of assembly
- Freedom to petition

At the 1787 Constitutional Convention, the framers argued vehemently over whether their new Constitution needed provisions that specifically protected individual rights.

On one hand, the anti-Federalists wanted a list of individual liberties—a Bill of Rights—to restrain the authority of the new national government. On the other hand, the Federalists argued that a national government could enhance rather than inhibit individual liberty. The Federalists believed the premise of the Constitution—that people grant rights to the government rather than the other way around—provided adequate protection for "natural" rights. The Federalists were also afraid that if the framers tried to list individual liberties in the Constitution, anything that wasn't listed would not be protected, that listing individual rights might actually lead to more limitations on personal freedom.

As a result of the anti-Federalist sentiment, and in response to calls from the states for specific protections for individual liberties, the Bill of Rights was proposed in the form of the first 10 amendments to the Constitution. Ratified in 1791 (although Georgia, Massachusetts, and Connecticut did not formally ratify the amendments until 1939), the Bill of Rights strives to establish a delicate balance within a democracy. Yes, the will of the majority should rule. But no, the majority should not be able to limit personal freedom as long as it doesn't intrude on other individuals or society. Individual rights should not be subject to the domination of the majority and should not be limited by a popular vote.

The First Amendment, also called the Great Amendment, is in many ways the cornerstone of America's free, open, and tolerant society. It's the basis of a democracy that prizes individual liberty. The amendment protects the freedom of religion, press, speech, assembly, and petition. It guarantees that Americans can share the information they need for a robust public debate on the issues and act on the issues.

> **WE THE PEOPLE**
>
> In the 1943 Supreme Court case *West Virginia State Board of Education* v. *Barnette*, Justice Robert Jackson noted that "if there is any fixed star in our constitutional constellation, it is that no official, high or petty, can prescribe what shall be orthodox in politics, nationalism, religion, or force citizens to confess by word or act their faith therein."

The First Amendment

It's important to note that the five freedoms protected by the First Amendment are not merely related. The way the framers presented them, in order, they build upon each other. The freedom of religion protects how you believe, think, and feel. Freedom of speech allows you to express your thoughts and beliefs. Freedom of the press guarantees your ability to spread the word more broadly about your thoughts and beliefs. Freedom of assembly protects your right to get together with other people to share views, debate, and plan. Freedom to petition gives citizens the right to join together to express opposition to government action and ask for changes and maybe compensation.

The five freedoms specifically protected in the First Amendment are not mutually exclusive, of course, so there has been considerable overlap in real-life cases. Freedom of religion is sometimes also freedom of speech, for example, and freedom of speech is sometimes also freedom of the press or freedom to petition. Taken together, the rights protected in the First Amendment are categorized as freedom of expression.

Beginning with "Congress shall make no law …," the First Amendment originally applied only to federal limitations on individual rights. However, the Fourteenth Amendment, ratified in 1868, granted equal protection under the laws to all citizens. Under the Fourteenth Amendment's Incorporation Doctrine, the Supreme Court eventually extended the protections of the First Amendment, along with virtually all the rest of the Bill of Rights, to apply to state actions, too.

Perhaps no other part of the Constitution reflects the changes we have seen in American government, society, and culture as clearly. As times have changed, our standards have changed for the way we look at many aspects of society, including what is obscene, what is offensive, what is dangerous, and what is a threat to national security.

Largely because of its tension between individual rights and the protection of society, the First Amendment remains controversial and is often the battleground for arguments over what is right and wrong, and what is good and bad, in our culture. That is why First Amendment cases are so often where legal scholars lock horns over the two widely different views of the Constitution in modern society: if you disagree with a ruling, you are more likely to say the "activist" court went too far in making a new law that was not intended by the Constitution; if you agree with a ruling, you are more likely to say the court did a proper job of interpreting the Constitution.

It frequently has been left to the Supreme Court, the court of last resort, to decide exactly what is or is not legal or illegal under the First Amendment. It is remarkable to think that so many of those decisions are made, and will be made, by nine middle-aged to elderly lawyers—and sometimes the most momentous cases are determined by 5–4 decisions. If one justice would change his or her vote, the result would be the opposite.

Indeed, it is not hard to find similar court cases, with comparable sets of facts and decided by the same nine justices, where one case has been decided 5–4 on one side of an issue and the other case has been decided 5–4 on the other side of the issue after a single justice changed votes.

Freedom of Religion

Many early colonists came to the New World to escape religious persecution, but once they got here, they themselves did not necessarily practice religious freedom or tolerance. Many early American communities ostracized and sometimes punished people for not following their religion or even their sect of a shared religion. They came to America to practice *their* religion, not to let you practice yours.

From Massachusetts to Virginia, the colonial Baptists seemed particularly prone to persecution. They were thrown in jail for offenses as varied as failing to follow the official Church of England teachings to refusing to pay taxes to support other churches preferred by colonial officials.

In 1663, the Charter of Rhode Island guaranteed religion freedom; in 1708, Connecticut guaranteed "full liberty of worship"; and by the time the framers were considering a new constitution, they were in general agreement that there would not be a national religion. Jefferson, Madison, and other framers talked up separation of church and state, using those words.

> **WE THE PEOPLE**
>
> "No man shall be compelled to frequent or support any religious worship, place, or ministry whatsoever."
>
> —Thomas Jefferson

The First Amendment guarantees the government will not prefer one religion over another. It also guarantees the government will not prefer religion in general over nonreligion or the lack of religion, and it will not prefer nonreligion over religion.

One example is a 1994 case in which the Supreme Court struck down a New York state law that outlined a school district conforming to the borders of Kiryas Joel, a settlement of Hasidic Jewish families, to create its own school district. The court said that action amounted to special treatment for a religious group and was, therefore, unconstitutional.

The protections for religion in the First Amendment are two-pronged. The Establishment Clause says "Congress shall make no law respecting an establishment of religion," while the Exercise Clause says "or prohibiting the free exercise thereof." The Establishment Clause is considered absolute; the government cannot prohibit you or anyone else from establishing or following your own religion.

There are many limitations, however, in the interpretations of the Exercise Clause: you can believe in your religion, but that does not give you the right to practice it any way you want. And there may be restrictions on what you can do in the name of your religion.

Religious Practices

The Exercise Clause covers religious practices. That might be something we do because our religion encourages or requires it, or it might be something we *don't* do because our religion *prohibits* it.

In one of the first religion cases to come before the Supreme Court, a Utah man asked the justices to overturn a federal law prohibiting polygamy, saying having more than one wife was part of his Mormon religion. The court upheld the polygamy law, reasoning that religion was not a license for extreme behavior. After all, some ancient religions allowed human sacrifice.

The Supreme Court considered a spate of First Amendment religion cases in the mid-twentieth century, many of them involving Jehovah's Witnesses appealing against local laws aimed at keeping them from practicing the "witness" part of their faith by going door to door and handing out leaflets. One law that was overturned required them to have permits; another let authorities charge them with littering for leaving their leaflets around town.

WHAT IT MEANS TO YOU

The freedom of religion, like the rest of the First Amendment, is designed primarily to protect beliefs, not actions. The government cannot punish you for what you think, but it can punish you for committing illegal acts because of what you think or believe.

In general, the courts must find a "compelling interest" for the government to overcome a religious practice, as in a 1972 case, *Wisconsin* v. *Yoder,* in which the Supreme Court said Amish children cannot be required to stay in school beyond the eighth grade if it violates their religion. On the other hand, in a 1990 case, the court denied the appeal of two workers who were fired for using peyote on the job, claiming it was part of their religion. The court said that does not give them immunity from "an otherwise valid law prohibiting conduct the State is free to regulate." A later court case struck down a Hialeah, Florida, ordinance banning ritual animal slaughter by Santeria followers while at the same time allowing kosher butcher shops to operate.

In recent years, the Exercise Clause has become the focal point of reaction to gay rights and equal marriage, especially since the U.S. Supreme Court struck down the federal Defense of Marriage Act in *Windsor* v. *United States* in 2013 (see Chapter 9) and legalized same-sex marriage in all 50 states in *Obergefell* v. *Hodges* in 2015 (see Chapter 13).

Those decisions recognizing the rights of people in same-sex marriages are in conflict with another Supreme Court decision, *Burwell* v. *Hobby Lobby Stores, Inc.* This 2014 decision held that employers could not be required to provide employees free access to contraception. The employers in the case argued that their religious beliefs against contraception prohibited them from enabling contraception for anyone else and that those beliefs were protected by their right to exercise their religion under the First Amendment. The question remains: does my right to have a gay wedding mean you have to sell me flowers? Or does my religious objection to gay marriage mean I don't have to sell you flowers?

> **WE THE PEOPLE**
>
> Justice Ruth Bader Ginsburg had long been a staunch liberal voice on the Supreme Court, but her 35-page dissent in *Hobby Lobby* helped turn her into a twenty-first-century feminist icon. Soon after she wrote it, "The Notorious RBG" began appearing on social media, T-shirts, coffee cups, and even a book of the same name. During a post-*Hobby Lobby* interview, Ginsburg said, "They have no constitutional right to foist that belief on the hundreds and hundreds of women who work for them and who don't share that belief."

Evolution

It never got to the Supreme Court, but a famous trial in 1925 in Dayton, Tennessee, drew the lines in the ongoing debate over teaching evolution and creationism—science versus religion—in public schools. In the so-called Scopes Monkey Trial, famed orator and four-time presidential candidate William Jennings Bryan led the prosecution of schoolteacher John Thomas Scopes for violating a state law against teaching evolution. Clarence Darrow, one of the most highly regarded defense attorneys in U.S. legal annals, represented Scopes in a trial that riveted the nation's attention. In the end, Scopes was convicted.

In 1968, the Supreme Court overturned an Arkansas law prohibiting the teaching of evolution. The court ruled that the law, which made it illegal "to teach the theory or doctrine that mankind ascended or descended from a lower order of animals," was a violation of the Establishment Clause.

In the 1987 case *Edwards* v. *Aguillard,* the Supreme Court struck down a Louisiana law that said if teachers talk about evolution, they also must talk about creationism.

In 2005, in *Kitzmiller* v. *Dover Area School District,* the Supreme Court held that it was an unconstitutional establishment of religion for schools to require the teaching of intelligent design.

Parochial Schools

Financial aid to private schools with religious affiliations has been and continues to be an issue. In a 1970 case, the court said religious organizations could be exempt from income and property taxes. The following year, it held that government financial aid to religious schools is permissible under the First Amendment, as long as the aid has a secular purpose, neither advances nor inhibits religion, and does not "excessively tangle" government and religion. However, local governments cannot pay part of the salaries of parochial school teachers and cannot "purchase" services from parochial schools as a way of providing financial support.

In one of the church-and-state questions that has not been fully decided, the Supreme Court has ruled that sometimes it may be permissible for state and local government authorities to provide financial aid to parents who send their children to parochial schools, provided the aid goes to the parents rather than to the religious schools.

In a pair of 1973 cases, the Supreme Court held that public funding could not be allocated to help low-income families pay their children's tuition at parochial schools. But that ruling was modified in a 1983 Minnesota case, *Mueller* v. *Allen,* which granted tax breaks to parents for sending their kids to private schools.

In a number of cases, the courts have said the First Amendment does not prevent government financial assistance to colleges and universities with religious affiliations.

In more recent cases, the high court has approved state use of federal money for a program providing educational materials and equipment to both public and private schools as well as a Cleveland school vouchers program. In the Cleveland case, opponents said it was unconstitutional government support for religious education, but the Supreme Court said vouchers, like tax breaks, were legal as long as they went to parents rather than to churches or church schools.

School Prayer

In 1962, the Supreme Court ruled that the New York Board of Regents violated the First Amendment by requiring a prayer, written to be nondenominational, to be recited in public schools. The following year, the court ruled that public schools cannot require daily Bible readings or recitations, including the Lord's Prayer. Justice Tom Clark wrote, "They are religious exercises, required by the States in violation of the command of the First Amendment that the Government maintain strict neutrality, neither aiding nor opposing religion."

A 1985 Supreme Court case overturned an Alabama law allowing schools to have a 1-minute period of silence at the start of the school day. It might have been permissible if the minute of silence was for nonreligious purposes—secular meditation, for example—but the court found that it was for prayer.

Subsequent cases have held that invocations at public school graduation ceremonies are unconstitutional, even if attendance is voluntary and the students vote to have an opening prayer. The same is true for student-initiated prayers before public school football games.

In 2000, a California father challenged a school district's practice of having students recite the Pledge of Allegiance. He said the phrase "under God" was akin to forcing his daughter to pray in school. A federal appeals court agreed with him in 2002, but the Supreme Court reversed that decision, not on First Amendment grounds but on a technicality—the father did not have custody of his daughter and, therefore, did not have legal standing to sue over her education.

WHAT IT MEANS TO YOU

The First Amendment does not prohibit prayer, Bible readings, or other expressions of religion in private schools—only in public schools that receive government funding from tax revenues.

Religious Displays

A religion-oriented display, such as a crèche or manger scene at Christmas, is not necessarily a violation of church and state. On a number of occasions, the Supreme Court has held that it is, depending on whether it seems to be presented to benefit or promote a particular view of religion, or whether it is part of a more secular display to celebrate the season. A manger scene in a county courthouse has been held unconstitutional, for example, while a Christmas tree and a menorah together have been allowed.

Similarly, displays of religious symbols such as the Ten Commandments may or may not violate the First Amendment. The court pointed out the distinction, with a pair of 5–4 rulings, in two cases in 2005. The cases were distinguished by a single swing vote—Justice David Souter. Souter said a Ten Commandments monument in a park at the state capitol in Austin, Texas, was okay because other nonreligious symbols of law and justice were present in the park as well. On the other hand, he said Ten Commandments plaques placed in Kentucky courthouses appeared to be religious symbols because they stood alone, rather than as part of a larger secular display.

One of the most highly publicized cases involving religious symbols began in 2001, when Alabama Chief Justice Roy Moore installed a large Ten Commandments monument in the state judicial building. The American Civil Liberties Union (ACLU) and others filed suit, claiming the monument violated the separation of church and state, and the federal courts ordered the monument removed. Moore refused and was removed from office—along with the monument. He appealed to the U.S. Supreme Court, which refused to take the case and let the lower court orders stand.

CASES

***Glassroth v. Moore* (2002):** Former Alabama Supreme Court Justice Roy Moore merely wanted to demonstrate his faith in God; he argued that the Ten Commandments were the moral foundation for the American legal system. The courts said the First Amendment would allow him to express his faith in many ways, but installing a 5,280-pound monument in the lobby of a public building was not one of them.

Freedom of Speech

We have a participatory democracy. Every citizen has a right, and maybe even a responsibility, to participate in civic affairs. That means we've got to share our thoughts, opinions, and ideas. We've got to communicate. We've got to talk. And that's why the First Amendment guarantees free speech.

Without freedom of speech, life would not only be boring, but we'd not be exposed to the theories and ideas—along with the criticisms and complaints—that make us think about how our government is doing and how our elected officials are representing us. Could they be doing a better job? Let's talk about it with other people and see what they think. That is freedom of speech.

Political Speech

Historically, governments put limits on free speech to maintain control of society and stay in power. If a king or dictator didn't like what people were saying, those people were tossed behind bars—or worse. That's what the English governors in the colonies did in the name of the king.

The First Amendment was supposed to keep that from happening, but it only took 7 years, until 1798, for Congress to pass the Alien and Sedition Act at the behest of President John Adams, who wanted a way to go after the people who were criticizing his government. It was an ironic piece of legislation, considering the country had been created not long before by a handful of radicals—including Adams himself—who criticized the government to the point of advocating and then leading a violent overthrow.

The act made it illegal to say or write anything "false, scandalous, or malicious" about the government—in other words, anything the government didn't like. The act expired 3 years later, and when Thomas Jefferson became president, he pardoned the 10 people who had been convicted of sedition.

Freedom of speech is not absolute; you cannot say anything you want, anytime, anywhere. And the definition of free speech, always evolving, often is defined more by what you are told you *cannot* say than by what you *can* say. Free speech, like other civil liberties, can be affected by the times, such as war or some other national crisis. From 1836 to 1844, for example, the House of Representatives had a gag rule preventing debate on abolition of slavery.

In 1917, Congress passed the Espionage Act, aimed at peace activists who tried to talk potential World War I recruits out of enlisting in the military. The following year another Sedition Act was enacted, making it a crime to speak or write anything negative about the government, the

Constitution, or the American flag. The Supreme Court upheld a series of convictions growing out of opposition to U.S. participation in the Great War, as it was called at the time.

Not everybody, however, thought it was a good idea to send people to prison for being peace activists during World War I. In a dissent in a Supreme Court case that upheld a portion of the Espionage Act against criticizing the government, Justice Oliver Wendell Holmes wrote that "the ultimate good desired is better reached by free trade in ideas—that the best test of truth is the power of the thought to get itself accepted in the competition of the market."

 WE THE PEOPLE

One of Oliver Wendell Holmes's frequent allies on the court, Justice Louis Brandeis, expanded on his colleague's "marketplace of ideas" principle in another opinion a few years later, suggesting that the answer to falsehoods and fallacies should be "more speech, not enforced silence."

Clear and Present Danger

In *Schenk* v. *United States* in 1919, which upheld the conviction of an activist passing out leaflets urging potential recruits not to join the military, Holmes enunciated a famous First Amendment doctrine: speech could be limited if it created a "clear and present danger" of criminal acts. In that case, Holmes also wrote one of the best-known misquotes in history. The commonly cited phrase is that free speech does not extend to "shouting fire in a crowded theater." Actually, Holmes wrote that the First Amendment does not protect "a man falsely shouting fire in a theater and causing a panic." He included "falsely," but not "crowded."

In response to the crackdown on free speech, the ACLU was formed in 1920 and could claim an early victory the following year when the Sedition Act was repealed. Just as Thomas Jefferson pardoned those convicted under the first Sedition Act more than a century earlier, Franklin Delano Roosevelt later issued presidential pardons to those convicted under the World War I Espionage and Sedition Acts.

The end of the war, however, did not end the tension between free speech and government interests, particularly in silencing critics such as anarchists and communists who advocated the overthrow of the government. In the 1925 case *Gitlow* v. *New York*, the Supreme Court ruled that the free speech guarantees of the First Amendment apply to state law via the Fourteenth Amendment but nonetheless upheld a pamphleteer's conviction under New York's antianarchy law.

The "clear and present danger" discussion has been revived in the age of global terror. Some political candidates, and a scant few constitutional scholars, have called for limiting the First Amendment's free speech protections—including shutting down some websites—to keep terrorist organizations from spreading propaganda, raising funds, recruiting new members, and planning new acts of violence. Those proposals to restrict free speech—along with proposals to limit immigration based on religion—have been widely scorned, but even the most vocal First Amendment defenders concede that heightened danger from terrorism very well could result in more limits on civil liberties.

CASES

Stromberg v. California **(1931):** In this case, the Supreme Court reversed the conviction of a young woman who had displayed a red flag to show her support for the Young Communist League. It was the first time the court regarded nonverbal, symbolic expression as free speech. But it wasn't the last.

Fighting Words

At one point, the Supreme Court ruled that "fighting words"—the kind of statement that might make anybody punch the speaker in the nose—were not free speech. However, the court later backed away from the idea that it's sometimes okay to resort to violence in response to someone else's statement. Instead, the court acknowledged that outrageous or inflammatory speech may be protected if it makes you think. In a 1949 case, Justice William O. Douglas wrote, "It may indeed best serve its high purpose when it induces a condition of unrest, creates dissatisfaction with conditions as they are, or even stirs people to anger."

In 1940, as World War II was heating up in Europe, the Supreme Court upheld a Pennsylvania law requiring children to salute the flag and recite the Pledge of Allegiance. "National unity is the basis of national security," Justice Felix Frankfurter wrote. But that decision was overturned 3 years later in another Jehovah's Witness case: kids were no longer required to pledge or salute at school. (It is worth noting that around the same time, the salute that schoolchildren used for the Pledge of Allegiance was changed to the hand over the heart. It had been a straight-arm, "Heil Hitler" salute, except with the palm up instead of down.)

With another war came another set of laws aimed at limiting free speech. In 1940, the United States enacted the Smith Act, formally the Alien and Registration Act, which again made it a crime to advocate the violent overthrow of the government. After World War II, the Smith Act became a Cold War tool for the government. It was used at the urging of J. Edgar Hoover, the director of the Federal Bureau of Investigation (FBI), to prosecute suspected communist activists. In 1951, the Supreme Court upheld a series of convictions under the Smith Act, ruling that it did not violate the First Amendment. The Smith Act technically remains on the books today.

The Vietnam War era sparked a flurry of First Amendment confrontations over free speech. In 1968, the Supreme Court upheld the conviction of a protestor who argued that burning his draft card was free speech, but the following year the court overturned the convictions of a group of Des Moines students who went to high school wearing black armbands to protest the war. In 1971, the court overturned the conviction of a protestor who wore a jacket bearing the words "F--- the Draft" into a courthouse.

The backlash against flag burning that began during the Vietnam protests has simmered since then. In 1989, Congress passed the Flag Protection Act, and soon after, the Supreme Court made two rulings, one voiding the new federal law and another striking down a comparable state law in Texas that said burning or otherwise abusing Old Glory is a legitimate expression of free speech.

Unpopular views, including those that are racist, may be protected by the umbrella of free speech, but there are limits. In a 1969 case, *Brandenburg* v. *Ohio,* the Supreme Court upheld the conviction of a Ku Klux Klan (KKK) member, saying his speech is not protected if it is "likely to incite or produce" violence. The court opinion noted that "the constitutional guarantees of free speech and free press do not permit a State to forbid or proscribe advocacy for the use of force or of law violation except where such advocacy is directed to inciting or producing imminent law-less action and is likely to incite or produce such action." In 2003, the high court ruled that a KKK cross-burning prohibition can be legal because it is so intimidating to black people, it effectively amounts to violence against them.

> **CASES**
>
> **Red Lion Broadcasting v. Federal Communications Commission (1969):** In this case, the Supreme Court endorsed the Federal Communications Commission's (FCC) "fairness doctrine," saying Congress and the FCC are authorized to require broadcasters to provide opportunities for opposing views to be aired in response to personal attacks and political editorializing. Later, however, the FCC and the courts abandoned the fairness doctrine. The "equal time" doctrine for political opponents remains in effect, although the Supreme Court has ruled that a TV station does not have to invite every candidate running in an election to participate in a televised debate.

In 1982 in *Board of Education* v. *Pico,* the Supreme Court held that officials cannot pull books off school library shelves merely because they disagree with the ideas in those books. The decision said "the right to receive ideas is a necessary predicate to the recipient's meaningful exercise of his own rights of speech, press, and political freedom."

However, just as the federal government can withhold grants from artists, the Supreme Court ruled in 1991 that the government can withhold funding from health centers that discuss abortion as a method of birth control. The discussion is free speech, but that doesn't mean the government has to support it with federal funding.

The early 1990s spawned a wave of so-called political correctness—the very phrase would seem to be a violation of at least the spirit and perhaps the letter of the First Amendment—that resulted in attempts around the country to ban "hate speech." Those efforts were largely snuffed out after a 1992 Supreme Court ruling overturned a local hate-speech ordinance.

Whistle-blowers, or people speaking up about misdeeds in their workplaces, do not enjoy any special protection under the First Amendment. Some statutes do protect whistle-blowers, but the courts have recognized reasons that employers, especially the government, might legally require reticence among their employees, too. Protecting national defense secrets is a clear-cut example.

In a May 2006 California case, *Garcetti* v. *Ceballos,* the Supreme Court rejected the First Amendment claim of an assistant district attorney who said he was passed over for a promotion because he criticized his boss in public. He said he was a whistle-blower, but the court said the Constitution does not protect "every statement a public employee makes in the course of doing his or her job."

Campaign finance laws have become a First Amendment issue in recent years. In the 1976 case *Buckley* v. *Valeo,* the Supreme Court upheld the part of the Federal Election Campaign Act that limited campaign contributions but struck down the part of the law that limited how much candidates can spend on their campaigns. Restricting campaign expenditures, the court held, was a restraint on freedom of expression.

Corporations as People

The next big campaign finance case was in 2010, when the Supreme Court held, in effect, that corporations are people, too—at least in terms of political donations.

In that case, a nonprofit corporation called Citizens United went to court to challenge Federal Elections Commission (FEC) rules that kept the group from advertising a documentary, *Hillary,* which was critical of Hillary Clinton during the 2008 presidential campaign. The FEC said the ads were prohibited by rules against corporations or unions spending money to influence elections within 60 days of a general election or 30 days of a primary. The Supreme Court ruled 5–4 in favor of Citizens United, saying corporations, just like people, have a First Amendment right to free speech, and spending money on a campaign is political speech. "The court has recognized that First Amendment protection extends to corporations," Justice Anthony Kennedy wrote in the majority decision. "The court has thus rejected the argument that political speech of corporations or other associations should be treated differently under the First Amendment simply because such associations are not 'natural persons.'"

Citizens United was complemented by another campaign finance decision in 2014, *McCutcheon* v. *Federal Election Commission,* which struck down federal rules limiting the amount of money individual entities, whether people or corporations, can donate in total during a 2-year election cycle. Limits remained on how much could be donated to individual candidates, removing the aggregate limits, but the changes in campaign finance law set the stage for the so-called PACs (political action committees) and super PACs that have brought virtually unlimited money into politics.

Obscenity

Obscenity is not protected by the First Amendment's guarantees of free speech. A series of federal and state laws approved in the latter part of the 1800s was the first widespread effort to control obscenity in American culture. Known as Comstock laws, after antiobscenity campaigner Anthony Comstock, the laws made it criminal to sell or distribute "obscene, lewd or lascivious" materials, including "any article or thing" providing information on contraception or abortion.

The federal law and many of the state Comstock laws remain on the books and are still used to prosecute those who sell obscene material, but the age-old question remains: what is obscene? After all, one man's pornography may be another man's artistic erotica.

 **WE THE PEOPLE**

> In 1964, Supreme Court Justice Potter Stewart spoke for most of us when he acknowledged that it was difficult to define pornography, but added, "I know it when I see it."

The courts have made a number of attempts to define obscenity and balance it against the guarantees of free speech. In the nineteenth century, the Supreme Court defined obscenity as material that would "deprave or corrupt those whose minds are open to such immoral influences." In other words, if material offended the most sensitive people in society—if it offended pretty much anyone—it was obscene.

The standards have loosened over the decades, but it has been a continual struggle to define when, where, how, and why words may be of "prurient interest," which means "too dirty" to those of us who do not sit on the U.S. Supreme Court.

But again, what is too dirty? Justice William Brennan offered the "utterly without redeeming social value" standard: something could be obscene, but if it had artistic or cultural value, it might be protected by the First Amendment.

A 1973 Supreme Court case, *Miller* v. *California*, offered a three-part test for whether speech is obscene:

- If the "average person applying contemporary community standards" would find that the material, taken as a whole, appeals to prurient interests.

- If the depiction or description is patently offensive sexual conduct that is defined and prohibited by state law.

- If, taken as a whole, the material lacks serious literary, artistic, political, or scientific value.

The current standards for obscenity do not include a national standard, except for child pornography. The courts have agreed that child pornography is never acceptable. In other types of obscenity, however, the courts are supposed to consider local or community standards.

The 1973 *Miller* provision for considering the literary, artistic, political, or scientific value allows for a nude stripper or live-sex performer in a bar to be regarded differently under the First Amendment than a nude actor appearing in *Hair*, a life study in an art gallery, or anatomical depictions in a medical journal. Another factor is the audience; material that can be viewed by children is treated differently from material restricted to adult eyes only, but even adult-only material can be obscene. The wider the audience, the more oversight: the FCC is allowed to regulate indecent speech because broadcasting's "uniquely pervasive presence" means that children might see or hear it. It is also legal for local governments to impose zoning restrictions that control where adult businesses may operate. A 1998 court case upheld federal requirements for the National Endowment for the Arts to consider decency standards when awarding grants to artists; merely denying government funding does not infringe upon an artist's freedom of expression.

WHAT IT MEANS TO YOU

The Supreme Court ruled in 1969 that "private possession of obscene material" is legal. Authorities cannot burst into your house and arrest you merely for possessing pornography. Justice Thurgood Marshall wrote, "If the First Amendment means anything, it means that a State has no business telling a man sitting in his own house what books he may read or what films he may watch."

As a society, we're still trying to figure out how to handle child pornography and the internet. The Supreme Court found the Child Pornography Prevention Act of 1996 unconstitutional in 1997; the court said it was overbroad, with the potential authority for law enforcement officials to punish legal speech in the name of protecting children.

A subsequent law, the Child Online Protection Act (COPA), also ran into a series of First Amendment setbacks in federal courts. The Supreme Court said there may be "a number of plausible, less restrictive alternatives," and said the government needed to justify COPA.

Campaigners for internet safety for kids could claim a victory, however, when the Supreme Court upheld the 1998 Children's Internet Protection Act, which withholds federal money from schools and libraries that do not have antipornography filtering software on their computers with internet access.

Freedom of the Press

Freedom of the press is closely linked to freedom of speech. If it is okay to say it, it's probably okay to publish it, too.

Our form of democracy relies on the press to perform the necessary but unofficial function of spreading around all that free speech so we have an informed citizenry capable of participating in the debates and electing the leaders we want to address the issues we care about. That's why the press is called the Fourth Estate, informally supplementing the three official branches of government.

Censorship

The First Amendment's guarantee of a free press, it should be noted, says nothing about press responsibility. The primary goal is to protect the press from government censorship, whether direct or indirect. But there are limits on what the press can do and penalties for violating the public trust conferred by the First Amendment. A good example is libel law, which allows individuals who are harmed by the press to sue for damages.

The 1735 trial of New York printer John Peter Zenger marked the beginning of the American free press. Zenger was jailed for publishing criticism of the royal governor, but a jury of colonists, responding to stirring arguments by defense attorney Alexander Hamilton, ignored the instructions of the governor's court and acquitted Zenger. It was an important milestone in showing the colonists the power of the press—and the law—in fighting imperial rule from London. In practical terms, the case also laid down early precedents for American law: a jury can decide what is libel and what isn't, and truth is a defense to libel. Later, in the Federalist Papers, Alexander Hamilton wrote, "The liberty of the press shall be inviolably preserved."

As with free speech, times of national crisis often provide stern tests for freedom of the press. During the Civil War, President Abraham Lincoln ordered temporary suspension of the *Chicago Tribune* and later two New York newspapers for printing stories he viewed as disloyal to the Union effort in the Civil War.

The Supreme Court's first free press case was decided in 1907, when the justices upheld the contempt conviction of a Denver publisher who had run criticisms of the Colorado Supreme Court.

In a 1931 case, *Near* v. *Minnesota,* the Supreme Court overturned a state court's *prior restraint* order on the grounds that the First Amendment was designed primarily to prohibit government censorship. That case also extended the protections of the First Amendment to the states through the Equal Protection Clause of the Fourteenth Amendment.

DEFINITION

Prior restraint is the term for preventing publication or broadcast. A plaintiff will ask a court to block the publication because of the potential harm it might cause, whether to national security or to a private individual or corporation.

A 1936 high court decision outlawed a state tax on advertising in newspapers with circulation of more than 20,000 a week. The court said such a tax could restrict the flow of "information to which the public is entitled in virtue of the constitutional guarantees." It could be a form of censorship, in other words.

Censorship has been permitted, however, in instances such as wartime—in 1941, Franklin Delano Roosevelt opened, with Congress's approval, an Office of Censorship—and there have been numerous examples of courts issuing gag orders to prevent pretrial publicity.

A major precedent for controlling pretrial publicity was the 1966 case *Sheppard* v. *Maxwell,* when the Supreme Court overturned the conviction of Dr. Sam Sheppard—the real-life inspiration for *The Fugitive* TV series and movie—on the grounds that newspaper publicity had kept him from getting a fair trial. Another example of censorship, sometimes in response to legal requirements but often voluntary self-censorship, is when the news media withholds the names of certain people involved in crimes, such as minors or rape victims.

CASES

New York Times Co. v. United States (1971): The Nixon administration tried to stop *The New York Times* and *The Washington Post* from publishing the so-called "Pentagon Papers," 7,000 pages of leaked documents recounting U.S. involvement in Vietnam. The Supreme Court decided by a 6-3 vote, with 9 separate opinions, that the injunctions the government sought amounted to prior restraint violating the First Amendment.

Libel

The case that shaped our modern law of libel—when someone sues for defamation, or damage to his or her reputation—was New York Times v. *Sullivan* in 1964. Previously, the main defense to libel allegations was truth: if you said your reputation had been damaged by something I wrote about you, I had to prove it was true. The *Sullivan* case, however, set new standards for people who are public officials. Instead of proving that the allegation was true, a defendant merely had to show that the allegation was not made with *actual malice*.

Actual malice is defined as knowledge that the allegation was false or reckless disregard for whether it was false or not. The court's reasoning was that society needs to be able to comment on and talk about public officials and that officials open themselves to criticism and commentary when they enter the public arena. If the press makes a mistake, the public official who has been wronged can collect money damages only by proving that the press either knew or should have known that the allegation was false.

The Supreme Court recognized that mistakes can be made in the press, particularly under deadline pressure, but reasoned that keeping accuracy standards too high could be a form of censorship and, therefore, a violation of the First Amendment. The "public official" standard for libel was subsequently expanded to include public figures, too, including celebrities.

Sometimes the best way to avoid libel damages, especially if you know what you're saying is false, is to be as outrageous as possible. In a 1988 case, evangelist Jerry Falwell sued *Hustler* magazine for running a fake liquor ad showing Falwell in a lewd pose. The Supreme Court rejected the libel suit on the grounds that it was legitimate political satire, which has played "a prominent role in public and political debate" in American history. In other cases, however, the court has made it clear that not only facts, but also opinions, can be the basis for a successful libel suit.

One of the continuing issues in the American press is where the role of reporter ends and the role of citizen begins. In a 1972 case, *Branzburg v. Hayes,* the Supreme Court said reporters are not exempt from the normal responsibilities of citizenship, including testifying before a grand jury, just because they are reporters. We've also seen, in recent cases such as the investigation into the leaking of a Central Intelligence Agency (CIA) spy's identity and the use of steroids in baseball, how reporters can be sent to jail—in theory indefinitely, since contempt of court need not carry a set term of imprisonment or even a maximum sentence—for refusing to provide law enforcement authorities and courts with information about confidential sources.

Reporters argue that freedom of the press allows them to protect their sources and that giving up their sources would discourage other whistle-blowers and leakers, but the courts have said that civic responsibility and the integrity of the legal system may be more important.

CASES

Miami Herald Publishing v. Tornillo **(1974):** Print publications are not subject to
the same "equal time" provisions required of broadcasters. In this case, the Supreme
Court struck down a Florida law requiring newspapers to give free rebuttal space
to political candidates they criticize. The ruling said an equal-time provision would
inhibit editorial decision-making—whether to print something or not.

School-funded student newspapers have presented a number of First Amendment dilemmas. The
courts generally have ruled that although student editors and reporters have First Amendment
rights, school officials can impose editorial controls as long as the decisions are justified for legitimate teaching and educational purposes.

Looking ahead, the rapid changes in communications technology in recent years are presenting
new challenges to the First Amendment and the concepts of freedom of the press. Instead of
being in an office that can be searched or seized or shut down, new technology allows almost
anyone to "publish" from almost anywhere. And the new world of self-publishing is forcing us
to rethink and redefine just who is a journalist and who is deserving of First Amendment free
press protection. Is a blogger a journalist? The rest of the world is watching China's attempts to
control the new media, including creating its own vast national intranet, limiting access to the
world wide web, and jailing surfers who visit sites deemed pornographic or politically subversive.

Freedom of Assembly

The freedom to assemble—to talk, march, plot against the government, or cheer for your team—
is closely linked to free speech. Also sometimes called the right of association, it means we can
hang out with whomever we want—mostly. We can form political parties, special interest groups,
clubs, and unions, but the First Amendment won't necessarily protect us if those organizations, or
some of the members we associate with, undertake illegal activities. Terrorist groups, for
example, can be banned.

As with other aspects of the First Amendment, the tension is between freedom of expression and
the need to protect society. It may be your right to organize a protest march, but the government
may have the right to require you to get a parade permit and follow a certain route at a certain
time in order to avoid snarling traffic and causing safety problems.

Throughout history, totalitarian governments have banned the right to assemble just as they
have banned free speech and the free press. And we're not talking about ancient history. In Iran
in 1978, amid fears about the exiled Ayatollah Khomeini returning to lead a revolt, the late

Shah's government banned any public gathering of more than two people. In 2001, amid fears of a Montagnard uprising, Vietnam banned gatherings of more than four people in its Central Highlands. In September 2006, Thailand banned gatherings of more than five people. If people cannot get together, repressive leaders reckon, they cannot plan a revolution.

On a smaller scale, American officials have sometimes limited the right of assembly—such as through parade permits—solely to discourage causes they do not agree with. The Supreme Court has overturned state laws against being a member of the communist party, ruling that "peaceable assembly for lawful discussion cannot be made a crime. The holding of meetings for peaceable political action cannot be proscribed." In 1958, the court ruled that the National Association for the Advancement of Colored People (NAACP) did not have to turn over its membership roster to authorities, and later that communist party members could be state employees in Arizona and public school teachers in New York.

CASES

> *Boy Scouts of America v. Dale* **(2000):** Sometimes the right of association can protect you from associating with people you don't want to be around. The Supreme Court, emphasizing that it did not agree or disagree with the Boy Scouts' position on gays, agreed in a 5-4 decision that the Scouts do not have to accept gay scoutmasters.

The suburbanization of America in the second half of the twentieth century led to a First Amendment debate over whether groups must be allowed to assemble—and speak—on private property such as malls and shopping centers. The reasoning is that malls have become the new town squares and village greens, where people historically would gather to talk about the issues of the day. The federal courts generally have said the right of association does not extend to private property and have sided with mall managers who want to keep out people chanting or distributing leaflets. In contrast, state courts have been more likely to recognize the "new town square" argument and give groups the right to assemble in malls as long as they behave themselves.

The tension between law enforcement and the right to assemble was in the headlines in the spring of 2003 when women's groups converged on Georgia to protest the no-females member-ship policy of the Augusta National Golf Club, the home of the Masters Tournament. Local authorities quickly made new rules requiring 20 days' notice for a permit to stage a public protest, leaving it up to the local sheriff to approve or deny permits and tell protesters when and where they could protest. The sheriff refused to let the women protest at the entrance to the club and instead moved them a half-mile away.

Freedom to Petition

This is the freedom to protest against the government, to ask for changes, and to ask that wrongs done in the name of the government be corrected. Sounds sort of like the Declaration of Independence, doesn't it? It gives everyday citizens the right to protest and to sue in a court of law to correct wrongs.

The right to petition has not been particularly controversial since the mid-nineteenth century, but in the decades before the Civil War, the House of Representatives had a rule—it was actually called the "gag rule"—that barred Congress from considering any petition that had anything to do with slavery.

In more modern times, the right to petition often overlaps with free speech and free assembly, and the courts sometimes prefer to focus on those or other constitutional rights when lawsuits are brought over the right to sue. For example, in 1963, the Supreme Court overturned a Virginia rule prohibiting people from soliciting lawyers and ruled it was permissible for the NAACP to seek attorneys to handle civil rights lawsuits. The right to petition was an issue, but the court decided the case on free speech and free association grounds.

In a 1971 Connecticut case, the Supreme Court said an indigent couple seeking a divorce should not have to pay the usual court fees. The couple had filed their appeal on the grounds of the right to petition, but the court instead said that denying them a divorce for financial reasons was a violation of their right to due process—the right to have their case heard fully and fairly.

The due process rationale, rather than the right to petition, also is why prisoners are allowed access to law libraries when working on their own appeals.

In 1980, the Supreme Court ruled in *Missouri* v. *National Organization for Women* that the state of Missouri could not claim damages from the National Organization for Women (NOW) because of economic damage resulting from a NOW boycott to protest opposition to the proposed Equal Rights Amendment. The court said the boycott was a form of petition and was, therefore, protected by the First Amendment.

In a 1981 case, the court made it clear that the right to petition, at least in terms of the right to sue, does not extend to frivolous claims. The justices found in favor of a property developer who complained that his plans to build a shopping center were being blocked by lawsuit after lawsuit filed by other property owners and existing shopping centers.

WE THE PEOPLE

"We have recognized this right to petition as one of the most precious of the liberties safeguarded by the Bill of Rights," Justice Sandra Day O'Connor wrote in a 2002 case, "and have explained that the right is implied by the very idea of a government, republican in form."

The Least You Need to Know

- The First Amendment protects freedom of expression, including freedom of religion, speech, and the press.
- Freedom of religion is the basis for the separation of church and state.
- The First Amendment protects your right to believe whatever you want, but your beliefs do not allow you to break laws or violate the rights of others.
- The First Amendment prohibits you from imposing your beliefs on others.
- The Constitution protects freedom of the press as a foundation of democracy.

The Second and Third Amendments: Arms and Armies

The Second Amendment, often cited for "the right to bear arms," is at the heart of the often-bitter national debate over gun control. It is one of the most controversial portions of the Bill of Rights.

The Third Amendment, which guarantees that citizens do not have to feed and shelter soldiers, is one of the least controversial parts of the Bill of Rights.

In This Chapter

- The Second Amendment: the right to bear arms
- The Militia Clause
- The Right to Arms Clause
- The gun control debate today
- The Third Amendment: quartering troops

Second Amendment: The Right to Bear Arms

"A well regulated militia, being necessary to the security of a free state, the right of the people to keep and bear arms, shall not be infringed."

Gun violence, and especially mass shootings with automatic weapons, have made the Second Amendment the centerpiece of a hot-button nationwide political controversy. The debate—the right of every American to own a gun versus society's desire to prevent violent crime—often appears intractable, particularly as people on the extremes dig in their heels.

Among Second Amendment absolutists, almost no restrictions on any aspect of gun ownership or use are acceptable. On the other side, gun control advocates say it's common sense to restrict the use of certain guns and keep all guns out of the hands of criminals and people who are unstable or potentially violent.

Yet even many of the most ardent opponents of guns in society don't want to take guns away from soldiers, police officers, private security people, hunters, and other individuals who meet rigorous licensing requirements.

The Second Amendment is divided into two clauses: the Militia Clause and the Right to Arms Clause. Various experts, depending on whether they are for or against more gun control, argue back and forth over which clause is more important. Does the amendment guarantee an absolute right for individuals to own guns? Or does it mean only that the states can form militias that may allow citizens to have firearms?

If the Militia Clause is more important, then perhaps the Right to Arms Clause has a limited meaning: that citizens have the right to bear arms only if they are part of the National Guard or some equivalent. If the Right to Arms Clause is superior, then perhaps the government has much less authority to make laws regulating the sale, possession, and use of guns.

Many scholars, citing the historical records dating back to the framers, argue that nothing indicates the framers ever intended guns to be owned only by members of an active militia. On the other hand, many modern gun control activists say times have changed, and the eighteenth-century Second Amendment guarantee of the right to own a gun is about as relevant today—that is to say, not very relevant—as the Third Amendment right not to feed and house soldiers.

"The right of self defense is the first law of nature: in most governments it has been the study of rulers to confine this right within the narrowest limits possible. Wherever standing armies are kept up, and the right of the people to keep and bear arms, is under any colour or pretext whatsoever, prohibited, liberty, if not already annihilated, is on the brink of destruction."

—Henry St. George Tucker, American Revolutionary gunrunner and legal scholar

The Militia Clause

The Articles of Confederation said the states should have militias but made no mention of individual gun ownership. At the Constitutional Convention in 1787, there were obvious reasons for including something about guns. Hunting was an important source of food for many people. Personal security was a factor in an era when society felt the need to protect itself not only from ordinary crime, such as armed robbery, but also from Indian attacks and slave uprisings in certain areas of the country.

But there also were political motivations for ensuring gun rights. Americans mistrusted standing armies. Europe had powerful standing armies whose main role, to Americans, seemed to be to keep monarchs in power. When they looked across the Atlantic, the Americans saw that virtually every monarchy in Europe had strict gun control laws, and the Americans believed it was to head off armed insurrections. After all, fresh in everyone's mind was the Revolutionary War, when the nation's independence had been earned through bloody victories fought largely by citizen soldiers using the muskets they grabbed off the mantelpiece or from the closet.

To early Americans, guns were more than a symbol of freedom. They *were* freedom. A well-armed citizenry within a state was a reminder and a warning not only to foreign countries but also to other states and the new federal government: don't tread on our inalienable rights.

The history of militias in America goes back to the seventeenth century, and eventually every colony had its own militia that required every able-bodied white male to be a member. But being a member didn't necessarily mean marching and carrying a rifle; there were other duties, such as fund-raising and record-keeping, a militiaman could do instead of actually picking up a gun—especially if he was rich or had political connections.

Massachusetts's militia, known as the *minutemen* for the way they could leave their shops and farms and be ready to fight in a minute, became the model for the other colonies. They were an inspiration for the growth of the militia across the colonies after firing "the shots heard 'round the world" to announce the war of independence against the redcoats at Lexington and Concord in 1775.

The importance of militias ebbed and flowed in the 1800s, depending on whether we were at war or not, but during the Civil War, states in both the North and South sent their militias into battle as units under their state flags. Indeed, rebel soldiers typically thought of themselves as fighting not for the Confederate States of America, but for old Virginia or old South Carolina. Every state's militia has evolved into its version of the modern National Guard, which began in the early 1900s in the populous northeastern states and gradually spread across the country to become today's professional, highly trained military force under shared state and federal control.

With our professional, full-time Army, Navy, Air Force, and Marines, society's current attitude toward a standing army and state militias is much different than it was in 1787. Most of us cannot imagine ever needing to grab a rifle off the mantle to defend ourselves against foreign invaders or occupying forces. But guns remain a part of American culture and heritage.

The Right to Arms Clause

Unlike some other provisions of the Bill of Rights, such as the right to free speech and the right to due process, the Second Amendment does not apply to the states under the Fourteenth Amendment's equal protection provisions. That means private organizations, such as housing associations, can ban guns. It also means states can be as restrictive or permissive as they want with their gun control laws. An estimated 20,000 local, state, and federal laws are already on the books controlling gun sales, possession, and use.

CASES

Lewis v. United States (1980): The Supreme Court ruled it was permissible under the Constitution for states to prohibit convicted felons from possessing firearms.

Evolving Law on Guns

Perhaps surprisingly, through much of U.S. history, the Second Amendment has been the subject of relatively little legal action. The courts, for the first two centuries of the republic, offered scant guidance on guns.

An exception from the era of Al Capone and the Untouchables was the 1939 case *United States* v. *Miller*. That case represented a challenge to a federal law that taxed machine guns and sawed-off shotguns—in effect making them illegal. The high court ruled that the law did not violate the Second Amendment because machine guns and sawed-off shotguns were not used by state militia nor in preserving the peace. Instead, those weapons were more commonly used by gangsters and armed robbers because they had a lot of firepower but could be hidden in clothes or small packages.

However, as the gun-control controversy heated up, more states and local jurisdictions passed gun-related laws, and more of those laws were challenged in court. In 1996 in *Hickman* v. *Block,* the U.S. Circuit Court of Appeals for the Western states held that the Second Amendment does not afford an individual right to gun ownership, rejecting an argument that even minor gun controls could eventually threaten the constitutional right to bear arms. In contrast, the Federal Appeals Court for Texas, Louisiana, and Mississippi ruled 3 years later in *United States* v. *Emerson* that it was a violation of Second Amendment rights for a court to prohibit someone from owning a gun as part of a marital restraining order.

Although the *Miller* case never mentioned either a collective or individual right to bear arms, for the next several decades, federal courts recognized only the collective right—the right of society to own guns—without engaging in any substantive legal analysis of an individual's rights or the government's authority to limit those rights. As a result of this, and the fact that the Second Amendment was not formally "incorporated" under the Fourteenth Amendment by a Supreme Court decision, the federal government and state and local governments had a relatively free hand in crafting legislation and regulations relating to gun ownership. Gun rights advocates were uneasy with the courts' recognition of a collective right only. They were afraid that meant the door was open to future decisions that could result in a complete constitutional prohibition of individual gun ownership.

That changed in 2008, when the Supreme Court struck down Washington, D.C.'s gun law in the case *District of Columbia* v. *Heller*. That law included a complete ban on handguns, and a requirement that all shotguns and rifles kept in the home be unloaded and either disassembled or kept under a trigger lock. In the 5–4 majority opinion, Justice Antonin Scalia wrote, "There seems to us no doubt, on the basis of text and history, that the Second Amendment conferred an individual right to keep and bear arms." Also: "The Second Amendment protects an individual right to possess a firearm unconnected with the service in a militia, and to use that arm for traditionally lawful purposes, such as self-defense within the home."

However, the court said that the right was not unlimited, setting the stage for ongoing legal challenges to state and federal gun laws. Also, because *Heller* involved only the District of Columbia, it did not address the question of whether the Second Amendment was "incorporated" under the Fourteenth Amendment and, therefore, applied to the States.

That question was resolved in the 2010 case, *McDonald* v. *Chicago*, when the court ruled that the Second Amendment was incorporated under the Due Process Clause of the Fourteenth Amendment. The court struck down Chicago's handgun ban, saying the right to bear arms is fundamental, and state and local laws must not violate that fundamental right.

WE THE PEOPLE

"The biggest hypocrites on gun control are those who live in upscale developments with armed security guards—and who want to keep other people from having guns to defend themselves. But what about lower-income people living in high-crime, inner-city neighborhoods? Should such people be kept unarmed and helpless so that limousine liberals can 'make a statement' by adding to the thousands of gun laws already on the books?"

—Thomas Sowell, legal scholar and commentator

Since *Heller* and *McDonald*, circuit courts have ruled on many Second Amendment challenges to gun control laws. So far, circuit courts have upheld laws relating to concealed carry, high-capacity magazine clips, and so-called "assault weapons."

Although there has not been a "circuit split" in any of these areas, it would not be surprising if they arise in the near future. If that happens, the Supreme Court will likely be called upon to further define how far the individual right to keep and bear arms extends.

WE THE PEOPLE

"We're not talking about banning or confiscating guns that people buy and own for hunting, collecting, or personal protection. The issue isn't whether someone is 'pro-gun' or 'anti-gun' but why there is a reluctance from some of our elected officials to take moderate steps that would make our homes and neighborhoods safer."

—Paul Helmke, director of the Brady Campaign to Prevent Gun Violence

The Third Amendment: Quartering Troops

"No soldier shall, in time of peace be quartered in any house, without the consent of the owner, nor in time of war, but in a manner to be prescribed by law."

While the Second Amendment is one of the most controversial parts of the Bill of Rights, the Third Amendment is one of the least controversial passages in the entire Constitution.

It seems antiquated today, the idea that we need an amendment—part of the Bill of Rights, no less—to keep the U.S. Army from forcing us to take in soldiers and give them room and board. But it wasn't such a crazy idea in 1787, when the framers of the Constitution could remember the English army invading their homes and forcing them to provide food and shelter.

The only significant case law relating to the Third Amendment came in *Engblom* v. *Carey* in 1982. The case grew out of a strike by New York prison officers in 1979. The guards lived in state housing that was part of their compensation package. But when they went on strike and members of the New York National Guard were called out to replace them in the prisons, New York officials evicted the prison guards and let the National Guard members live in the state housing.

The prison guards who went on strike and then were tossed out of their homes sued in federal court on the Third Amendment grounds. The U.S. District Court threw out their case, and they appealed. The U.S. Court of Appeals for the Second Circuit (the case never made it to the Supreme Court) ruled that the National Guard could be considered soldiers under the Third Amendment and said the prison guards might actually have a case.

The case went back to the district court, which found for the state (the defendant, Carey, was the governor of New York) again on different grounds. The prison guards appealed again, but this time their appeal was denied, and that was the end of the case.

The Least You Need to Know

- The Second Amendment says "the right of people to keep and bear arms shall not be infringed."
- The Second Amendment has not kept many gun laws from being implemented and enforced by local, state, and federal governments.
- The debate over gun control balances two issues: the historic right of law-abiding citizens to own guns for hunting or self-defense, and society's desire to keep guns out of the hands of criminals.
- Because the issue is such a political hot potato, it seems unlikely that either a new Second Amendment or a Supreme Court ruling will resolve this controversy any time in the near future.
- Much less controversial, the Third Amendment guarantees we do not have to feed and shelter soldiers in our homes.

CHAPTER 8

The Fourth Amendment: Unreasonable Searches and Seizures

The Fourth Amendment is one of the most cherished legal concepts in our democracy. It is a cornerstone of the right to privacy and sets the boundaries for what law enforcement authorities can do in terms of stopping you, entering your home or workplace or motor vehicle, and searching you and your property. The Fourth Amendment is a buffer between personal privacy and police power, but the rules that have been handed down by the courts a bit at a time are often controversial and confusing.

Those rules try to balance society's desire for the protection of individual rights against society's desire to ensure criminals are caught and convicted. Look at it this way: the Fourth Amendment is aimed at protecting all of us, but the only people who directly benefit are those who get away with committing crimes because of procedural errors in the criminal justice system.

In This Chapter

- Foundations of the Fourth Amendment
- Unreasonable searches and seizures
- The exclusionary rule
- What about privacy?
- Stop and frisk

This chapter explains how the courts have interpreted and enforced the Fourth Amendment to strengthen individual rights in society—your rights—but also highlights the limits to your rights both in the courtroom and out on the streets.

The Fourth Amendment Foundations

"The right of the people to be secure in the persons, houses, papers and effects, against unreasonable searches and seizures, shall not be violated, and no Warrants shall issue, but upon probable cause, supported by Oath or affirmation, and particularly describing the place to be searched, and the person or things to be seized."

Look at the opening phrase of the Fourth Amendment: "The right of the people to be secure in their persons, houses, papers and effects …." The Fourth Amendment is all about privacy—your right to privacy. It's an ancient concept, still evolving in many ways, but the basic premise is that governments should leave people alone unless it can prove they're doing something wrong.

English History

Like much of the Constitution, the Fourth Amendment is rooted in English common law—the rules that evolved over the centuries as Europe emerged from the Dark Ages into the Renaissance and toward the Industrial Age. The rights of individuals gradually became more important as kings and queens and their governments recognized it was easier to keep the rabble somewhat mollified than put down rebellions. Our Fourth Amendment, the part of the Constitution that protects us from illegal searches and seizures by authorities, is rooted in the English principle that "a man's home is his castle."

That actual language was used in a British court case in 1603. A citizen challenged the right of the crown's agents to break into his home and search for evidence he had not paid his tax bill in full. Until that time, the king's men could do pretty much whatever they wanted to whomever they wanted, no questions asked. In a remarkable departure from the acceptance of the monarch as all-powerful, the court declared that a homeowner does have the right to defend against unlawful entry by the king's agents. It was a huge victory for personal liberty—in theory, at least. In practical terms, the impact was not immediate. The court also said the king's men still had the right to enter and search, including breaking down doors and smashing locks, to do the king's will. And even if authorities conducted unlawful searches, the evidence they seized could still be used in court.

A system of *warrants* developed: legal orders, requested by law enforcement authorities and approved by judges, which allowed law officers to search and seize people and property. Originally, these were "general warrants," so named because they were so general and vague. With a general warrant, a law officer could break into almost anyone's house and look for pretty much anything.

Eventually, English law moved toward requiring more specifics in warrants. Law officers seeking warrants had to identify the premises they wanted to enter, who they wanted to search, and what they wanted to seize. Further challenges in English courts laid down another important principle that came to guide our Fourth Amendment: the requirement for *probable cause*. It wasn't enough to apply for a warrant with specific names and addresses. If the king's men were going to enter a man's home, whether a castle or a hovel, they had to have probable cause—a good reason to believe a crime had been committed, evidence of the crime was in the house, or the homeowner had been involved in the crime.

> **DEFINITION**
>
> A **warrant** is a document that serves as a legal permission slip granted by a judge or magistrate allowing a law enforcement officer to take a legal action—in the case of the Fourth Amendment, to carry out an arrest, search, or seizure. **Probable cause** is the legal justification for an arrest, search, or seizure, based on sufficient reason to think a crime has been committed, a certain person has committed a crime, or certain property may be evidence of a crime.

In 1886, the U.S. Supreme Court hailed the concept of probable cause for arrest, search, and seizure as "one of the permanent monuments" of British law and said it no doubt had inspired the founding fathers who framed the Constitution.

Early America

If England had followed its own common law and court cases in the New World, we might still be living under the Union Jack. The colonists might never have rebelled, and the United States might never have been created. Instead, the British imposed much harsher legal rules on the American colonies than they did on their citizens back home.

As so often happens in history, money was at the heart of the story. The British had an empire to keep afloat. They relied on the people and the vast resources of the American colonies to pay for it all, largely through trade and taxes. For example, to protect their trade deficit, the British required that the colonies buy and import certain raw materials, products, and goods from England instead of making or growing their own more quickly, easily, and cheaply. Plus, the British taxed everything coming and going.

Cheating on taxes became a way of life for the colonists—except they called it avoiding unfair taxation without representation. The British called it smuggling and used general warrants—with no specifics in terms of people, places, or evidence to be searched or seized—to find evidence, send offenders to prison, and confiscate their property in the name of the Crown. These warrants were called "writs of assistance," meaning the colonists were supposed to assist the authorities in their searches and investigations. You could be arrested, for example, if you didn't assist the tax men by snooping on and reporting your neighbor.

If someone broke into your house, you could not appeal to anyone. As the British campaign against tax evaders became more aggressive, with blanket searches of neighborhoods often door to door, the colonists became more outraged.

In 1775, Americans picked up their rifles and undertook the Revolution with a simple goal: to create a government based on law, not people. They wanted their lives to be regulated by laws that applied to everyone, not by the whims of kings and queens or their appointed sheriffs. In nondemocratic nations, a law enforcement official can't break the law, because he *is* the law. In our democratic system, a law enforcement official who oversteps legal boundaries becomes a law-breaker himself.

WE THE PEOPLE

In 1761, James Otis went to court on behalf of 63 Boston merchants to argue that the writs of assistance were illegal under England's own law. Otis lost the case, but John Adams later said Otis's argument was the real start of the rebellion against England.

After the Constitutional Convention of 1787, when the framers agreed to amend the original Constitution with a Bill of Rights, James Madison stepped up and took the lead. Madison, a member of the first House of Representatives who was to become the fourth president of the United States, figured the 13 states would be more likely to ratify the amendments in the Bill of Rights if the ideas and language were already familiar to them. His home state, Virginia, already had a provision against illegal searches and seizures written into its constitution, so Madison adapted it as the proposed Fourth Amendment.

Searches and Seizures

Today the American rules for search and seizure are remarkably similar, both in the spirit and in the letter of the law, to the procedures outlined by James Otis in 1761. To get a search warrant, authorities have to go before a neutral judge or magistrate—he or she can't be a district attorney or someone else on the prosecuting side of the criminal justice system—and either testify under oath or produce a sworn, written affidavit that lays out the specifics of the proposed search.

The specifics may include the place and the people to be searched, perhaps the time the search will be conducted, and what the authorities are looking for. The search warrant is approved if the judge or magistrate finds probable cause that a crime may have been committed, the person named in the warrant may have committed the crime, and there may be evidence on the person or property to be searched.

The search warrant cannot be general, like the old British writs of assistance in the 1700s. If the police have a warrant to search your backyard only, they cannot use it to search your house. If the search warrant says they are looking for stolen TVs, they cannot look in desk drawers to go through your papers.

However, police are allowed to seize contraband or evidence of other crimes. For example, if the warrant says they are searching your house for stolen TVs but they see an AK-47, they can arrest you on weapons charges. Police officers using a warrant can go beyond the scope of the warrant under certain circumstances, such as to protect their own safety or the safety of others, if evidence is in *plain view,* if they need to act quickly to prevent the destruction of evidence, or if the evidence they've found leads them elsewhere in the house or yard.

DEFINITION

Plain view is the rule that allows evidence to be seized if the police can see it from a public place or in a private place during a lawful search.

The Fourth Amendment also allows searches without warrants. Indeed, most arrests, searches, and seizures occur without warrants. However, those undertaken without warrants must not be "unreasonable" under the Fourth Amendment—and deciding just what is unreasonable has kept our courts busy for many years. That tension between individual rights and protecting society results in an ever-evolving process.

Time is often a factor in the court's reckoning on whether the police should get a search warrant or just go ahead and do the search. For example, let's say a police officer walked past your window, happened to look in, and saw your hydroponic greenhouse full of thriving young marijuana plants. It doesn't look like those plants, or their still-ripening buds and seeds, are going anywhere soon. So the courts likely would say there's time for the police to go get a search warrant and come back.

WHAT IT MEANS TO YOU

The police can break down your door if they're investigating a serious crime, have "clear" probable cause to think someone inside did the crime, and think the suspect might be armed or about to escape.

The Exclusionary Rule

The Fourth Amendment had little effect for more than a century after it was ratified. Yes, it declared that unreasonable searches and seizures were illegal without warrants and probable cause, but there were no legal definitions to set the boundaries. Furthermore, even if a search or seizure was unreasonable, the evidence could still be used. The Fourth Amendment was, in effect, merely advisory.

In 1914, however, the Supreme Court issued a landmark decision in *Weeks* v. *United States*. Fremont Weeks was convicted on gambling charges after authorities—without warrants—searched his home and business and found lottery tickets in his mail. Weeks appealed, and the Supreme Court unanimously ruled that not only had his Fourth Amendment rights been violated, but also that the evidence seized in the illegal searches could not be used against him. With the evidence inadmissible, Weeks's conviction was overturned.

Weeks created the exclusionary rule, the rule that prohibits courts from considering evidence that has been obtained illegally. The exclusionary rule gave the Fourth Amendment a sharp new spur to keep the police in line: evidence that is illegally obtained must be excluded. *Weeks* gave defense attorneys the power to file a pretrial *motion to suppress* evidence that is illegally obtained. If evidence is ruled inadmissible, prosecutors cannot present it, judges cannot consider it, and juries cannot even see or hear about it.

> **DEFINITION**
>
> A **motion to suppress** is a request made by a defense attorney before a judge, usually before trial, to suppress or declare evidence inadmissible under the exclusionary rule.

Fruit of the Poisonous Tree

The Supreme Court made it clear: the goal of the exclusionary rule was to deter law enforcement authorities from conducting unlawful searches and seizures. The logic was that if the evidence they gathered from unconstitutional action was not allowed in court, and if the convictions they gained by going too far were overturned, the police would be more likely to follow the rules.

For decades, the exclusionary rule applied only to federal cases. It was up to the individual states to decide how to handle illegal searches and seizures and whether to exclude evidence obtained unlawfully. In 1961, however, the Supreme Court extended the exclusionary rule to the states in the *Mapp* case, described later. The court said the exclusionary rule now applied to the states in determining whether the police could enter without a warrant and whether the evidence obtained in a subsequent search was admissible.

The high court held that states do not have to stick strictly to the rules of the Fourth Amendment, but they cannot give their citizens less protection—a lowered expectation of privacy—than the Fourth Amendment. They can give *more* protection against unlawful searches and seizures, in other words, but not *less*.

The courts have ruled that unlawful searches result not only in the exclusion of evidence seized directly, but also of evidence that was discovered later or separately—as long as it was a result of the initial violation of the Fourth Amendment. This kind of evidence is called "the fruit of the poisonous tree." An extension of the exclusionary rule, this doctrine suppresses not only evidence seized in an unlawful search, but also any subsequent evidence that might be uncovered because of the search.

Suppose the police come into your house looking for stolen cell phones, but they don't have a warrant or probable cause. They find some stolen phones, and they see a note scrawled on a blackboard: "Deliver E to Smith." As part of a separate investigation, they go find Smith, gather evidence that you are selling ecstasy, come back with a proper warrant, and arrest you.

A court rules first that the stolen cell phones cannot be used against you because the original search was a violation of the Fourth Amendment. In addition, everything about the ecstasy—Smith's testimony, the police finding the drugs in your home, and even your confession, if you made one—is inadmissible as fruit of the poisonous tree because the police never would have gone in that direction if they had not violated your rights in the first place.

The Legal Technicality

Naturally, public opinion does not applaud Supreme Court rulings that might let a criminal go free, no matter what individual rights are being protected. On one hand, sure, it is a noble goal to protect individual rights. On the other hand, we want to put away the bad guys. We have a certain amount of sympathy for someone whose rights have been abused by law enforcement authorities, but many of us are outraged at the idea of crooks walking and feel even more sympathy for their victims.

The provisions of the Fourth Amendment, particularly the exclusionary rule, have come to fall under the scorned catch-all phrase *legal technicality*. When unlawfully obtained evidence is excluded and a suspect gets off, we are told the case has been dismissed "on a technicality." Many of us have come to regard technicalities as loopholes created by the courts and exploited by criminals.

WHAT IT MEANS TO YOU

The courts have held that if a private person, someone not connected to the authorities, seizes evidence and hands it to the police, it is admissible. That includes nosy neighbors and private security officers (who outnumber real police by about three to one, incidentally).

In 1957, a bomb went off on the porch of the home of Don King, a Cleveland numbers racketeer who, years later, after time in prison, became the preeminent boxing promoter in the world. Police investigating the bombing went to the home of Dollree Mapp, the ex-wife of a boxer, looking for a suspect. The police showed her a piece of paper they said was a warrant. She grabbed the piece of paper and stuffed it "down her bosom," as the court so delicately described it. The cops wrestled with her, got the piece of paper back, and proceeded to search the house. They apparently didn't find any evidence of the bombing, but they did find some "lewd and lascivious material"—dirty books and homemade pornography, apparently, including sketches—down in the basement.

The police arrested Mapp on obscenity charges. She appealed the conviction on First Amendment grounds, saying her right to free speech allowed her to have erotica in her own home. The Supreme Court reversed her conviction, but not on First Amendment grounds. Instead, the court said the police had violated her Fourth Amendment rights. The police might have had a stronger case, but they could not produce the warrant, saying it had been lost. Moreover, the court extended the exclusionary rule to the states. The dirty books were out as evidence, and Dollree Mapp was once again a free woman. Moreover, state, county, and local police had to abide by the Fourth Amendment or see their cases thrown out of court.

WE THE PEOPLE

In the *Mapp* case (*Mapp* v. *Ohio*), extending the exclusionary rule to the states, Justice Tom Clark wrote, "Nothing can destroy a government more quickly than its failure to observe its own laws, or worse, its disregard of their charter of its own existence ...."

Privacy

The Fourth Amendment is all about privacy, but it protects you only when you have a reasonable expectation of privacy. You expect to be secure and have privacy in your home, and that's reasonable. You may expect some degree of privacy at your workplace, too, perhaps, but probably not as much as at home. The same with your car: there is some expectation of privacy, but not as much as at home. Both at work and in your car, people are more likely to see you.

There is a presumption against any expectation of privacy in most public places; you can't reasonably claim you expect privacy at a crowded concert, midfield in a football stadium, or while you're using your laptop at the local coffee hangout. But there are exceptions. The courts have ruled, for example, that, yes (thank goodness), there is a reasonable expectation of privacy in a public restroom, and law enforcement authorities cannot hide cameras in there to see just what you're doing and whether it's illegal. Here's one more significant point about privacy: the courts say there is no expectation of privacy in illegal acts, wherever they occur.

A key part of the whole issue of privacy concerns the plain view doctrine. If something is in plain view, the police don't need a warrant to seize it. If you're pulled over for running a stop sign, and the police see a bong on the floor of your car, you're probably going to get busted for that, too. If you're sunbathing nude behind a tall fence and nobody can see you, you have a reasonable expectation of privacy. But if you open the fence gate so kids on their way home from kindergarten can see you, you've given up your expectation of privacy and are fair game for an indecent exposure charge.

In recent years, the Supreme Court has broadened its vision, so to speak, in determining just what is in plain view and what isn't. A good example is the 1986 case *California v. Ciraolo*. The Santa Clara cops got an anonymous tip a guy was growing marijuana, but they couldn't be sure—not sure enough to have probable cause and get a warrant—because of the tall fences around his garden. So the cops got a small plane, cruised over the pot plot at about 1,000 feet, and got a warrant because they had seen the marijuana from the air. The Supreme Court ruled that the search was legal because it was "nonintrusive" and "took place within public navigable airspace." Chief Justice Warren Burger wrote, "Any member of the public flying in this airspace who glanced down could have seen everything that these officers observed."

WE THE PEOPLE

The increase in the use personal drones is posing nettlesome privacy questions. Who can fly a drone? Where can it be flown? Does it matter if the drone carries a small camera? If someone flies one of those quadcopters over my property, can I shoot it down? These and other questions are looming. The Supreme Court heard its first significant drone case in early 2016. In *EPIC* v. *FAA*, the Electronic Privacy Information Center (EPIC), along with dozens of other organizations, is petitioning the Federal Aviation Administration (FAA) to set privacy rules on drone use with the public's input.

A much-cited case on privacy expectations came from California and was decided by the Supreme Court in 1988. The police suspected Billy Greenwood of dealing drugs but didn't have enough evidence to get a warrant. They couldn't show a judge they had probable cause to toss his place. So the police waited until garbage day and went through the garbage Greenwood left out by the curb. Bingo. They found enough evidence of drug use and drug dealing to get a judge to give them a warrant. They then searched the house and found drugs.

Greenwood appealed that the search warrant had been improperly issued because his garbage was private. The court said, in a word, rubbish. Greenwood had no reasonable expectation of privacy for trash he had thrown out on the street. Any member of the public could have gone through his garbage the same way the police did. The decision noted that the bags were "readily accessible to animals, children, scavengers, snoops, and other members of the public"—not to mention narcs.

One of the biggest challenges for law enforcement and the judicial system has been keeping up with technology. In 1928, the Supreme Court ruled that wiretapping was not a violation of the Fourth Amendment's right to privacy—as long as the bug was planted outside the home, not inside.

That changed in 1967, in the case of Charles Katz, a bookie who habitually made gambling-related calls from Los Angeles to Miami and Boston. He did a lot of his business from a phone booth—one of those old glass-and-metal boxes out on the sidewalk, with the door that folded shut behind you. The feds tapped the outside of the phone booth and nailed Katz. He argued that the phone booth was a "constitutionally protected" area. The court disagreed but threw out the case against him anyway, citing his expectation of privacy. "The Fourth Amendment protects people, not places," Justice Potter Stewart wrote.

A few recent court decisions, however, make it clear that the Supreme Court intends to keep an eye on how the authorities use new technology. In a case decided in 2001, a federal agent suspected that Danny Kyllo was growing marijuana. But he was apparently growing the herb indoors, and the agent did not have probable cause for a search warrant. To show probable cause, he used thermal imaging to indicate there were high-intensity heat lamps inside—the kind sometimes used to give marijuana plants a growth spurt.

The Supreme Court narrowly ruled that the search was unconstitutional because the heat waves were not in plain view. Justice Antonin Scalia noted that when "the government uses a device that is not in general public use to explore details of the home that would previously have been unknowable without physical intrusion, the surveillance is a 'search' and is presumptively unreasonable without a warrant."

The courts have outlined a number of instances when a warrant may not be needed and the standards for probable cause may be less, including the following:

- When the evidence is in plain view
- When someone in authority has given consent
- When police are in hot pursuit of a suspect

- When necessary to prevent destruction of evidence

- During emergencies or exigent circumstances

- When police stop and frisk someone

- When needed for airport security

- During sobriety roadblocks

- During work-related drug tests

- When needed for public school students and prisoners

- When police act in good faith even though a warrant is faulty

If a police officer wants to enter your home or business and doesn't have a warrant, you can ask that he or she get a warrant, and you can verbally object. But don't try to physically block the officer's entry. For one thing, the officer may have probable cause you don't know about. For another, whether or not the officer is entering illegally, you could be charged with interfering with police.

If the police stop you on the street and you push back physically, or if you are disrespectful verbally, you probably will be arrested. Even if you were innocent of whatever they were investigating, the charges for not cooperating may stick. And even if you are released with apologies later, you probably won't be able to sue for damages. So keep your cool around the cops.

> 👆 **WHAT IT MEANS TO YOU**
>
> The police can lawfully stop motorists merely for driving through a neighborhood known for prostitution, especially if the police notice a car is moving slowly, repeatedly circling the block, or stopping so the driver can engage in curbside conversation. It usually doesn't do any good to tell the cops you were just asking for directions.

Consent

A search and subsequent seizure are not an issue if the authorities are operating with consent. If someone in control, maybe a relative or a roommate, says it's okay to come in and search the place, the police don't need a warrant. A spouse who shares a home can give authorities consent to search. A suspect's roommate can allow police inside an apartment to search but not in the suspect's private bedroom. Under ordinary circumstances, police should have a warrant before getting a landlord or hotel manager to unlock a rented room.

Sometimes we give implied consent merely by moving around in public, and in some cases, the courts have said the public's security interests override the need for individual warrants. No warrants are necessarily needed, for example, to search passengers going through airport security, job applicants who provide evidence for drug tests, someone on parole, or prisoners in their cells. Government employees have a lower expectation of privacy than private employees, and courts have given government supervisors broad leeway in poking through their staff's offices, desks, and filing cabinets. Students give up some of their privacy rights every time they walk into a public school.

In a 1985 New Jersey case, a 14-year-old freshman girl, "TLO," was caught smoking in the restroom at her public school. She denied that she smoked, but when the assistant principal asked for her purse, he opened it and found marijuana, rolling papers, and a list of students and how much money they owed her. It looked like she was a dealer. The school called her parents and the police.

TLO was suspended from school for 10 days and sentenced to a year's probation for juvenile delinquency. She appealed on the grounds that the search of her purse and seizure of her pot was a violation of the Fourth Amendment. The court ruled that authorities, including assistant principals, have a lesser standard for searching students in public schools. Instead of probable cause, they need only a *reasonable suspicion* of a crime to undertake a search, and under that standard, TLO's search was legal.

📖 **DEFINITION**

> **Reasonable suspicion** isn't as stringent as probable cause; this lower standard for conducting searches is allowed in certain cases where the courts have said that it made sense for the authorities to suspect wrongdoing and act without a warrant.

Here's a final point related to consent: while third parties can consent to search areas under their control, third parties cannot object to a search or seek to have evidence excluded on a suspect's behalf. A passenger in a car or a guest in a home cannot object if the police are otherwise lawfully conducting a search of the vehicle or house.

Good Faith

Just because a warrant is faulty doesn't mean the defendant will get off. In recent years, the courts have carved out a "good faith" exception so evidence is admissible as long as the police officers who found it honestly believe the warrant was properly issued and they had probable cause.

In a 1984 case, a defendant named Alberto Leon was the target of a drug bust. An informant gave information about him to the police, who did surveillance on him and then went to court and filed an affidavit to show probable cause. They got the search warrant and recovered drugs from Leon, and he was convicted on federal charges. On appeal, the court found that the affidavit supplied by the police was insufficient; the warrant never should have been issued because there was no probable cause. However, the court did not exclude the evidence or overturn the conviction. Justice Byron White wrote, "In such a case where the police were acting in good faith, the exclusion of valid evidence has no deterrent effect and exacts too high a price from society."

The court said the exclusionary rule is not a right, but rather a remedy to deter illegal police conduct. If it is not deterring illegal police conduct (the police thought they were doing everything aboveboard), the evidence stays in. Many principles of law are based on a cost-benefit analysis, and in *United States* v. *Leon*, the high court said the cost of the exclusionary rule outweighed the benefit to society.

Jimmy Hoffa, the onetime labor leader with organized crime ties, disappeared mysteriously and was never found. His body is reputedly buried somewhere in the New Jersey Meadowlands, perhaps under the old Giants Stadium. But Hoffa lives on, in a way, through a Supreme Court decision. During one of his many legal travails, Hoffa was placed in a cell with another man. As they chatted, Hoffa said more than he should have. The cellmate turned out to be an undercover cop, and Hoffa's comments were used against him. Hoffa appealed, but the Supreme Court said he had no expectation that his conversation was private, "however strongly a defendant may trust an apparent colleague."

Stop and Frisk

Obviously, the requirements of the Fourth Amendment have a huge impact on the way police actually do their work out on the streets. In recent years, the courts have been gradually giving back some of the leeway cops gave up under stricter interpretations of the Fourth Amendment. For example, stop-and-frisk cases have had a lot to do with chipping away at the standards of probable cause in favor of the on-the-street standard of reasonable suspicion.

The courts seem intent on helping the police do the job of policing, in part by sometimes considering not only the circumstances, but also the experience and judgment of the police officer on the scene. The thinking is that a veteran cop actually may be the best judge of whether someone should be a suspect or not. The courts call it the *totality of circumstances*.

DEFINITION

Totality of circumstances is the concept handed down by the courts allowing them to more deeply review search-and-seizure cases to consider, among other factors, the experience and judgment of the police officers involved.

Critics on the civil liberties side of the equation might be more likely to call it letting the cops act on their biases. However you look it at, the courts have made a little bit of room under the Fourth Amendment for cops to play hunches.

An important case for stop and frisk is *Ohio* v. *Terry,* decided by the Supreme Court in 1968. John W. Terry and a couple other guys were spotted in an area of Cleveland where the police had been having a lot of trouble with pickpockets and shoplifters. A police officer thought maybe they were casing a jewelry store. The police stopped the guys, patted them down, and found they were carrying guns.

Terry was convicted of carrying a concealed weapon and appealed, claiming the search was unlawful because the cops had no probable cause for stopping him; he hadn't been breaking any laws. And he argued the search was illegal because he hadn't been arrested yet. Terry probably went to the Supreme Court thinking his chances of having the search declared unconstitutional were pretty good. After all, until then, the rule was that until someone was arrested, the police needed probable cause to do a search.

The Supreme Court disagreed, however, and fine-tuned the rules in favor of the police. The high court held that the search was legal because a "reasonably prudent man" would have been warranted in believing Terry "was armed and thus presented a threat to the officer's safety while he was investigating his suspicious behavior." Chief Justice Earl Warren's decision held that the Fourth Amendment allows for sometimes giving the benefit of the doubt to the police officer in order to protect the officer's and the public's safety. "The officer need not be absolutely certain that the individual is armed," Warren wrote. "The issue is whether the reasonably prudent man in the circumstances would be warranted in the belief that his safety or others' was in danger."

Police authority expanded further a few years later in another case, when police patted down a man pulled over on suspicion of driving with a revoked license. The pat down, ostensibly for weapons, revealed marijuana cigarettes. The Supreme Court upheld the drug conviction.

WHAT IT MEANS TO YOU

If you are pulled over for a traffic offense, you can be ordered to step out of the car and be patted down if the officer is concerned you might have a weapon. Your passengers can be frisked, too. The police also can search the inside of your car—but not the trunk, not until they impound the car or get a warrant.

To Knock or Not

Ordinarily, authorities are required to "knock and announce" before they enter a home. An example of the legal rationale can be seen in a 1995 U.S. Supreme Court case, *Wilson* v. *Arkansas,* which began when Sharlene Wilson sold drugs to an undercover Arkansas state police officer. The police got warrants to search her house and arrest her. They arrived at the house and found the main door open. There was a screen door, and it was unlocked, so the police walked in, identified themselves, and said they had a warrant. Wilson was arrested and convicted on drug charges. She then appealed on the grounds that the police should have knocked before they came in and should have announced themselves before they came in, not after.

The high court agreed with her, saying yes, the cops should have knocked and announced. "Given the longstanding common-law endorsement of the practice of announcement, and the wealth of founding-era commentaries, constitutional provisions, statutes, and cases espousing or supporting the knock-and-announce principle … the Amendment's framers thought that whether officers announced their presence and authority before entering a dwelling was among the factors to be considered in assessing a search's reasonableness." However, the court also emphasized that the way the police officers entered could have been considered legal if they had good reasons for not knocking first.

Authorities can get warrants that specifically allow them to enter without knocking first, but usually only after convincing the judge or magistrate that it's for their own safety, or to prevent a suspect from escaping or destroying evidence. In the 1997 Wisconsin case *Richards* v. *Wisconsin,* police suspected a man named Steiney Richards of dealing cocaine from his hotel room. A policeman knocked on the door and said he was a hotel custodian. Richards started to open the door, but when he saw a uniformed police officer, he slammed the door shut.

The officers broke down the door and grabbed Richards before he could escape. They also found coke and cash in the bathroom. Richards was convicted, but he appealed on the grounds that the officers violated the Fourth Amendment by using deception—the phony identification as a hotel custodian—and then forcing their way into his room. The Supreme Court, however, ruled that the officers could legally break down the door as soon as Richards slammed it in their faces. That was a pretty good indication, the court said, that Richards was trying to escape, flush the evidence, or both.

In a 1998 case, the *United States* v. *Ramirez,* the police were looking for a dangerous prison escapee named Alan Shelby. A federal agent, acting on a tip from an informant, saw a guy who looked like the escaped prisoner at a home in Boring, Oregon. Agents got a "no-knock warrant" and came back to the home during the night. They broke a window to get in and woke up the man sleeping inside—Hernan Ramirez. Startled, Ramirez grabbed a gun and fired it into the ceiling. The police found no Shelby, but they found more guns and arrested Ramirez.

The trial court refused to allow the guns into evidence on the grounds that the agents should have knocked and did not have justification for destroying property—breaking the window—to gain entry. The decision was upheld on appeal, but the Bureau of Alcohol, Tobacco, Firearms, and Explosives appealed to the Supreme Court. The high court unanimously overturned the verdict and said the guns were in as evidence. The court said breaking the window was justified because the officers had a "reasonable suspicion" to think that knocking and announcing might be dangerous, futile, or inhibit their investigation.

WE THE PEOPLE

In *United States* v. *Ramirez,* Chief Justice William Rehnquist said that even if the officers had violated the Fourth Amendment, the evidence was still admissible. "Excessive or unnecessary destruction of property in the course of a search may violate the Fourth Amendment," Rehnquist wrote, "even though the entry itself is lawful and the fruits of the search not subject to suppression."

Here's one more no-knock case: *Brigham City* v. *Stuart,* decided in the spring of 2006. There probably aren't a lot of really loud all-night parties in Brigham City, Utah, so it makes sense that the police responded promptly when a neighbor called in a complaint around 3 A.M. The officers went to the front door and pounded but got no answer, apparently because the music and voices inside were so loud.

The officers walked up the driveway, saw juveniles drinking in the backyard, and entered the yard. Looking into the house, they saw a juvenile punch an adult in the face. While the adult was spitting blood into the sink, the police entered the home, shouting to identify themselves. After a period of scuffling and shouting, and angry protests from partygoers, the police finally calmed things down and made a number of arrests, including for providing alcohol to minors.

The defendants argued that their Fourth Amendment rights had been violated. The Supreme Court disagreed. The officers had probable cause to enter the backyard when they saw the juveniles drinking, and seeing the attack inside provided enough of an emergency for them to enter the house without knocking first. Besides, they tried to announce themselves but the music was too loud.

The Least You Need to Know

- The police do not necessarily need a warrant to search your home, office, yard, car, garage, or barn.

- If the police want to search your home or office, ask to see a warrant—politely and calmly.

- Don't resist, physically or verbally.

- If you have questions, ask if you may have a lawyer present, or check with a lawyer later.

The Fifth Amendment: Due Process

The Fifth Amendment is one of the Constitution's bulwarks of individual liberty against the powers of police and prosecutors. It restrains the forces of law and order throughout the criminal process, from the moment an individual is suspected of a crime.

The Fifth Amendment

"No person shall be held to answer for a capital or otherwise infamous crime, unless on a presentment or indictment of a grand jury, except in cases arising in the land or naval forces, or in the militia, when in actual service in time of war or public danger; nor shall any person be subject for the same offense to be twice put in jeopardy of life or limb; nor shall be compelled in any criminal case to be a witness against himself; nor be deprived of life, liberty, or property, without due process of law; nor shall private property be taken for public use, without just compensation."

The Fifth Amendment protects you against having to give evidence against yourself. When you "take the Fifth," you are refusing to provide possible evidence against yourself, but the Fifth Amendment also gave us the Miranda ruling we hear on all the TV cop shows: "You have the right to remain silent …."

However, the Fifth Amendment contains several other important provisions for protecting your rights. It is the source of the double jeopardy doctrine, which prevents authorities from trying you twice for the same crime, and it requires that people accused of serious crimes be indicted by a grand jury before they can be prosecuted. The Fifth Amendment also guarantees "due process," or that the government will follow the law and procedural rules in taking your freedom or property, and that you'll be fairly compensated if the government condemns and takes it over under eminent domain.

The Fifth Amendment originally applied only to federal law, but most of its requirements now apply to the states, too, under the provisions of the Equal Protection Clause of the Fourteenth Amendment.

Grand Jury Indictments

"No person shall be held to answer for a capital or otherwise infamous crime, unless on a presentment or indictment of a grand jury …."

One of the historic cornerstones of the criminal justice system is the Fifth Amendment's requirement that an indictment be returned by a grand jury before the government can prosecute a defendant on serious criminal charges. In effect, the grand jury decides whether the prosecution has enough evidence to bring a defendant to trial. It is an ancient legal concept, going back to English common law in the twelfth century, to prevent a king or his minions from prosecuting someone for no good reason. Designed to prevent prosecutions born out of political, religious, business, or personal motivations, it was one of the first checks on government power in what has become our system of checks and balances.

After all, throwing a rival in prison or chopping off his head was a good way for a nobleman to take over a rival's land, steal his wife, or get him to stop saying things the nobleman didn't like. The idea was to give some regular citizens a chance to say, "Hey, wait, this isn't fair!"

Most people are familiar with the kind of jury, traditionally 12 people, that hears the evidence in criminal trials, goes off to deliberate in closed session, and then comes back to the courtroom with a verdict: guilty or not guilty. In legal terms, that type of jury is called a *petit jury*.

The *grand jury* is different. Like a regular jury, a grand jury is made of people from the community who receive a summons to report for jury duty. But a grand jury is larger, usually 23 people. A grand jury may be convened to consider just one case, which is what usually happens when a special prosecutor has been appointed to conduct a complex and often high-level government scandal, such as the Whitewater investigation of the Clintons or the inquiry into possible leaks that revealed the identify of an undercover CIA operative related to the search for weapons of mass destruction before the Iraq war. On a local level, however, a grand jury is more likely to be appointed to serve over a period of several weeks, being called into session to consider not one but several different cases during its terms.

Instead of a judge presiding, a prosecutor, such as a U.S. attorney in federal courts or a district attorney in state courts, leads or directs the proceedings presenting the case against the defendant to the grand jury.

The Fifth Amendment's requirements for grand jury indictments for serious crimes—generally agreed to be any offense that carries a potential prison sentence—applies to federal crimes only. Unlike many other requirements in the Bill of Rights, the Supreme Court has never extended the grand jury rules to the state courts. As a practical matter, however, state criminal courts either have their own comparable grand jury requirements or a similar process called a *preliminary hearing.* In a preliminary hearing, the prosecutor presents evidence to a judge to decide whether there is enough of a case against an accused person to bring an indictment and go to trial.

WHAT IT MEANS TO YOU

If you are called to serve, the amount of time you spend on a grand jury depends on where you are and what kind of court it is. State grand jurors typically serve for a matter of weeks, while federal grand jurors often serve for months. In either case, you might be called into session almost daily or only a few times a month, depending on the caseload.

Another big difference between grand juries and regular juries is that the strict rules of evidence don't apply in grand jury proceedings as they do in a trial; for example, a prosecutor is allowed to lead a witness or use hearsay as evidence. The accused person may attend a grand jury session, but he or she does not have an attorney present and is not allowed to present evidence or ask questions of witnesses. Unlike trial jurors, who are required to sit quietly and pay attention, grand jurors are allowed to directly ask their own questions of witnesses. And while the Fourth Amendment's exclusionary rule prevents a trial jury from considering or even hearing anything about evidence that was acquired in violation of a defendant's rights, grand jurors can hear and consider evidence that was obtained illegally.

While members of a jury at a criminal trial are instructed to find a defendant not guilty unless they agree that guilt is "beyond reasonable doubt," members of a grand jury have a lower standard. They can indict (or "return an indictment against") an accused person if they find "probable cause" that the accused person committed the crime.

The indictment is a formal legal document that gives the prosecution the green light to proceed. When an indictment is returned, an accused person is "bound over" to the criminal courts for trial.

As you might imagine, prosecutors don't like to take a case to a grand jury unless they're pretty certain they will get an indictment. And the great latitude they are allowed—hearsay, illegal evidence, probable cause, and so on—lets prosecutors lead grand juries to almost any indictment they want.

WE THE PEOPLE

An old saying around the courthouses of America is that a good prosecutor can get a grand jury to indict a ham sandwich. When a Texas prosecutor indicted former House Republican Leader Tom DeLay on conspiracy charges that led him to resign in 2005, one of his supporters, Florida Congresswoman Ileana Ros-Lehtinen, told reporters, "This is a ham sandwich indictment and we just ask, where's the beef?"

Grand jury proceedings have always been held in secret for a couple reasons: one, to ensure the authorities, whether the nobleman of yesteryear or the government prosecutors of today, would not seek revenge against the members of the grand jury, and two, to avoid publicity or other repercussions that might be unfair to witnesses or to the accused person.

The secrecy requirements of the grand jury system have become more controversial in recent times. Some states allow the release and publication of grand jury testimony in certain circumstances after a criminal case is completed, but some jurisdictions have imposed harsh penalties against those who spill a grand jury's secrets.

For example, the two San Francisco newspaper reporters who broke the story about baseball player Barry Bonds's links to a steroid drug operation were threatened with jail time for refusing to reveal how they got Bonds's testimony and other transcripts from the grand jury. It was a case of the right to free speech versus the need to protect grand jury secrecy. Charges against the reporters were dropped after a suspected steroid dealer's defense attorney pleaded guilty to releasing the grand jury testimony, but for a time, it looked like the reporters might spend more time behind bars than the dealers or users or anyone else connected with the case.

Double Jeopardy

"… nor shall any person be subject for the same offense to be twice put in jeopardy of life or limb …"

Double jeopardy is not only the second half of a venerable television trivia program, it also is a venerable legal concept that, like the grand jury requirement, is designed to limit government harassment of citizens. The idea is simple: you should not have to stand trial twice for the same offense. If you are found not guilty by a judge or jury, the government cannot try you again for the same thing. In fact, you cannot be tried a second time even if you were convicted. The government cannot lose a case against you and then bring a new charge for the same crime. Nor can the government get a conviction against you and then bring another charge against you for the same crime in hopes of adding to your punishment.

Back in the day, the concept of double jeopardy applied only to capital cases—crimes that carried the death penalty—in both English common law and the American colonies. In the United States, it applied only to federal criminal cases until 1969, when the Supreme Court decided it was one of those rights that applied to state law, too. Instead of applying only to capital crimes, the Fifth Amendment's language concerning any case that would put a defendant "in jeopardy of life or limb" means double jeopardy now generally applies for any offense that carries a potential prison sentence.

CASES

Brown v. Ohio **(1977):** The defendant was convicted of operating a motor vehicle without the owner's permission. The prosecutor subsequently brought new charges—stealing the car—against the defendant. The defendant was convicted and appealed. The Supreme Court ruled that both charges were based on the same joyride, and the second conviction was overturned.

The Supreme Court has offered these reasons for the rules against allowing authorities to try citizens twice for the same act:

- By sheer use of its superior legal firepower—time, money, investigators, lawyers—the prosecution can wear down the defense and convict an innocent person.

- People can suffer in many ways, from financial to emotional, from having to defend themselves repeatedly.

- Public respect for the criminal justice system will wane if prosecutors are allowed to pick on people instead of letting them settle their debts to society once and for all.

- Prosecutors could develop too much power, and too much potential for abusing that power, if they can drag people they don't like back into court over and over.

- Judges would be able to pile on unduly harsh sentences, one on top of the other, for the same offense.

You can be charged with more than one offense for any particular act, but you cannot be punished for it more than once. Suppose someone kills another person. Depending on the prosecutor's assessment of the case, the defendant might be charged with various levels of the crime: manslaughter, second-degree murder, first-degree murder. A jury hearing the evidence and determining the facts of the case can find the defendant guilty of any one of the charges, but not more than one. If you beat up someone (battery) who then dies (murder), you can be charged with both battery and murder, but you can be convicted of only one.

CASES

Ashe v. Swenson **(1970):** In this case, a guy who robbed a poker game was charged with robbing only one of the seven players. He was acquitted, so the prosecution brought charges against him for robbing the second player, and he was convicted. The U.S. Supreme Court overturned the conviction on double jeopardy grounds.

It is possible, however, to be charged for the same act in different jurisdictions. A state court might find a defendant not guilty of murder, but a separate proceeding then could be brought in federal court to convict the person of violating the victim's civil rights—death being the ultimate violation of someone's civil rights. And sometimes a civil case, in which the typical standard is "a preponderance of the evidence," may succeed despite the failure of a criminal prosecution, where the standard for conviction is "beyond a reasonable doubt." For example, take the case of former football star O. J. Simpson, who was accused of killing his estranged wife. He was found not guilty at a criminal trial. But his wife's family sued in civil court, and Simpson was found to be responsible for her death and ordered to pay monetary damages.

Mistrials are not covered by double jeopardy, nor are most convictions overturned on appeal. If you are convicted, you appeal, and the appeals court overturns the conviction, you don't necessarily walk; you're probably going to be retried.

And if a judge declares a mistrial because of a hung jury or because of juror misconduct, the prosecution can bring the case against you again. One distressing wrinkle for criminal defense lawyers came in a 2012 U.S. Supreme Court case, *Blueford* v. *Arkansas,* decided by a 6–3 vote, which held prosecutors could reboot the whole case when a jury acquits a defendant on some charges and is hung on others and a mistrial is declared. The high court ruled that prosecutors can retry the defendant on all the charges, including the ones for which the defendant was acquitted.

It is important to remember that double jeopardy does not apply to cases in civil court—noncriminal cases, in other words. You can be sued in civil court, win, and be sued all over again by the same person for the same thing in the same court. And if you were acquitted in criminal court, you can still be sued in civil court for the consequences of your action. You won't be going to prison, but you can be ordered to pay damages to a plaintiff who claims he or she was wronged and suffered financial losses because of it.

WE THE PEOPLE

The glove didn't fit, so the jury did acquit. But when O. J. Simpson got off after being charged with two murders, double jeopardy didn't keep him from being sued in civil court by the Brown and Goldman families. A civil court jury found that Simpson had killed Nicole Brown Simpson and Ronald Goldman and ordered him to pay the families $33.5 million.

Self-Incrimination

"... nor shall any person ... be compelled in any criminal case to be a witness against himself ..."

The Fifth Amendment is best known for guaranteeing the right to silence—you cannot be forced to give evidence against yourself. The right against self-incrimination, however, is a relatively new one in legal history. Originally, any confession, no matter how the authorities got it—even by torture—was admissible in court.

Confessions

An important case against self-incrimination was brought by John Lilburne in England in 1637. A Puritan activist put on trial for smuggling antigovernment pamphlets into the country, he refused to answer questions by the Star Chamber, a notoriously harsh court. He was whipped for his stubbornness, but the case led Parliament to abolish the Star Chamber and to agree that citizens should not be forced to give evidence against themselves.

Even in colonial America, the Puritan settlers in Massachusetts, who faced the same sort of oppression from authorities on the other side of the Atlantic, permitted torture as a means of extracting confessions from the accused. Not until the eighteenth century did English common law, in Great Britain and subsequently in the colonies, embrace the notion that it might be a good thing to disallow confessions obtained by coercion, extortion, or trickery.

As a practical matter, of course, police in America had a long history of pushing that particular envelope. The "rubber hose treatment" (rubber hoses supposedly left fewer marks and less evidence of police misconduct) was a cliché for a reason. So was giving a suspect "the third degree" to gain a confession, or "sweating it out of him."

WHAT IT MEANS TO YOU

If you think something about yourself—something you know, something you've done—could conceivably be used against you in a criminal proceeding, you do not have to divulge that information.

Gradually, the federal courts led the way in forcing the police not to abuse suspects, primarily by reversing the convictions in cases when the police stepped over the line. In a 1936 case in Mississippi, three black men were accused of killing a white plantation owner, and the police readily confirmed that the men had been whipped to encourage them to confess. The Supreme Court overturned the convictions on Fifth Amendment grounds. The high court also reversed a conviction in a 1940 Florida case in which a defendant finally confessed after being interrogated for 5 days. The same thing happened in a 1944 case in Tennessee, in which a defendant confessed after being grilled pretty much nonstop under hot lights for 36 hours.

In these and other cases, the court reasoned that a prolonged interrogation made a confession inadmissible because it was unreliable: defendants would say whatever the authorities wanted them to say just to get the questions to stop, or get a slice of pizza, or get that blazing hot and incredibly bright light out of their face.

The Self-Incrimination Clause of the Fifth Amendment forces prosecutors to come up with independent evidence, something other than the accused person's confession, to secure a conviction. Make no mistake, the Fifth Amendment does not diminish the weight of a voluntary confession, and in fact the willing confession is still the biggest single piece of evidence in many if not most criminal prosecutions. Once an accused person has signed that confession, a plea bargain—pleading guilty to a slightly lesser charge or in exchange for a more lenient sentence—that avoids the time and expense of a trial is often a perfunctory matter.

 CASES

> ***Hiibel v. Sixth Judicial District Court of Nevada* (2004):** In this case, the U.S. Supreme Court ruled that you have to give the police your name if they ask. Neither the right to free speech under the First Amendment nor the right to silence under the Fifth Amendment applies. It's reasonable for the authorities to ask you your name, and simply giving your name is not necessarily regarded as incriminating.

Taking the Fifth

The Fifth Amendment's protections against self-incrimination apply in state or federal court and anywhere else you have to testify under oath, including in civil proceedings. That's why, back in the 1950s, when the House Un-American Activities Committee was handing out subpoenas to anyone and everyone rumored to have any links to communists or communism, those Hollywood celebrities took the Fifth:

> Q: Are you now or have you ever been a member of the communist party?

> A: On the advice of counsel, I respectfully refuse to answer on the grounds that my answer might incriminate me.

Whether they are hearings on organized crime or the Enron collapse, it's become a familiar scene: the witness in the hot seat ducking the question. Intellectually, we know the witness is exercising a constitutional right we all share, but it doesn't exactly inspire confidence in someone's integrity or innocence—even when a witness such as Enron's late chairman, Ken Lay, tried to convince a congressional hearing he really would like to answer all those pesky questions and clear everything up but his doggone lawyers just won't let him, darn it.

Taking the Fifth in a civil proceeding beats outright lying for one simple reason: lying under oath is perjury, and that's criminal. You might not go to jail for whatever it is you have to testify about, but if you lie about it, you might go to jail for committing perjury. For example, former Bush administration aide Lewis "Scooter" Libby was implicated in the scandal over the outing of Valerie Plame as a CIA agent, but he was never charged with the crime of revealing her name. Instead, he was charged with and convicted of lying to a grand jury about what he told reporters about Plame. Going further back, President Bill Clinton initially denied having relations with Monica Lewinsky, but he later admitted it rather than lie under oath and face perjury charges.

But don't think the Fifth Amendment comes into play only in headline-grabbing cases. In 2014, a Pennsylvania man suspected of poaching deer out of season was fined $150 under a state law that requires people to answer a game warden's questions. The man, Larry Coble, decided to fight the fine. He got a lawyer and spent a lot more than $150 to go to court and appeal on the grounds that answering the game warden's questions would violate his Fifth Amendment right against incriminating himself. The local district attorney agreed with Coble, and the state did not object when the case was thrown out of court.

Meanwhile, be aware that the courts have been steadily chipping away at the right to silence. Depending on the circumstances, and how and when you speak to the police, your statements still might be used against you if you have not received a Miranda warning. And in a 5–4 ruling in a 2013 case, *Salinas* v. *Texas,* the Supreme Court said that under certain circumstances, yes, a suspect's silence actually can be used against him in court.

WHAT IT MEANS TO YOU

It is a well-established principle: a jury is not supposed to draw an inference of guilt if a defendant has exercised the right to silence. But what about you? What do you think of a person who takes the Fifth? Do you think, *Hmm, that person is exercising an inalienable right?* Or do you think, *Hmm, that's somebody who's been doing something wrong?*

Immunity

If you agree to testify against someone in exchange for immunity from prosecution, you give up your right to silence. There are two kinds of immunity: *transactional* and *use immunity*.

In transactional immunity, you cannot be prosecuted for anything relating to your testimony. In use immunity, you still can be prosecuted, but the testimony you provided in exchange for immunity cannot be used against you.

The Miranda Warning

No doubt the most far-reaching aspect of the Fifth Amendment's protection against self-incrimination—even more than pleading the Fifth—is the right to remain silent and the requirement that police inform a suspect of that right at the time of arrest. These are the rights outlined in the well-known Miranda warning:

> You have the right to remain silent.

> You have the right to consult an attorney before and during questioning.

> If you cannot afford an attorney, the court will appoint one for you for free.

> Any statements you make to the police can and will be used as evidence against you in a court of law.

Ernesto Miranda was a guy who'd been in a lot of trouble when he was picked up by the police for robbery, kidnapping, and rape in Arizona in 1963. He confessed, signed a statement admitting his guilt, and was convicted, but he appealed. The appeal made it before the Supreme Court in 1966 and became the best known of a series of controversial cases decided by the court under Chief Justice Earl Warren. Chief Justice Warren, himself a former prosecutor, wrote the Miranda decision himself. He said Miranda's Fifth Amendment right against self-incrimination had been violated and spelled out the warning word for word.

Critics said the Warren court was tipping the scales of justice too far in favor of the accused and endangering society by making it harder for the police to do their job. Supporters, notably the American Civil Liberties Union (ACLU), welcomed constitutional interpretations that aimed to protect individual rights. (In his decision, Warren rejected the ACLU's suggestion that every police station have a lawyer either on duty or nearby, so every suspect brought in could see a lawyer immediately.)

The warning has survived a number of challenges in recent years, including one in 2000 when Chief Justice William Rehnquist, a notably conservative jurist, voted to uphold the warning and noted that Miranda warnings "have become part of our national culture." But critics, including Justice Antonin Scalia, maintain that the Warren court overstepped its authority in 1966 and that the Constitution doesn't require such a warning. They hold out hope that the Miranda decision may someday be reversed.

Legal authorities are virtually unanimous: a suspect has little or nothing to gain by making any comment to police before consulting with an attorney. Still, studies show that despite the mandatory Miranda warnings, many suspects do talk with the police before consulting an attorney.

Confessions obtained without a proper Miranda warning cannot be used as evidence under the exclusionary rule. But an inadmissible confession doesn't prohibit the prosecution from using other evidence. In fact, that's what happened to Ernesto Miranda. On appeal, the Supreme Court overturned his conviction on the grounds of an inadmissible confession and sent the case back for retrial. Prosecutors in Arizona then retried Miranda and convicted him using other evidence.

WE THE PEOPLE

Ernesto Miranda served several years for rape and kidnapping. After his release, he made pocket change selling autographed copies of the Miranda warning. He was stabbed to death in a bar fight in Phoenix in 1976.

One of the keys to the Miranda ruling and the admissibility of confessions is whether a suspect has been arrested or taken into custody. To ask questions in what the courts call a "custodial interrogation," the police must administer the Miranda warning first. The Supreme Court has said "by custodial interrogation, we mean questioning initiated by law enforcement officers after a person has been taken into custody or otherwise deprived of his freedom of action in any significant way."

A number of cases have tried to define exactly when a suspect is in custody. Simply being in a police station—taking a ride downtown, as they say on the cop shows—is not necessarily being in custody. If you can leave, you're not in custody. Sometimes, of course, a suspect is not sure whether he can leave or not. The police don't necessarily need to declare you're under arrest. If you cannot leave, or if it's reasonable for you to believe you cannot leave, you're in custody.

WHAT IT MEANS TO YOU

You don't need to be in custody, and the police don't need to be asking you questions, for anything you say to be used against you. Sometimes two police officers will discuss a case in front of a suspect in the hopes the suspect will just have to interject something. It's not deception, and the evidence is admissible.

The information you provide on your federal income tax returns can be used against you. In a 1927 case, the Supreme Court ruled that a taxpayer could not plead the Fifth Amendment's protections against self-incrimination when the information on his tax return—he said he was a professional gambler—was used against him at his trial for trying to fix sporting events. "If the form of return provided called for answers that the defendant was privileged from making," the court held, "he could have raised the objection in the return, but could not on that account refuse to make any return at all. We are not called on to decide what, if anything, he might have withheld."

Companies cannot claim the Fifth Amendment to withhold records from the authorities. The courts have ruled that the right against self-incrimination protects only "natural persons"—real human beings, in other words.

Even if a confession is inadmissible on Fifth Amendment grounds, it can still end up being used against a defendant under certain circumstances. For example, let's say a defendant is on trial, his confession is inadmissible, but there is other evidence. If the defendant takes the stand to deny committing the crime, he opens the door to what he did or said, and the prosecution can then use the confession to impeach that testimony.

WHAT IT MEANS TO YOU

You cannot be forced to testify against your spouse, and your spouse cannot be forced to testify against you. But the rules are less well defined, from case to case and especially from state to state, over when and whether you can prevent your spouse from testifying against you. Someone who truly wants to put his or her spouse away often gets the chance in court.

Due Process of Law

"... nor be deprived of life, liberty, or property, without due process of law ..."

Due process of law is hard to define, but it's a powerful legal doctrine. It's an all-encompassing concept that means you cannot be harmed by loss of freedom or property unless the rules of the justice system have been followed and your rights have not been violated.

The principle was expressed in the Magna Carta this way: "No free man shall be seized, or imprisoned, or disseised, or outlawed, or exiled, or injured in any way ... except by the lawful judgment of his peers, or by the law of the land." That last phrase, "the law of the land," was the due process part. When a government sets up rules, the rules have to be reasonable, and it has to follow them.

In many ways, due process honors the rule of law. Society insists that the government play by the rules and treat everyone fairly. Due process also goes to entitlement: we have inalienable rights and we're entitled to them all the time, not just when it's convenient for the government to respect them. Society and society's customs have a lot to do with determining what is fair, what we're entitled to, and what due process means.

Due process originally applied only to the federal government under the Fifth Amendment, but the Fourteenth Amendment extended its protections to the states, too.

Legal scholars make a distinction between *procedural* and *substantive* due process. Procedural due process is the "how" of the law. How was a law approved? How is it applied? How does it affect the public? If the answer to any of those "how" questions is not acceptable—if there are violations of our rights—the law may be unconstitutional. Substantive due process is the "why" of the law. Why was the law passed? Why does it make sense? Why is it fair? If the answer to any of those "why" questions is not acceptable—if there are violations of our rights—the law may be unconstitutional.

In practical terms, though, most of us don't need to know the difference between substantive and procedural due process. We merely need to know that laws have to be fair, and they have to be enforced fairly.

One of the biggest due process decisions in recent years came in *United States* v. *Windsor* in 2013, when the Supreme Court struck down the federal Defense of Marriage Act (DOMA) by a 5–4 vote. DOMA had restricted the legal definition of marriage—and spousal benefits under federal law—to heterosexual unions. The case was brought by Edith Windsor and Thea Spyer, an elderly New York couple who had been legally married in Canada in 2007. When Spyer died in 2009 and Windsor inherited her estate, Windsor went to court to be allowed to claim the federal estate tax exemption for surviving spouses. Under DOMA, however, the Internal Revenue Service could not recognize Windsor as a legal spouse, so she was not eligible for the tax break. The Supreme Court found that Edith Windsor was indeed eligible for the tax break and declared DOMA unconstitutional under the Due Process Clause.

WE THE PEOPLE

In his majority decision in the *Windsor* case, citing the Due Process Clause, Justice Anthony Kennedy wrote: "The federal statute is invalid, for no legitimate purpose overcomes the purpose and effect to disparage and to injure those whom the State, by its marriage laws, sought to protect in personhood and dignity."

The *Windsor* decision paved the way for the subsequent 2015 decision in the *Obergefell* case, which made same-sex marriage legal in all 50 states. (*Obergefell* v. *Hodges* is discussed in Chapter 13.)

Here are a few other examples of the many types of cases pertaining to individual rights that can hinge on whether due process was followed in enacting or administering a law:

- Death penalty cases
- Affirmative action cases
- Privacy cases
- Voting rights cases

Eminent Domain

"... nor shall private property be taken for public use, without just compensation."

The concept of eminent domain—that the government can take away a person's private property for public use—is another principle that has evolved through the ages from English common law. Back in the day, the Crown could take away a landowner's property without compensation, but the Fifth Amendment requires "just compensation."

Eminent domain played a big role in the building of American society dating back to colonial times. If a new road or bridge was needed to help open the frontier for economic development, it didn't make sense to go miles out of the way to build around someone's private property. It made more sense to declare eminent domain over the needed property—condemn it, in other words— and then appropriate it for public use.

During the Revolutionary War, both sides seized property—land and supplies—from citizens, against their will and without compensation. After independence, some states seized the property of loyalists who had supported Britain in the war, and some states had few qualms about taking over property inside their borders that was owned by residents of other states.

The Eminent Domain Clause is one of the Constitution's classic balancing acts: what's good for society versus what's good for the individual. On one hand, it makes sense to allow the government to take possession of private property—usually land but it can be personal property, too—if it will benefit the general public. On the other hand, if and when that happens, the property owner should be fairly compensated for the loss.

As with any balancing of different interests, there are bound to be tensions. In America, we've been arguing for a long time—and continue to argue—over exactly just what is in the public interest and exactly what is fair compensation.

The general agreement on the Fifth Amendment's provisions, which have been applied by the Supreme Court to the states, too, is that "just compensation" usually means fair market value—what a property owner could get for the property by selling it on the open market. In theory, it should be pretty easy to figure out what property is worth: simply have it appraised. But what if the property is worth more to its current owner than the appraised value? What if the property owner has plans for the property that will make it more valuable? What if the property has sentimental value, such as a family homestead or a historic site?

 WE THE PEOPLE

> The concept of eminent domain has long been a target for conservatives and libertarians. Adam Millsap, a research fellow for the State and Local Policy Project for the Mercatus Center at George Mason University, summed up one objection in 2015: "The use of eminent domain does require that the property holder receive 'just compensation,' which is usually interpreted as the market price for the property under the assumption of a willing seller and a willing buyer engaging in a good-faith negotiation. But remember, eminent domain is only used when a property owner is not a willing seller. So the government negotiates with a phantom representative seller, who is treated as if they value the property no more than a disinterested buyer would."

Sometimes an eminent domain case can cause problems not only for the owner whose property has been seized, but for other people, too. Suppose the county decides a new highway has to come through your neighbor's backyard and pays him to pull up and move out. What about you? You may not technically be eligible for compensation—it wasn't your property that was taken away—but your peaceful little haven in the country may not be worth as much if it's across from an on-ramp. If zoning laws change and you're suddenly under the flight pattern for a new airport, should you be compensated? Probably. Maybe. But not necessarily. And how much? The courts will decide based on the particular facts you present when you sue.

The definition of "for public use" also remains contentious. The courts always have left it to Congress to decide, and there's usually little debate if eminent domain is used by the government for a purpose that directly benefits the public and provides open access to the public. Anybody can use a highway or an airport or a school or a park, for instance; those are examples of private property being turned into public property.

But eminent domain also has been used to seize property that will not actually be public. The courts have said only that there must be a benefit to the public, even if that benefit seems to be indirect and seems to directly benefit certain individuals. In a 2005 case from Connecticut,

Kelo v. *City of New London,* the Supreme Court held, in a controversial 5–4 decision, that it was permissible for the city to take over property from one private owner so it could be used for private development, including a resort, hotel, conference center, shops, restaurants, offices, and apartments. Justice Paul Stevens, delivering the majority opinion in the *Kelo* case, wrote, "The city has carefully formulated a development plan that it believes will provide appreciable benefits to the community, including, but not limited to, new jobs and increased tax revenue."

Dissenting, Justice Sandra Day O'Connor warned that the danger was that rich people would be able to benefit from eminent domain as governments took away land from poor people: "Any property may not be taken for the benefit of another private party, but the fallout from this decision will not be random. The beneficiaries are likely to be those citizens with disproportionate influence and power in the political process, including large corporations and development firms." She urged the court, futilely, to stick to a strict interpretation of "for the public use" in the Fifth Amendment.

Not long after that decision, a libertarian activist asked the town council in Weare, New Hampshire, to use eminent domain to take over the home of David Souter, who was one of the five justices in the majority in the Supreme Court decision. The activist said he would turn the property into a hotel—the Lost Liberty Hotel, no less—and it would have the same benefits, including new jobs and local tax payments, as the property development in the New London case. At last report, the town council had no plans to turn the justice's home into a hotel.

The Least You Need to Know

- You cannot be forced to give any evidence against yourself, and neither can your spouse.
- You have the right to remain silent—and if you're ever in the position, you probably should use it.
- Grand jury testimony is secret, and the rules are different from a regular trial.
- If the government does something that affects the value of your property, you may have a case for compensation.

CHAPTER 10

The Sixth and Seventh Amendments: Fair Trials

The Sixth Amendment guarantees criminal defendants the right to a fair trial. It ensures defendants are brought to trial soon after they are charged, their trials are held in public, they have a fair and impartial jury, they can confront the witnesses against them, and they can compel potentially helpful witnesses to appear and testify.

The Seventh Amendment extends many of the same rights to litigants in civil cases.

In This Chapter

- A public and speedy trial
- An impartial jury
- Witnesses for and against
- The right to counsel
- Juries in civil trials

The Sixth Amendment: Juries in Criminal Trials

"In all criminal prosecutions, the accused shall enjoy the right to a speedy and public trial, by an impartial jury of the State and district wherein the crime shall have been committed, which district shall have been previously ascertained, to be confronted with the witnesses against him, to have compulsory process for obtaining witnesses in his favor, and to have the assistance of counsel for his defense."

The concept of the speedy trial goes back to the Magna Carta, the concept of an impartial jury goes back even farther, and the concept of a public trial goes back to the Bible.

The Sixth Amendment's provisions for fair trials in criminal cases are part of the bedrock of individual rights. Its provisions aim to protect individuals, but they also strengthen society. Fair trials prevent governments from persecuting individuals or classes of people but also assure everybody they won't be persecuted. Fair trials give people confidence in their judicial system and their government.

The Speedy Trial Clause

It's not fair for the government to charge you with a crime and then not give you a chance to clear your name as soon as possible. The longer an accusation hangs over your head, the more it hurts you, the more people believe you did it, and the more it hurts your ability to defend yourself.

By the same token, the government sometimes wants speedy trials, too. Defendants who really are crooks can commit more crimes if they're not locked away; long delays increase the chances they will jump bail; and if they might be reformed or rehabilitated, long delays may keep them from getting treatment that might help. In the big picture, citizens are never happy with a government that locks up people without giving them a chance to tell their side of the story.

In the United States, the speedy trial became an issue as caseloads grew with the rise in crime in the 1960s. Dockets became more clogged, and lawyers began filing and winning appeals on behalf of defendants who had to wait too long to go to trial. Few hard-and-fast rules have emerged amid the ensuing court decisions and legislation, however, so even today it is often difficult to say exactly how long is too long.

In general, the clock starts running at the time of arrest. But the Supreme Court has ruled that there are no specific time limits, and how long is too long depends on a number of factors. As usual, there is a balancing act: the defendant's constitutional right to a fair trial versus factors such as the reason for delay, the length of the delay, whether the defendant pushed for a speedy trial, and whether delays affected the outcome of the trial.

On one hand, the mere fact of a delay does not necessarily overcome the public's interest in seeing justice done. On the other hand, a defendant whose trial has been delayed doesn't necessarily need to show any harm from the delay. But one thing is pretty clear: when the courts do find that a defendant has been denied the right to a speedy trial, the charges are dropped or the conviction is overturned.

> **WHAT IT MEANS TO YOU**
>
> The federal Speedy Trial Act of 1974 sets forth a timetable: there must be an indictment within 30 days of arrest, an arraignment within 10 days of indictment, and a trial within 60 days of arraignment. Many states have comparable rules, but the state deadlines are usually less stringent, providing more time for grinding the various legal gears.

No matter what deadlines apply, many exceptions waive those deadlines without objection from defendants. Indeed, the defendants typically are responsible for many of the delays, largely through filing motions that let them find and gather witnesses and do research that will help their defense. In practical terms, defendants often don't want a speedy trial because it can close the window of opportunity for a plea bargain; the longer the delay, the longer the attorneys have a chance to work out a deal.

In addition, judges and lawyers routinely accommodate each other's schedules, including for personal reasons. For example, if a prosecuting attorney asks to put off a trial for a week because of a long-scheduled family vacation, the judge ordinarily will agree and the defense attorney ordinarily will not object.

The Public Trial Clause

Our form of democracy is deeply rooted in the concept that government should be conducted in the open—including public trials. Historically, public trials have been seen as a safeguard against a government using secret trials to persecute individuals or groups of people. The Spanish Inquisition and England's Star Chamber are notorious examples of judicial proceedings that were conducted out of the public view. The original 13 states either had their own legal guarantees for public trials by the time the Sixth Amendment was ratified in 1791, or they enacted them soon after.

A trial open to the public is more likely to be fair. It discourages perjury, makes judges or lawyers less likely to bend the rules or do anything inappropriate, and reduces the chances that decisions will be made arbitrarily or as a result of prejudice. The public trial is also a First Amendment issue; the press should be able to attend and report on government proceedings, particularly if those proceedings might take away someone's liberty or property.

The right to a public trial in criminal cases is not absolute, but because it is such an ingrained concept in our system, the Supreme Court has not been asked to consider many cases on public trials. The courts have ruled that the Sixth Amendment does not extend to the right to televise a trial, although individual jurisdictions can set their own rules for when and whether trials may be broadcast. Juveniles are not guaranteed the right to a public trial, and neither are defendants in the military justice system.

Despite the presumption that all trials should be public, judges can close court proceedings for a number of reasons, including when witnesses or jurors might be afraid to be identified—as in cases involving organized crime or terrorism—or in cases involving victims of sex crimes or juveniles who might be unduly harmed if their identities became public. Judges can decide on a case-by-case basis and consider intimidation, trauma, embarrassment, common decency, and other factors. Those same factors can lead a judge not to close a trial but to impose a gag order that keeps the participants—and sometimes the media—from identifying victims, defendants, or witnesses.

Sometimes a judge may close part of a court proceeding but not the whole thing. In the 1984 case *Waller* v. *Georgia,* police used legal wiretaps to gather evidence on illegal gambling, and the defendants filed a motion to suppress the wiretap evidence. A number of people not on trial were mentioned on the wiretaps, including suspects who might have been tipped off about the possible evidence against them, so the court barred the public from the suppression hearing.

On appeal, the Supreme Court noted that the suppression hearings were closed for 7 days, but the evidence from the wiretaps against other people took only 2 hours. In a unanimous decision, the high court said the Sixth Amendment right to a public trial is "no less pressing in a hearing to suppress wrongfully seized evidence." The justices agreed there could be instances when trials and hearings can be closed to the public, but only in specific cases when there is no alternative.

Either the prosecution or the defense can ask a judge to close a trial or hearing. In either case, the judge must consider whether the defendant's right to a fair trial would be endangered in open court, and whether there are any reasonable alternatives to closing the courtroom to the public. If a judge does decide to close a trial, the press can object—and so can the public—on First Amendment grounds.

The Impartial Jury Clause

This clause shores up the Constitution's Article III guarantees for jury trials and can be traced back to the Magna Carta, when the noblemen wanted to ensure that, if King John's government charged them with crimes, they would be tried before a jury of their peers—other noblemen, presumably, who might be sympathetic.

The framers of the Constitution viewed the impartial jury as a way to protect citizens against overly aggressive prosecutors or incompetent judges. The participation of ordinary citizens brought checks and balances to the everyday working of the judicial system and kept prosecutors and judges from having too much authority.

Historically in English common law, jurors were chosen for their wisdom and good judgment—and often because they knew a lot about the case at hand. Who better to understand what the case was about and render a fair decision than someone who knew the defendant, the prosecutor, and the particulars of the alleged crime?

In contrast, today's juries often seem to be selected for their *lack* of knowledge about the case. The less they know, in theory, the more able they are to make an impartial judgment. Ironically, some lawyers who want jurors to know nothing about a case complain after they lose that the jurors were too dim to understand their erudite arguments.

WE THE PEOPLE

Juvenile proceedings often pose exceptions to the principles that apply to open trials for adults. Journalist Kathleen Culliton, in a research feature for Reporters Committee for Freedom of the Press, wrote: "Compared with the rest of the American judicial system, juvenile courts operate underwater, beneath varying layers of secrecy. It is that way largely because it has always been. … Courts across the country have repeatedly declined to find a First Amendment-based right of public access to the juvenile system. … Broadly put, a delinquency proceeding is not considered a criminal prosecution, but a hybrid beast bearing features of both the civil and criminal systems. So judges have been free to reject the firm body of law that generally holds open courtroom doors in criminal trials."

In terms of what a jury is supposed to do under the Sixth Amendment, it's important to note that the jury is not expected to know anything about the law. In a jury trial, the judge administers the law and the jury determines the facts. That's why a jury, for example, is not asked to determine whether a confession is admissible and why, if a confession is ruled inadmissible, a jury is not even told about it.

A jury's decisions about the facts of a case—who, what, when, where, why, and how—are not carved in stone, but almost. When a conviction is appealed, the appeals court typically looks only at whether the law was carried about properly and fairly. Appeals courts do not ordinarily consider whether the jury decided the facts properly.

Let's say you are accused of stealing your neighbor's garden gnome. You claim it's a case of mistaken identity—another neighbor, not you, stole the gnome—but the jury finds you guilty. You appeal your conviction. The appeals court cannot even consider whether it really was a case of mistaken identity, but the court can overturn the conviction if authorities did not follow proper procedures for the lineup that identified you as the gnome-napper.

To meet the Sixth Amendment's requirements for a fair trial and an impartial jury, the courts have developed a system of jury selection. Just as the noblemen who pushed the Magna Carta on King John wanted to have a jury that might give them a break, today's *voir dire* process, from the French "to see, to speak," allows the prosecution, defense lawyers, and judge to question prospective jurors and exclude them if there is a chance they might be biased.

Prospective jurors can be dismissed "for cause" for knowing too much about the case, for knowing people involved, or for having opinions or experiences that might color their judgment. The opposing attorneys also may have a set number of "peremptory" challenges that allow them to reject jurors for any reason or no reason. It is okay for a juror to have opinions, as long as the judge believes the juror can still consider the case fairly. Typically, prospective jurors are required to show that they can …

- Put aside whatever they have read or heard about the case.

- Listen to evidence with an open mind.

- Deliver an impartial verdict.

WHAT IT MEANS TO YOU

If you have been a victim of a similar crime and tell the judge and lawyers during the jury selection process that the experience would keep you from considering the case fairly, there is almost no chance you will end up on the jury. But don't make up anything or exaggerate: you're under oath, and lying is perjury.

Naturally, opposing lawyers try to gauge which prospective jurors will be more sympathetic to their case. Lawyers may ask jurors about personal prejudice in a civil rights case or how they feel about the death penalty in a capital case.

In a 1968 case, *Witherspoon* v. *Illinois,* the Supreme Court held that a defendant's right to an impartial jury was violated during the jury selection process when prospective jurors were rejected if they said they were against the death penalty. The high court said a jury cannot be "organized to return a verdict of death" and said the jurors who oppose the death penalty also should have been asked if they could nonetheless follow the law and impose the death penalty if it was applicable in that particular case.

> ✏️ **CASES**
>
> In 2016, the Supreme Court in *Hurst* v. *Florida* struck down Florida's death penalty. The opinion by Justice Sonia Sotomayor, citing a 2002 ruling in *Ring* v. *Arizona*, held that the Sixth Amendment requires a jury, not a judge only, to find each fact necessary to impose a death sentence. "Like Arizona at the time of *Ring*, Florida does not require the jury to make critical findings necessary to impose the death penalty," Sotomayor wrote. "Rather, Florida requires a judge to find these facts." And that, she concluded, violates the Sixth Amendment.

The Sixth Amendment does not specify that a jury must have 12 members. Indeed, the Supreme Court has said in a number of cases over the years that having 12-member juries appears to be an "accident of history" dating back to feudal times. Rather than any specific number, a jury is supposed to be large enough to …

- Foster group deliberations.

- Resist outside intimidation.

- Represent the community at large.

In a 1970 case, *Williams* v. *Florida*, the Supreme Court said a jury does not have to be 12 members. Justice Byron White wrote, "In short, neither currently available evidence nor theory suggests that the 12-man jury is necessarily more advantageous to the defendant than a jury composed of fewer members." The courts have held that six-member juries do not necessarily violate the Sixth Amendment.

Jury decisions need not be unanimous, but the courts have frowned on anything less than unanimous decisions for six-member juries. In general, the more serious the charge, the more the courts prefer larger juries and more unanimity. The Supreme Court has overturned a conviction on a 5–1 verdict that carried a prison term and upheld another conviction on a 9–3 verdict.

A jury is supposed to be a reasonable cross-section of the community and has been found to be partial if it excludes any specific group or class of people within the community. But it is not easy for a defendant to get a conviction overturned by claiming a jury was not impartial because of bias in the selection process. The defendant must prove a distinctive group in the community was excluded, the exclusion was not fair and reasonable, and the exclusion was systematic.

> **CASES**
>
> ***Taylor v. Louisiana* (1975):** A defendant convicted of kidnapping said he did not get a fair trial because Louisiana required women to register to serve on juries. If they didn't sign up, they weren't called. The Supreme Court reversed the conviction, noting, "It can no longer be held that women as a class may be excluded from jury service or given automatic exemptions based solely on sex ...."

Pretrial publicity also can prejudice a jury. Trials ordinarily are to be held in the district where the alleged crime was committed, but if the courts find that publicity tainted the jury pool so it is impossible to empanel an impartial jury in a specific area, the trial can be moved—a change of venue—to an area where prospective jurors are less likely to have heard or read about the case and formed an opinion.

> **CASES**
>
> ***Sheppard v. Maxwell* (1966):** The Supreme Court reversed the conviction of Sam Sheppard, a Cleveland physician accused of murdering his wife, Marilyn. The court cited pretrial publicity, including news stories calling Sheppard a liar, for depriving him of his Sixth Amendment right to a fair trial. The case inspired the television series *The Fugitive* and later the movie of the same name.

A jury also can be biased by what happens once the trial starts—by the actions of the judge, lawyers, defendant, witnesses, or even other jurors. When that happens, jurors can be instructed to ignore whatever they saw or heard that might keep them from deliberating fairly. If whatever they saw or heard is nonetheless likely to influence their deliberations, the judge will declare a mistrial.

In December 2006, the Supreme Court ruled that a federal appeals court erred in granting a new trial to an accused murderer after the victim's relatives came to court every day wearing badges with a photo of the dead man. The appeals court said the badges prejudiced the jury and ordered a new trial. The Supreme Court disagreed and reinstated the conviction, but on technical grounds rather than specifically because of the badges. The unanimous opinion by Justice Clarence Thomas said the question of whether the badges were prejudicial remains "an open question in our jurisprudence," to be decided in the future.

In general, a defendant has the right to a jury trial for any offense that carries a potential penalty of more than 6 months in jail. That does not apply, however, if a defendant is charged with a series of offenses with penalties that would extend to more than 6 months if convicted on all counts. There must be at least one charge that carries a potential sentence of 6 months or more.

Like other principal aspects of the Sixth Amendment, the impartial jury clause applies to states through the Fourteenth Amendment. The Supreme Court extended this protection in 1968 in *Duncan* v. *Louisiana,* a case that began 2 years earlier when a young black man named Duncan was driving down a Louisiana highway and noticed two of his cousins with a group of young white men alongside the road. Fearful that his cousins were being harassed because they had recently complained about racial bias in local schools, the young man pulled his car over and asked his cousins to get into his car and leave with him.

The white youths said Duncan slapped one of them. Duncan and his cousins denied it, but Duncan was arrested and charged with battery—a misdemeanor in Louisiana, but punishable by up to 2 years in prison. Duncan was convicted by a judge and sentenced to 60 days in jail, but he appealed on the grounds that he was denied right to a jury trial. The Supreme Court agreed, overturning the conviction on the grounds that the Sixth Amendment applies to state law, too.

There is no constitutional right to a trial before a judge only—a bench trial, it's called—but courts routinely allow defendants to waive the right to a jury trial. The rule of thumb is that you ask for a bench trial only if you think a judge might be more sympathetic to your case than a jury of your peers—for example, if your case is particularly complex or if you are particularly unpopular in the community.

The Confrontation Clause

The Sixth Amendment guarantees defendants in criminal proceedings the right to confront the witnesses against them, to look them in the eye and ask them questions. The Confrontation Clause is aimed to prevent defendants from being convicted on the basis of *ex parte* statements, affidavits, or depositions that were made outside court.

The history of this principle supposedly dates back to Sir Walter Raleigh, the Elizabethan-era adventurer who supposedly took off his cloak and threw it in the mud so Good Queen Bess would not soil the royal shoes. After the queen died and Sir Walter no longer had her protection, his legal troubles began. His enemies and rivals made statements about him, including allegations of conspiracy. Those statements were taken into evidence at Sir Walter's trial, even though the accusers were not required to appear and testify in person. He spent years in the Tower of London and finally was beheaded in 1618.

As part of the Confrontation Clause, defendants are entitled—but not required—to attend their own trials. However, defendants can be removed from the courtroom or restrained for disrupting court proceedings. For example, Bobby Seale's outbursts led him to be shackled and gagged at the 1969 trial of the Chicago Eight (which became the Chicago Seven when Seale's trial was separated). More recently, Saddam Hussein was removed from portions of his 2005–2006 trials in Baghdad.

The Confrontation Clause gives defendants the right to cross-examine witnesses—to test their credibility in front of the judge and jury, to hear what they have to say and how they say it, to view their demeanor, and to consider their body language. That makes sense in our judicial system, an adversarial process that pits the prosecution and defense against each other in a competition.

> **WE THE PEOPLE**
>
> One of America's best-known legal scholars, professor John Henry Wigmore, called the right to cross-examine "the greatest legal engine ever invented for the discovery of truth."

Other criminal justice systems, such as those in France, Spain, and Italy, rely less on competition—which side has the better legal team—and more on a prosecutor who is, in theory at least, less interested in winning convictions than in seeking truth and fairness. Our system, with its emphasis on individual rights, prefers the adversarial contest to putting more trust in the government to do what is right.

As a result, lawyers in our system try to get jurors to disbelieve, distrust, or at least dislike prosecution witnesses. They use strategies to bother opposing witnesses: they move around the courtroom, they change the pace or tone of questioning, they look for contradictions and inconsistencies, they try to get witnesses to misspeak or get flustered. Sometimes they attack the character of witnesses; even if a witness isn't lying, a lawyer may make points with a jury by pointing out that the witnesses might have reason to lie.

The O. J. Simpson trial, remember, eventually hinged on the prosecution witnesses. The jury didn't like the witnesses, and Simpson was acquitted. If you're a law student or lawyer who wants to see a masterful cross-examination, look up David Boies's cross-examination of Bill Gates and other Microsoft executives in their antitrust trial.

This part of the Sixth Amendment is where hearsay is a factor. Unlike the accusations against Sir Walter Raleigh, statements made outside of court proceedings today are usually inadmissible. You're allowed the right to confront the witnesses against you, but you cannot confront them if they are not in court.

It is worth noting, however, that the hearsay rule is not universal. Hearsay can be admissible in civil cases, and even in criminal cases there are exceptions. In a 1980 landmark case, *Ohio* v. *Roberts,* the Supreme Court set forth conditions for allowing hearsay: the prosecution must show it has tried to produce the witness and show good reason why the witness will not appear, and if a witness cannot appear, the prosecution must show that the hearsay is reliable and trustworthy.

The "dying declaration" is a widely accepted exception to the hearsay rule, under the theory that people who think they are dying—they don't actually have to die—are probably going to tell the truth. In addition, forensic expert testimony is sometimes allowed in response to hypothetical questions. Some states allow dying declarations to be admitted as evidence in all or most trials, but in federal courts, the dying declaration is admissible only in civil cases and homicide cases.

WE THE PEOPLE

In American courts, the dying declaration goes back to 1770, at the murder trial of British soldiers accused of shooting down colonial citizens in the Boston Massacre. One of the victims, Patrick Carr, told authorities with his dying gasp that the crowd had provoked the soldiers. His testimony helped the defense attorney, John Adams, get charges reduced or dismissed against the soldiers.

There are exceptions to the way cross-examinations can be conducted, too. They don't always have to be face to face in front of the judge and jury, especially if the witness would be traumatized by the presence of the defendant. The Supreme Court has ruled, for instance, that children testifying in sexual abuse cases do not necessarily have to face the defendants. The kids can testify behind a screen or via closed-circuit TV or videoconference. Even if there is no face-to-face confrontation with the defendant, however, the judge and jury still get to see the witness, and the defendant still has the right to cross-examine.

The Sixth Amendment has been at the heart of recent controversy over how the United States should prosecute suspected terrorists, and the Supreme Court gave mixed results to the George W. Bush administration. The Supreme Court refused to consider a case that challenged the administration policy of withholding names and other information about people taken into custody after the September 11, 2001, attacks on the World Trade Center and the Pentagon.

In the summer of 2006, however, the Supreme Court struck down the administration's plans for prosecuting suspected terrorists held at Guantanamo Bay Naval Base. The 5–3 decision did not say the military tribunals were necessarily unconstitutional but did say some of the aspects of the administration's plans for the tribunals were violations of the Sixth Amendment. The administration classified suspected terrorists as "enemy combatants" and planned to prosecute them in military tribunals—exempt from the Sixth Amendment's requirements for trial by jury. Plans for the tribunals included allowing hearsay evidence, and in some cases, the defendants would not be able to cross-examine witnesses, have legal counsel, protest their incarceration in federal court, see the evidence against them, or even attend their own trials. Congress reacted quickly, and in the autumn of 2006 sent President Bush legislation aimed at legalizing the military tribunals.

That Supreme Court decision on the military tribunals could turn out to be a significant constitutional footnote regarding the separation of powers and the system of checks and balances. The Bush administration argued that the Supreme Court did not even have the power to consider whether the tribunals were legal. The administration also said the sweeping antiterrorism authority Congress granted the president after the 2001 attacks gave Bush—and subsequent presidents—broad powers that were beyond review by the courts. The Supreme Court disagreed, obviously.

The Compulsory Process Clause

The Sixth Amendment not only guarantees the right to cross-examine witnesses who testify against you, but also gives you the power to call witnesses who might testify in your favor—and to force them to appear in court even if they are reluctant.

This right also extends to state courts, thanks to the Supreme Court's 1967 decision in *Washington v. Texas.* In that case, a defendant charged with murder wanted to call a defense witness who had already been convicted of participating in the same murder. Texas authorities said no, citing a state law that prohibited people charged in connection with the same crime from testifying on each other's behalf. Without the testimony, the defendant was convicted but then appealed. The Supreme Court reversed the conviction, saying the defendant's Sixth Amendment right to call witnesses had been violated.

The clerk of the court issues a subpoena and then it's served on the witness by a law enforcement officer or process server. There's no charge to the defendant. Defendants can compel almost anyone to testify, as long as they can show that the testimony will be material to the case and favorable to their arguments. A judge will reject the request for a subpoena if it seems like the witnesses are being called merely to prolong the proceedings. If a judge decides the testimony is redundant, the witness is out.

WHAT IT MEANS TO YOU

You might not be involved, and you might not want to get involved, but if you are served with a subpoena to testify, you have to appear and testify. You have a legal right to challenge the subpoena, but don't expect to get out of it. The best policy is to show up, take the oath, and tell the truth.

Witnesses also can be disallowed if the side calling them didn't give the other side notice those witnesses would be called. Court rules do not ordinarily permit surprise witnesses or any sort of surprise evidence, and both the prosecution and the defense normally are required to show each other pretty much their entire case before the trial begins. This helps ensure a fair trial, but as a practical matter, it also speeds up the judicial process by encouraging plea bargaining. If you know the other side has the smoking gun, you're probably going to want to make a deal for a lesser charge if you can.

Witnesses can also be disallowed if they are too important to testify. From George Washington to Richard Nixon to Bill Clinton to George W. Bush, American presidents have claimed that their jobs make them exempt from testifying, supplying evidence, or otherwise responding to subpoenas due to their executive privilege.

During the Watergate investigations, John Dean and other aides to President Richard Nixon offered conflicting testimony before Congress. Someone was committing perjury. Another aide revealed that Nixon had been taping conversations in the Oval Office, so the Watergate special prosecutor subpoenaed the tapes. Nixon refused, citing executive privilege, and the case went to the Supreme Court in the summer of 1974.

WE THE PEOPLE

The first president to claim executive privilege was George Washington, who rejected a House demand in 1796 that he turn over papers relating to the Jay Treaty with England. Washington ducked a constitutional confrontation by agreeing to turn over the documents to the Senate, the chamber that ratifies treaties.

The high court ruled that executive privilege was a legitimate claim by the president even though it was not specifically mentioned in the Constitution. However, in a unanimous decision that cited several constitutional grounds, including the Sixth Amendment, the Supreme Court ordered Nixon to turn over the Oval Office tapes.

What if Nixon had refused to comply with the Supreme Court's decision? What if he had burned the tapes in a bonfire on the South Lawn? What if he had called out the troops to surround the White House and prevent anyone from coming and getting the tapes or presenting him with articles of impeachment? Two weeks after the Supreme Court's decision, he turned over the tapes. Four days later, he resigned rather than face impeachment and possible removal from office. But the hypothetical—what if he hadn't?—shows just how tenuous our democracy can be, and how it hinges on a society's willingness to follow the rule of law.

More recently, Dick Cheney claimed executive privilege applies to vice presidents, too. In 2002, Congress's General Accounting Office (now called the Government Accountability Office) asked him for more information on his National Energy Policy Development Group as part of an inquiry into the oil industry's influence on government policies. Cheney's office refused on the grounds that executive privilege applies to vice presidents.

Assistance of Counsel

The Fifth Amendment's Miranda warning requires authorities to tell people who are being arrested that they have the right to an attorney, but the actual right to an attorney stems from the Sixth Amendment. You don't have to accept an attorney's help; you can represent yourself. But courts can deny a defendant the right to represent himself if it seems like he will be incompetent or disruptive.

The landmark case, from the height of the Great Depression, is officially in the law books as *Powell* v. *Alabama,* but it's more widely known as the Scottsboro Boys case. In March 1931, when it was common for jobless young men to strike out from home and ride the rails, a group of black hoboes got into a fight aboard a freight train passing through Alabama. The black hoboes won the fight and tossed most of the white hoboes off the train outside the town of Stevenson. The white hoboes told the stationmaster at Stevenson what had happened, and the stationmaster messaged ahead to the next stop, Scottsboro. The sheriff organized a posse, stopped the train, and pulled off the nine black men on board. Two white women were on the train, and they told the authorities, apparently under prodding, that they had been gang-raped.

The men were taken to the Scottsboro jail, and the National Guard was called out to maintain order and prevent a lynching as word of the alleged rapes spread. The men were charged with rape, a crime that carried the death penalty, but none of them was allowed to have an attorney or even contact relatives, all of whom lived in other states. They still did not have an attorney on the day of the trial, when the judge finally appointed two local lawyers to represent them, but the lawyers had no chance to prepare a case or even talk with the young men.

Doctors who examined the women testified there was no evidence of rape, but all nine men were convicted, and eight of the nine were sentenced to death. The state courts in Alabama rejected their appeals, and the case went to the U.S. Supreme Court.

The high court overturned the convictions and ordered new trials on the grounds of the Sixth Amendment. The court's 7–2 opinion held: "No attempt was made to investigate …. Defendants were immediately hurried to trial …. [A] defendant, charged with a serious crime, must not be stripped of his right to have sufficient time to advise with counsel and prepare his defense." The court ruled that the right to counsel was part of the "fundamental principles of liberty and justice which lie at the base of all our civil and political institutions." The Scottsboro decision was the first in a string of Supreme Court cases over the ensuing decades that guaranteed the right to counsel at no expense to the defendant, not only in capital cases but in all serious criminal cases.

The Seventh Amendment: Juries in Civil Trials

"In Suits at common law, where the value in controversy shall exceed twenty dollars, the right of trial by jury shall be preserved, and no fact tried by a jury shall be otherwise re-examined in any Court of the United States, other than according to the rules of the common law."

The framers considered extending Article III's guarantees of a jury trial to civil cases as well as criminal cases. But it didn't come up until late in the Constitutional Convention, after a long, hot summer of hard work, and it may have been voted down simply because the men were all eager to go home.

There was widespread support for the idea, however, including among the states. Congress approved the proposed Seventh Amendment without debate, and the right to a jury trial in civil cases became part of the Bill of Rights.

The Constitution does not extend the right to a jury trial in civil cases to the states, but as a practical matter, the states have comparable rules with varying requirements for the nature of the lawsuit and the amount of money damages at stake. In general, the Seventh Amendment has been interpreted to hold that the right to a jury does not include an "equity" lawsuit—an action seeking not money damages but nonmonetary relief, such as an injunction or some other type of "performance" order in which a court tells someone they must or must not do something.

The Least You Need to Know

- You have the right to a jury trial in serious criminal cases.
- You have the right to a jury trial in many civil cases.
- You have the right to defend yourself in court.
- You have the right to cross-examine hostile witnesses.
- You have the right to subpoena witnesses at no expense to you.

The Eighth Amendment: Bail and Punishment

"Excessive bail shall not be required, nor excessive fines imposed, nor cruel and unusual punishments inflicted."

The Eighth Amendment's vague language has led to confusing and conflicting court rulings over the years, especially with shifts in society's standards and the makeup of the Supreme Court. What does "excessive" mean? What is "cruel and unusual"? And do the standards apply differently to different types of defendants? Children? People with mental disabilities?

In This Chapter

- The Eighth Amendment
- Excessive bail and fines
- Cruel and unusual punishment

In particular, there's been a lot of uncertainty over the death penalty. Most of us don't like it, but many of us think it is necessary, and all of us think it should be administered fairly. Society's attitudes have been reflected in the convoluted and sometimes contradictory Supreme Court rulings.

Excessive Bail and Fines

In Olde England, the same sheriff who arrested you had the right to decide whether you should be released on bail, and the king could have you arrested and confined without bail. The unfairness was obvious, and Parliament nicked away at the power to withhold bail until 1689, when the English Bill of Rights declared that if bail was granted, it could not be excessive.

Our Eighth Amendment says pretty much the same thing. There is no right to be granted bail and released pending trial, but if bail is granted, the amount cannot be unreasonable for meeting the purpose of granting bail. The primary purpose of granting bail is to ensure the defendant shows up in court to face the charges. You're less likely to skip town if it means you're going to take a serious financial hit.

In considering bail, judges are supposed to balance the amount of bail—or whether to grant bail—against the severity of the crime.

In a 1987 case, *United States* v. *Salerno,* the Supreme Court held that denying bail and keeping a defendant in jail prior to trial is not necessarily a violation of the Eighth Amendment. However, the court said the government must prove the defendant might be a danger to the community. Chief Justice William Rehnquist's opinion said the rule for bail is that "the government's proposed conditions of release or detention not be 'excessive' in light of the perceived evil."

In many cases, particularly for less serious crimes, or when a defendant has an otherwise relatively clean criminal record and strong ties to the community, pretrial release is granted "on recognizance," or without any financial commitment. The defendant is released after promising to appear at the trial or the next scheduled hearing.

When charges are serious, however, especially for any sort of homicide, or when the defendant is considered a flight risk, the judge often requires bail in the form of a financial bond. A defense attorney ordinarily wants the sum to be as low as possible, of course, while the prosecutor may seek higher bail. Because the primary purpose of the bail is to guarantee appearance, the judge may set the bond much higher for a rich person, although the Supreme Court has held that judges do not necessarily need to consider a defendant's financial status.

> **WHAT IT MEANS TO YOU**
>
> If bail is set at $100,000, the court may require only a percentage, often 10 percent, to be put down in cash. If the defendant does not show up, however, the entire amount is forfeited and a warrant is issued for the defendant as a fugitive. If you put up your assets to guarantee someone's bail, you could lose your house if he or she doesn't show up for trial.

When a crime is particularly serious and the defendant is a flight risk likely to skip town, the judge may deny bail altogether. Besides guaranteeing appearance, a prosecutor also can argue that the defendant should be kept in custody as a matter of preventive detention—to keep him or her from committing further crimes.

This is a tricky area because our judicial system is based on the presumption of innocence and on penalizing people not for what they *might* do but only for what they actually *have* done. Someone has to be a pretty bad person for a judge to deny bail on the grounds that society is safer if he or she remains behind bars while awaiting trial.

Sometimes, besides money, judges will set conditions for bail, such as requiring a defendant to stay away from victims, witnesses, or the scene of the crime.

Cruel and Unusual Punishment

One person's idea of cruel might be another person's idea of tough love. It's the same dilemma whether raising kids or punishing society's wrongdoers. And while strict constructionists think the Constitution should be interpreted as closely as possible to the original intentions of the framers in 1787, the Eighth Amendment is an example of how the Constitution is flexible, bending to changes in society. After all, pretty much everyone agrees that society's views on punishment have changed. As the Supreme Court ruled in one case, the standard for cruel and unusual "must draw its meaning from the evolving standards of decency that mark the progress of a maturing society."

One literal interpretation has not changed much over the years, however. The *and* is important in the phrase *cruel and unusual punishment*. The courts have ruled, to varying degrees, that punishment can be cruel. Punishment also can be unusual. But it's not supposed to be both.

Supreme Court rulings in the nineteenth century made it clear that some forms of punishment would always be unconstitutional as cruel and unusual, including drawing and quartering, beheading, burning alive, and disemboweling. Death by hanging and by firing squad were permissible, however, in part because those were the common ways states executed criminals. Even if it was cruel, it wasn't unusual.

One of the decisions that reflected changing views in society came in a 1962 case, *Robinson v. California*. The Supreme Court determined a 90-day sentence for being a drug addict was cruel and unusual punishment because drug addiction "is apparently an illness," and authorities were trying to punish the defendant for an illness rather than for a specific criminal act.

In recent years, court cases have challenged long sentences for relatively minor crimes, or for minors. For example, the Supreme Court has ruled that minors can no longer be sentenced to life in prison without the chance of parole except for homicides. Such sentences, the court ruled, violate the Eighth Amendment as cruel and unusual punishment.

It's important to remember that sentences are supposed to meet the acceptable goals of punishment—retribution and deterrence—and that punishment is excessive if it does not fulfill those purposes or if it's out of proportion to the severity of the crime.

Three Strikes and You're Out

The "three strikes and you're out" laws many states have enacted in recent years have prompted a range of court rulings.

The Supreme Court upheld a mandatory life sentence for a three-time loser even though his three nonviolent felonies netted him barely $200.

In another case, however, the court overturned the conviction of a guy who wrote a $100 bad check. Under state recidivism laws, he received a mandatory life sentence without the chance for parole. The court said it was cruel and unusual that he had no chance for parole, while the defendant in the previous case at least had a chance at parole after 12 years in prison.

In a third case, the Supreme Court said a life sentence without the possibility of parole for a repeat offender is not necessarily cruel and unusual, particularly considering that offender had a long record of violent crime and the most recent conviction was for possession of more than 600 grams of cocaine.

In a 1983 case, *Solem v. Helm*, the Supreme Court for the first time said the length of a sentence in and of itself could be cruel and unusual if it was "disproportionate" to the severity of the crime. The court has waxed and waned on this "proportionality" test over the years, but it often seems to come back to three factors:

- The gravity of the offense and the harshness of the penalty

- Sentences imposed on other criminals in the same jurisdiction

- Sentences imposed for the same crime in other jurisdictions

On numerous occasions, lower courts, both state and federal, have held that conditions in certain prisons or entire prison systems violate prisoners' protections against cruel and unusual punishment. The Supreme Court in general has endorsed the power of the courts to step in, but at the same time has indicated that courts need to proceed with caution when coming in conflict with the states or the federal executive branch over how prisons are run.

CASES

Trop v. Dulles (1958): In this case, the Supreme Court ruled that punishing a citizen by taking away citizenship is a cruel and unusual punishment. The high court called it worse than torture, "total destruction of the individual's status in organized society," and "a fate forbidden by the principle of civilized treatment guaranteed by the Eighth Amendment."

The Death Penalty

Capital punishment has always been part of the American criminal justice system, even as much of the rest of the world has moved away from the death penalty. The American Civil Liberties Union (ACLU), long an opponent of the death penalty, says the vast majority of the court-imposed executions in the world today occur in four countries: China, Iran, Saudi Arabia, and the United States.

The Supreme Court has had many opportunities to declare the death penalty unconstitutional, and it has overturned a number of convictions based on the way death sentences were handed down. But the court has never said capital punishment itself is cruel and unusual. "Whatever the arguments may be against capital punishment," the court held in a case in the 1950s, "the death penalty has been employed throughout our history and, in a day when it is still widely accepted, it cannot be said to violate the constitutional concept of cruelty."

But several factors have led courts and juries to be more careful about applying the death penalty in the twenty-first century. A number of studies, reviewing evidence, claims that dozens of people have been executed even though they were not guilty of the crimes for which they were convicted. Postconviction work by the Innocence Project and other groups of lawyers who oppose the death penalty has overturned a number of death penalty convictions. Advances in the use of technology, particularly DNA analysis, have helped lawyers review and question death penalty convictions. New studies have cast more doubt on the veracity and reliability of eyewitness testimony. Many other developed countries have banned the death penalty. And some right-to-life advocates have rejected the inconsistency of opposing abortion but supporting the death penalty.

But the recent increasing unease over the death penalty—a growing number of states either has outlawed the death penalty or simply stopped imposing it—is nothing new in America. Concern about the death penalty led many states to suspend executions in the 1960s, and during a period from 1967 to 1976, there were no court-ordered executions in the United States.

In a 1972 landmark case, *Furman* v. *Georgia,* a narrowly divided court effectively struck down every existing state death penalty. The 5–4 majority was divided over whether the death penalty was always unconstitutional as cruel and unusual and whether it could be legal if the states could come up with capital punishment procedures that were not random and capricious and did not discriminate against blacks and poor people.

In the *Furman* decision, the Supreme Court laid down restrictions on punishment, declaring any form of punishment is unconstitutional if it is …

- Degrading to human dignity—as in torture.

- A severe punishment obviously inflicted in a wholly arbitrary fashion.

- A severe punishment clearly and totally rejected throughout society.

- A severe punishment that is patently unnecessary.

WE THE PEOPLE

In the *Furman* case, Justice Potter Stewart criticized the random application of capital punishment in America this way: "These death sentences are cruel and unusual in the same way that being struck by lightning is cruel and unusual."

The criticisms and guidelines laid down by the high court in the *Furman* decision gave the states a road map for rewriting their capital punishment laws. In the following months, 35 states, starting with Florida, passed new death penalty laws that aimed to remove the arbitrary and irrational aspects of their old laws.

One of the key aspects was the two-part trial: first a jury would decide whether the defendant was guilty of the crime and then it would decide whether the defendant should be sentenced to death. Relying on suggestions from court decisions, the new procedure ensured that judges and juries considered a defendant individually and personally and weighed any mitigating factors. Because death is a unique punishment, the court ruled, the death penalty needs to be considered on a case-by-case basis, with thought given to each defendant's individual circumstances and the particular details of each case.

Before any more executions took place, the Supreme Court reconsidered a series of cases based on new death penalty laws passed by several states. The justices have remained mindful that the reasons for any penalty, including a death sentence, are retribution and deterrence, and that it may be preferable for state legislatures to lay out the particulars. As a result, the Supreme Court issued a series of opinions in 1976, including *Gregg* v. *Georgia,* which opened the door for executions to resume.

Today, each state's death penalty process includes the following:

- Standards for the sentencing authority, whether judge or jury, to evaluate both the circumstances of the offense and the character of the accused

- A two-part trial for considering first guilt and second the sentence

- Automatic appeal of both the conviction and the sentence to the state supreme court

Subsequent Supreme Court decisions have narrowed the range of crimes that carry the death penalty and expanded the range of reasons for sentencing defendants to life in prison instead of execution. For example, rape was a capital crime in many states, but a 1977 Supreme Court case, *Coker* v. *Georgia,* said the death sentence was cruel and unusual punishment for the rape of an adult female. The court seemed to be saying that the death penalty may be imposed only for the intentional killing of another person.

In recent years, however, proposals have been made in some states to execute repeat child molesters. The courts also have become more attuned to racial bias in the way the death penalty has been applied and to the quality of legal representation in those cases.

CASES

The ACLU says 455 men were executed for rape in the United States between 1930 and 1967. Of them, 405—almost 90 percent—were black.

Three cases before the Supreme Court in 2002 looked at the quality of representation provided to defendants who were charged with capital crimes but could not afford their own attorneys. In two cases, the high court rejected appeals from death row, once holding that a defendant's rights were not violated when his lawyer skipped the closing argument to the jury, and another time when a defendant was assigned a lawyer who had represented the victim in an earlier case.

However, the Supreme Court did overturn the Texas murder conviction of a gay man whose court-appointed lawyer slept through parts of the trial. The prosecution, which had argued in favor of the death penalty on the grounds that prison was not such a severe punishment for a gay man, futilely claimed the defense lawyer snoozed only in *unimportant* parts of the trial.

Other recent Supreme Court cases have determined that the states cannot impose an automatic death penalty for certain crimes, such as the murder of a police officer or for prison inmates who are already serving life sentences without the chance of parole. The Supreme Court also has made it more difficult for states to impose the death penalty on defendants accused of felony murder—for example, when they participate in a crime in which someone is killed but they don't actually pull the trigger themselves.

Other rulings have said the insane and the mentally handicapped can no longer be executed, and a 2005 case, *Roper* v. *Simmons,* prohibits states from executing defendants whose crimes were committed before they turned 18 years old.

For a time, it appeared the Supreme Court was moving away from "victim impact statements," but recent decisions have opened the door for judges and juries to consider the character of victims as well as defendants.

In recent years, the Supreme Court has repeatedly refused to outlaw lethal injection as cruel and unusual punishment. But it is clear that the death penalty is far from a settled issue in American jurisprudence.

In 2015, in a 5–4 vote in *Glossip* v. *Oklahoma,* the Supreme Court upheld Oklahoma's use of the controversial lethal injection drug midazolam despite headlines and lawsuits blaming the drug for several executions that apparently caused pain to the prisoner and took longer than expected. A striking part of the court's decision was a long, passionate dissent by Justices Stephen Breyer and Ruth Bader Ginsburg, which indicated they believe any application of the death penalty may be cruel and unusual punishment. "I believe it highly likely that the death penalty violates the Eighth Amendment," Justice Breyer wrote. "At the very least, the court should call for a full briefing on the basic question."

The Least You Need to Know

- If you are arrested and brought before a judge, you have the right to be released on bail.
- Sentences are supposed to match the crime committed.
- The Supreme Court has never ruled that the death penalty is cruel and unusual punishment.
- The Supreme Court has, however, been concerned about ensuring the death penalty is carried out as fairly as possible.
- The Supreme Court has yet to rule on whether execution by lethal injection is cruel and unusual.

CHAPTER 12

The Ninth Through Twelfth Amendments: The Political System

The last two amendments of the Bill of Rights—the Ninth and Tenth—were aimed at providing flexibility in the Constitution. The framers did not want future American leaders, legislators, or judges to say, "You don't have the right to do that because it isn't mentioned in the Constitution."

Instead, the Ninth Amendment said that just because a particular right isn't mentioned doesn't mean it doesn't apply or that the government can abridge that right. The Tenth Amendment said any authority not granted to the federal government in the Constitution is reserved to the people or the states.

The Eleventh Amendment protects states' sovereignty by prohibiting them from being sued in federal court. And the Twelfth Amendment separated the campaigns for president and vice president while keeping the same qualifications for both offices.

In This Chapter

- The Ninth Amendment: unenumerated rights
- The Tenth Amendment: states' rights
- The Eleventh Amendment: suing states
- The Twelfth Amendment: electing a president

The Ninth Amendment: Unenumerated Rights

"The enumeration in the Constitution, of certain rights, shall not be constructed to deny or disparage others retained by the people."

Other parts of the Constitution, and especially the Bill of Rights, specify or "enumerate" particular rights, such as free speech and fair trial. But the framers of the Constitution did not think they had all the answers. In effect, this amendment says, "In case someone raises a right we didn't list, it can still be valid. The government cannot take away a right from the people just because we didn't mention it."

The seeds of the amendment were planted in the Constitutional Convention, when anti-Federalists argued for a Bill of Rights to limit national government. The Federalists did not want a written Bill of Rights included in the Constitution for the same reason: to limit the power of the central government. They were afraid that if the Constitution included a written list of individual rights the government could not abridge, anything not on the list might be considered fair game for government limits or controls.

James Madison, leading the Federalist movement, put it this way: "It has been objected also against a bill of rights, that, by enumerating particular exceptions to the grant of power, it would disparage those rights which were not placed in the enumeration; and it might follow by implication, that those rights which were not singled out, were intended to be assigned into the hands of the General Government, and were consequently insecure."

The anti-Federalists got their promise of a Bill of Rights, of course, in part as a compromise to gather support for the Constitution from the states during the ratification process. As part of the compromise, the Ninth Amendment was created.

Imagine a group of individuals has a big basket of rights. The Bill of Rights plucked out a few of those rights—free speech, fair trial, and so on—and held them up: these are shiny examples of the kinds of inherent, inalienable, individual rights the new government cannot limit. The Ninth Amendment says there are other rights in the basket, too, beyond the ones plucked out for the Bill of Rights. They are just as inalienable, and just as valid, even if they are not specifically mentioned anywhere in the Constitution, including the Bill of Rights.

The Ninth Amendment was an afterthought in the development of constitutional law for most of the United States' first two centuries, but it has had some flurries of controversy in recent years.

Today, some say it is meaningless, while others say it is crucial to democracy. Some say it grants many rights; others say it is merely a guide for how to read the Constitution. Some say it defends fundamental rights; others say it allows activist judges to reach any decision they want for social, political, or even personal reasons.

Privacy

Much of the controversy centers around the right to privacy. The right to privacy is not specifically mentioned anywhere in the Constitution, but few people would say there is no such thing. We all have the right to be left alone, especially from government interference in our personal lives. Court rulings have found the parts of the First, Third, Fourth, and Fifth Amendments—the right to speak our minds, for example, and the right not to give evidence against ourselves—pertain to the right of privacy.

The Ninth Amendment stepped to the forefront in a 1965 case *Griswold* v. *Connecticut,* after the director of Planned Parenthood in Connecticut teamed up with a Yale medical professor to open a birth control clinic in New Haven. They were arrested, tried, and fined $100 under Connecticut's 1879 law banning contraceptives. They appealed, the state courts rejected their appeal, and they took their case to the Supreme Court.

The Supreme Court overturned the convictions and declared the law unconstitutional, along with similar anticontraceptive laws in other states, on the grounds it violated the marital right to privacy. The majority opinion cited "zones of privacy" guaranteed by the Constitution, including the Ninth Amendment, while a concurring opinion by Justice Arthur Goldberg flatly said that because privacy was not covered elsewhere in the Constitution, it was an individual right protected by the Ninth Amendment.

WE THE PEOPLE

Justice Goldberg's often-quoted concurring opinion in *Griswold* v. *Connecticut* said in part: "To hold that a right so basic and fundamental and so deep-rooted in our society as the right of privacy in marriage may be infringed because that right is not guaranteed in so many words by the first eight amendments to the Constitution is to ignore the Ninth Amendment and to give it no effect whatsoever."

Birth Control and Abortion

Most of the subsequent Supreme Court decisions on privacy have confirmed there is a right to privacy but have shied away from finding it in the Ninth Amendment. In a 1972 case, *Eisenstadt v. Baird,* the Supreme Court ruled that unmarried couples could legally use contraceptives, too. In *Roe* v. *Wade,* the case that set the parameters for legal abortions in 1973, the Supreme Court rejected a lower court's reasoning that said reproductive rights were part of the privacy protections of the Ninth Amendment. Instead, the Supreme Court said a woman's right to abortion is protected by due process.

Here's the specific court language on privacy from the majority opinion in the Roe case: "This right of privacy, whether it be founded in the Fourteenth Amendment's concept of personal liberty and restrictions upon state action, as we feel it is, or, as the district court determined, in the Ninth Amendment's reservation of rights to the people, is broad enough to encompass a women's decision whether or not to terminate her pregnancy."

Another case that looked at privacy, *Planned Parenthood* v. *Casey* in 1992, narrowly upheld *Roe* v. *Wade* but allowed Pennsylvania to impose restrictions, such as a 24-hour waiting period and parental consent for minors. Again, that case found the right to privacy in the Fourteenth Amendment rather than the Ninth.

Another significant privacy case in recent years includes *Lawrence* v. *Texas.* Police, acting on a call from a neighbor who reported a man with a gun, entered a home, found two men having anal sex, and arrested them for violating Texas's antisodomy law. After being fined $200 each, they appealed. The Supreme Court overturned their conviction in 2003 and tossed out the Texas law along with the remaining handful of antisodomy laws in other states. Incidentally, the neighbor who had called the cops with the fake weapons report was arrested and spent 15 days in jail.

WE THE PEOPLE

Arguing to uphold the Texas antisodomy law, Justice Antonin Scalia dissented: "Let me be clear that I have nothing against homosexuals, or any other group, promoting their agenda through normal democratic means. Social perceptions of sexual and other morality change over time, and every group has the right to persuade its fellow citizens that its view of such matters is the best ...."

The privacy cases brought it onto the constitutional stage briefly, but the Ninth Amendment now seems to be back in the wings again, not playing a major part. Some constitutional scholars believe the Ninth Amendment may become a factor in the development of American law in the future, but perhaps only if and when the courts stop thinking about it in terms of preserving individual liberty instead of particular individual rights.

The Tenth Amendment: States' Rights

"The powers not delegated to the United States by the Constitution, nor prohibited by it to the States, are reserved for the States respectively, or to the people."

Just as the Ninth Amendment sought to preserve individual rights, the Tenth Amendment preserves states' rights not specifically mentioned in the Constitution. Consequently, some describe this amendment as the essence of federalism: the national government has certain powers listed in the Constitution, and that's it; everything else can and should be up to the states.

The Tenth Amendment, growing out of the original states' unease about having another out-of-touch, faraway government replace British rule, was requested by the states to protect their own self-identity and self-rule at a time when it was much more meaningful to say you were a Virginian or a New Yorker than it was to say you were an American. Often called the "states' rights" amendment, it is cited by those who believe that the federal government's primary—and perhaps only—role is to defend the shores and deliver the mail.

WE THE PEOPLE

Thomas Jefferson summed up the spirit of the Tenth Amendment this way: "The States should be left to do whatever they can do as well as the federal government."

The Tenth Amendment was viewed as being very important when the nation was new, and it was seen as a brake on growing federal power—particularly taxing power and police power. But it has become less significant over time. Tension between the Tenth Amendment and the Constitution's Commerce Clause generally has evolved in favor of the Commerce Clause, giving the government broad authority to oversee and regulate all manner of activity among citizens, whether across state lines or not.

In the first half of the twentieth century, there was still enough life left in the Tenth Amendment for the Supreme Court to strike down a range of congressional controls on the states, including the imposition of taxes on products from factories that relied on child labor, coal, poultry, grain futures, and other agricultural products. Other court rulings, however, upheld the federal government's authority to regulate interstate transportation of lottery tickets and transporting women across state lines for immoral purposes.

The Tenth Amendment was the rationale for a 1918 Supreme Court decision that gave the states "nullification" authority over congressional legislation that violated state authority. But that decision was overturned in a 1941 case, *United States* v. *Darby,* which all but dumped the Tenth Amendment into the constitutional wastebasket. Justice Harlan Stone wrote:

> "The amendment states but a truism that all is retained which has not been surrendered. There is nothing in the history of its adoption to suggest that it was more than declaratory of the relationship between the national and state governments as it had been established by the Constitution before the amendment or that its purpose was other than to allay fears that the new national government might seek to exercise powers not granted, and that the states might not be able to exercise fully their reserved powers."

The *Darby* decision also made it clear that the Commerce Clause, giving the federal government broad authority over anything it defines as commerce, is the one that matters in modern law: "The power of Congress over interstate commerce is complete in itself, may be exercised to the utmost extent, and acknowledges no limitations other than are prescribed by the Constitution."

The concept of "states' rights" also fell into disfavor during the second half of the twentieth century when it became a rallying cry among foes of the civil rights movement in Southern states, who argued that the individual states should be allowed to require that African Americans sit in the back of the bus.

The concept of states' rights had a brief revival in a 1976 case before the Supreme Court, *National League of Cities* v. *Usery.* The court ruled against the federal government's attempts to set requirements for working hours and wages for certain local and state employees but did not specifically mention the Tenth Amendment. In any event, the ruling was overturned in a 1985 case, *Garcia* v. *San Antonio Metropolitan Transit Authority,* which said states retain their sovereignty only to the extent they have not given up their powers and transferred them to the federal government via the Constitution. Some interpret this ruling as saying that merely by being part of the United States, the individual states have ceded their authority to the federal government.

One line of reasoning in that case said any states' rights challenge should be a political rather than a judicial issue. The rationale: the Tenth Amendment prohibits Congress from passing laws that are a burden on the states, but the people have given Congress the authority to make laws, so if a law is burdensome, it is up to the people to elect members of Congress who will change it.

In a 1992 case, *New York* v. *United States,* the Supreme Court threw out federal regulations that required the states to clean up low-level radioactive waste that failed to meet federal standards. The court said the U.S. government cannot force a state to administer federal regulations. Similarly, another Supreme Court opinion in 1997, *Printz* v. *United States,* threw out the Brady Handgun Violence Prevention Act's requirements that state and local officials conduct background searches on people who are buying handguns.

In general, however, the federal government has become more and more dominant in our everyday lives, and the differences between being a Virginian and a New Yorker are not as meaningful as the similarities in being American. States are in theory still free to buck federal laws, but there is often a high price. For example, Congress in effect mandated lower speed limits for the entire nation and a national minimum drinking age of 21 by threatening to withhold highway funds for any state that did not fall in line.

The Tenth Amendment isn't what it used to be, but it still could be a factor in future decisions balancing state and federal powers, particularly in terms of antiterrorist programs. For example, can the federal government require the states to enforce new federal immigration procedures?

The Eleventh Amendment: Suing States

"The Judicial power of the United States shall not be construed to extend to any suit in law or equity, commenced or prosecuted against one of the United States by Citizens of another State, or by Citizens or Subjects of any Foreign State."

This amendment, like the Tenth, reflected the independence and autonomy the original states enjoyed and wanted to preserve in the new union. In effect, it was aimed at giving them a measure of *sovereign immunity,* a phrase that dates to the English principle that the king had to agree to any lawsuit filed against him. If he didn't agree, there could be no lawsuit. The Eleventh Amendment was aimed at providing a similar insulation from lawsuits for the individual states.

The amendment was proposed, approved by Congress, and ratified by the states in quick sequence as a result of a 1793 Supreme Court case. In that case, *Chisholm* v. *Georgia,* two residents of South Carolina said they were owed money by the State of Georgia under a contract for supplies during the Revolutionary War. Georgia said it could not be sued by residents of another state, but the Supreme Court disagreed.

Georgia's leaders were angry, and the state legislature passed a law saying anyone who came to Georgia to collect the debt could be hanged. The leaders of other states were afraid the same thing could happen to them, that they could be sued by residents of other states and the federal courts would end up deciding the cases.

The Eleventh Amendment was passed to overcome the court decision and bar lawsuits against states by nonresidents. In an 1890 case, *Hans* v. *Louisiana,* the Supreme Court launched a series of decisions holding that not only are nonresident citizens barred from suing states, but also, resident citizens are barred from suing their own states in federal court.

The Eleventh Amendment is generally viewed as barring cases brought *in law*, seeking monetary damages, but case law has established that the federal courts can take cases against the states *in equity*, seeking nonmonetary relief or "performance" such as injunctions ordering someone to do something or not to do something. The courts have done some legal tap dancing here. For example, there is the line of reasoning that says suing a state official is not the same as suing the state because if a state official is violating the law, he or she is not acting on behalf of the state.

> **DEFINITION**
>
> The Eleventh Amendment bars suits against states *in law* or *in equity*. In legal language, a suit **in law** is one that seeks monetary damages. In contrast, a suit **in equity** seeks a court order, such as injunction, that orders a specific action to be taken or sometimes bars a specific action from being taken.

Cases in recent years have yielded mixed results. One said there can be Fourteenth Amendment grounds for limiting state sovereign immunity, and another said Article I's Bankruptcy Clause can, too. But other recent cases have bolstered states' immunity, including one that said states do not have to respond to private complaints filed with federal agencies.

The Twelfth Amendment: Picking the President

"The Electors shall meet in their respective states, and vote by ballot for President and Vice-President, one of whom, at least, shall not be an inhabitant of the same state with themselves; they shall name in their ballots the person voted for as President, and in distinct ballots the person voted for as Vice-President, and they shall make distinct lists of all persons voted for as President, and of all persons voted for as Vice-President, and of the number of votes for each, which lists they shall sign and certify, and transmit sealed to the seat of the government of the United States, directed to the President of the Senate;

"The President of the Senate shall, in the presence of the Senate and House of Representatives, open all the certificates and the votes shall then be counted; The person having the greatest number of votes for President, shall be the President, if such number be a majority of the whole number of Electors appointed; and if no person have such majority, then from the persons having the highest numbers not exceeding three on the list of those voted for as President, the House of Representatives shall choose immediately, by ballot, the President. But in choosing the President, the votes shall be taken by states, the representation from each state having one vote; a quorum for this purpose shall consist of a member or members from two-thirds of the states, and a majority of all the states shall be necessary to a choice. And if the House of Representatives shall not choose a President whenever the right of choice shall devolve upon them, before the fourth day of March next following, then the Vice-President shall act as the President, as in the case of the death or other constitutional disability of the President.

"The person having the greatest number of votes as Vice-President, shall be the Vice-President, if such number be a majority of the whole number of Electors appointed, and if no person have a majority, then from the two highest numbers on the list, the Senate shall choose the Vice-President; a quorum for the purpose shall consist of two-thirds of the whole number of Senators, and a majority of the whole number shall be necessary to a choice. But no person constitutionally ineligible to the office of President shall be eligible to that of Vice-President of the United States."

The Twelfth Amendment was drafted to replace the part of Article II (Clause 3 of Section 1) that laid out the process for selecting the president and vice president. Originally, that clause called for members of the Electoral College to vote for their top two choices for president. The majority winner would be president and the second-place finisher would be vice president. In the election of 1796, this resulted in a president from one party and a vice president from another, but it was the following election, in 1800, that led to amending Article II.

A majority of the Electoral College expected to elect Thomas Jefferson as president and Aaron Burr as vice president in 1800. A deal was worked out: all the Jefferson–Burr supporters would vote for both men, but one elector would leave Burr off the ballot so he would finish second. The plan went awry, however, and Jefferson and Burr ended up with the same number of votes. That threw the election to the House of Representatives, where each state had one vote. The House was deadlocked for a week before Jefferson finally was declared president, in large part thanks to Alexander Hamilton's tireless campaigning against Burr.

WE THE PEOPLE

Aaron Burr was furious at the scurrilous things Alexander Hamilton said about him in 1800 when Burr wanted to be president and again in 1804 when Burr lost a campaign for governor of New York. After the 1804 loss, Burr challenged Hamilton to a duel. Hamilton fired first and missed. Burr's shot hit Hamilton in the abdomen, and he died the next day.

The Twelfth Amendment changed the Electoral College procedure so that instead of submitting one ballot with two names, electors now each submit two ballots, one for president and one for vice president. The candidate with a majority of the vote is elected.

If no candidate for president gets a majority in the Electoral College, the election is thrown to the House. The House then votes by state among the top three vote-getters. If no candidate for vice president gets a majority, the Senate votes by state from the top two vote-getters. If the House cannot declare a winner of the presidential race by inauguration day—March 4 when the Twelfth Amendment was ratified, or January 20 now—the newly elected vice president serves as acting president until the election is resolved.

The Twelfth Amendment also requires the vice president to have the same qualifications as the president: 35 years old, natural-born citizen, and a resident of the United States for at least 14 years.

The Twelfth Amendment does not prohibit a president and a vice president from being elected from the same state, but voters in the Electoral College cannot vote for two candidates from their own states. In other words, an elector from Ohio can vote for either a presidential candidate or a vice presidential candidate from Ohio—but only one of them, not both.

In 2000, Republican nominee George W. Bush, then the governor of Texas, chose Dick Cheney, then a Texas businessman, as his running mate. Cheney changed his residence to Wyoming, where he grew up and was elected to Congress, to ensure Texas electors would be able to vote for both him and Bush.

WE THE PEOPLE

In the 1824 presidential race, Andrew Jackson had 99 of the 131 Electoral College votes needed for a majority. John Quincy Adams had 84 votes, and two other candidates combined for 78 votes. Jackson expected to be elected by the House, but Adams got the support of 13 of the 23 states and became president.

The Least You Need to Know

- The Ninth Amendment protects individual rights not specifically mentioned elsewhere in the Constitution, including—maybe—the right to privacy.
- If no presidential candidate wins a majority in the Electoral College, the election is thrown to the House of Representatives.
- The vice president must meet the same qualifications for office as the president, including being 35 years old and a natural-born citizen.
- The president and vice president can be from the same state. But if they are, Electoral College voters from that state can vote for only one of them.

CHAPTER 13

The Thirteenth Through Fifteenth Amendments: Civil Rights

The three amendments that combine to form a constitutional bulwark for civil rights were ratified in the years following the Civil War and are known as the Reconstruction Amendments.

The Thirteenth Amendment formalized President Abraham Lincoln's Emancipation Proclamation, making slavery illegal as part of the law of the land. The Fourteenth Amendment aimed to ensure every citizen is treated the same under the law, no matter what race or economic standing, and has turned out to be one of the most far-reaching parts of the Constitution for protecting the individual regardless of race or creed. The Fifteenth Amendment not only guaranteed the right to vote, but also banned authorities from putting up obstacles such as registration requirements that might be discriminatory against minorities and the poor or uneducated.

In This Chapter

The Thirteenth Amendment: Abolishing Slavery

"Neither slavery nor involuntary servitude, except as a punishment for crime whereof the party shall have been duly convicted, shall exist within the United States, or any place subject to their jurisdiction."

"Congress shall have power to enforce this article by appropriate legislation."

In 1641, Massachusetts became the first of the American colonies to legalize slavery. By July 4, 1776, slavery was legal in all 13 original states.

In one of its most infamous decisions, the Supreme Court held that slavery was legal in 1857. The *Dred Scott* decision, formally *Scott* v. *Sandford,* came in the case of a lifelong slave claiming his freedom. Historically and legally, if a runaway slave could make it to a free state or territory, he or she was free. Dred Scott argued that because his owner had taken him to a jurisdiction where slavery was outlawed, he was free.

The Supreme Court, in a blatantly political decision designed to head off a confrontation between slave and free states, rejected Scott's argument. The court not only held that slavery was legal, but also reversed longstanding legal precedent and said Scott was still a slave, even in a free state. The reasoning behind the case was due process: setting a slave free would deprive an owner of his property. Even worse, the Supreme Court ruled that people of African descent, whether slave or not, could not be American citizens because they were inferior.

Protesting the *Dred Scott* decision, abolitionist leader Frederick Douglass pointed out that the Constitution said "We the people," not "We the *white* people." He added, "Slavery lives in this country not because of any paper Constitution, but in the moral blindness of the American people, who persuade themselves that they are safe, though the rights of others may be struck down."

WE THE PEOPLE

The Supreme Court decision that said Dred Scott was still a slave was handed down in March 1857. Two months later, the sons of his first owner purchased the freedom of Scott and his family. Scott died the following year, apparently of tuberculosis.

The Civil War

The Supreme Court apparently hoped the *Dred Scott* decision would defuse tensions between slave owners and abolitionists, and between slave states and free states. It didn't. In fact, it fanned the flames that led to the Civil War.

In 1858, the year following the decision, Abraham Lincoln, while debating Stephen Douglas for a U.S. Senate seat from Illinois, made the speech—"A house divided against itself cannot stand"—that helped turn him into a national figure. Lincoln lost that race, but he won the Republican presidential nomination and then the election in 1860.

Lincoln was against slavery, and the Confederate states, comparing themselves to the American colonies less than a century earlier, declared independence. Lincoln took pains to make war against the Confederacy not on the grounds of slavery—it had been ruled legal by the Supreme Court, after all—but because the rebel states had violated our constitutional form of government by seceding. To Lincoln, it ostensibly was not a war of slavery but of secession. In August 1862, Lincoln defined the war this way: "My paramount object in this struggle is to save the Union, and it is not either to save or destroy slavery. If I could save the Union without freeing any slave, I would do it; and if I could save it by freeing some and leaving others alone I would also do that."

The war began in 1861, and it was not until January 1, 1863, that Lincoln's Emancipation Proclamation, based on his assumption of war powers, went into effect. It may be worth noting that the Emancipation Proclamation actually freed relatively few slaves—those in the Union states, or who had escaped to Union states.

Reconstruction

Even before the Civil War ended, when it became clear that the Union would prevail, Lincoln and his advisers agreed that a constitutional amendment was needed to overturn the *Dred Scott* decision and prevent any state—or the federal government—from again legalizing slavery. Lincoln also saw the proposed Thirteenth Amendment as a political move to demoralize the South in the last throes of the war.

Amid pitched battles in Congress—the Republicans were for it, the Democrats against it—the Thirteenth Amendment was approved in February 1865. The war formally ended with the signing of the treaty at Appomattox, Virginia, in April, and the amendment was ratified later in the year. A number of states refused to ratify the amendment in 1865. The last state to ratify it was Mississippi in 1995.

In an 1873 case, the Supreme Court, by then made up of a roster considerably different from the justices who came up with the *Dred Scott* decision 16 years earlier, ruled that the Thirteenth Amendment prohibited all types of involuntary servitude, not solely the slavery of people of African descent. "If Mexican *peonage* or the Chinese coolie labor system shall develop slavery of the Mexican or Chinese race within our territory, this amendment may safely be trusted to make it void," the court held.

DEFINITION

Not quite slavery, **peonage** is enforced servitude that forces a person to work against his or her will to pay off a debt or some other obligation. A key factor, even if there is no real legal obligation, is whether the person in servitude has been led to believe the debt must be worked off.

The nation and the Supreme Court took a broad view of civil rights in the years immediately after the Civil War, during the period known as Reconstruction, when the South was in effect ruled by Northern occupying forces. At first, the courts seemed to be moving toward identifying and eliminating symbols and manifestations—"badges and incidents"—of slavery, including many different types of discrimination against blacks.

For example, there was concerted effort to keep former slave owners from keeping their former slaves working for them in conditions comparable to slavery, including sharecropper arrangements. Under these arrangements, a former slave might be granted property—40 acres and a mule was typical—but then would be charged exorbitant fees for rent, seeds, food, furniture, and equipment. Every year the sharecropper would fall farther behind and deeper into servitude— a form of post–Civil War slavery that carried the threat of jail for nonpayment.

But the advances against involuntary servitude slowed when the federal forces withdrew from the South in 1877 and many areas began institutionalizing discrimination in the form of so-called Black Codes and Jim Crow laws.

Another notorious Supreme Court case came in 1896: *Plessy* v. *Ferguson,* which ushered in the "separate but equal" doctrine, holding that under the Thirteenth and Fourteenth amendments (see the following section) the states had to ensure that blacks and whites had the same benefits in society; however, they did not need to ensure that blacks and whites enjoyed those benefits shoulder to shoulder or had access to them together. It was not until 1968 that the Supreme Court made it clear that a black family had the right to move in next door to a white family: "At the very least, the freedom that Congress is empowered to secure under the Thirteenth Amendment includes the freedom to buy whatever a white man can buy, the right to live wherever a white man can live."

Under the Thirteenth Amendment, the courts will not order "specific performance"—requiring you to do what you agreed to do—if you violate a personal services employment contract. For example, athletes who sign a contract but refuse to play for their teams can be liable for money damages but cannot be forced to play. In addition, mandatory military service is not considered involuntary servitude under the Thirteenth Amendment.

The Fourteenth Amendment: Due Process and Equal Protection

"All persons born or naturalized in the United States, and subject to the jurisdiction thereof, are citizens of the United States and of the State wherein they reside. No State shall make or enforce any law which shall abridge the privileges or immunities of citizens of the United States; nor shall any State deprive any person of life, liberty, or property, without due process of law; nor deny to any person within its jurisdiction the equal protection of the laws.

"Representatives shall be apportioned among the several States according to their respective numbers, counting the whole number of persons in each State, excluding Indians not taxed. But when the right to vote at any election for the choice of electors for President and Vice-President of the United States, Representatives in Congress, the Executive and Judicial officers of a State, or the members of the Legislature thereof, is denied to any of the male inhabitants of such State, being twenty-one years of age, and citizens of the United States, or in any way abridged, except for participation in rebellion, or other crime, the basis of representation therein shall be reduced in the proportion which the number of such male citizens shall bear to the whole number of male citizens twenty-one years of age in such State.

"No person shall be a Senator or Representative in Congress, or elector of President and Vice-President, or hold any office, civil or military, under the United States, or under any State, who, having previously taken an oath, as a member of Congress, or as an officer of the United States, or as a member of any State legislature, or as an executive or judicial officer of any State, to support the

Constitution of the United States, shall have engaged in insurrection or rebellion against the same, or given aid or comfort to the enemies thereof. But Congress may by a vote of two-thirds of each House, remove such disability.

"The validity of the public debt of the United States, authorized by law, including debts incurred for payment of pensions and bounties for services in suppressing insurrection or rebellion, shall not be questioned. But neither the United States nor any State shall assume or pay any debt or obligation incurred in aid of insurrection or rebellion against the United States, or any claim for the loss or emancipation of any slave; but all such debts, obligations and claims shall be held illegal and void.

"The Congress shall have the power to enforce, by appropriate legislation, the provisions of this article."

In 1868, 3 years after the Thirteenth Amendment outlawed slavery, the Fourteenth Amendment was ratified to help wipe out the inequality and discrimination that lingered after slavery. The Fourteenth Amendment also struck down the part of the original Constitution that counted a slave as three fifths of a person for allocating seats for the House of Representatives and members of the Electoral College. It also blocked the former Confederate states and their citizens from filing lawsuits seeking compensation for damage to their property during the Civil War, including claims their freed slaves represented property losses.

Citizenship

Beyond those historical artifacts, the continuing impact of the Fourteenth Amendment comes from that brief opening paragraph, which begins: "All persons born or naturalized in the United States … are citizens of the United States."

The Constitution does not define citizenship, but it has been interpreted to give the same rights to both natural-born and naturalized citizens, or people from other countries who become American citizens. Natural-born citizens include children born within the United States and children born outside the United States but whose parents are U.S. citizens. Neither the Constitution nor the Supreme Court has said so explicitly, but the longtime practice has been to regard any baby born in the United States as a natural-born citizen, including those whose parents are in the country illegally.

There have been and no doubt will continue to be proposals in Congress to require at least one parent to be an American citizen for a baby to be a citizen from birth, but wholesale changes in the rules of citizenship seem unlikely in the foreseeable future. As a nation of immigrants, our culture, tradition, and laws have always held a bias toward making it easier rather than harder for newcomers to become citizens.

WHAT IT MEANS TO YOU

Many people think Americans who are born with dual citizenship with another country "have to choose" at age 18 or at some other point. Not true. Some countries do prohibit dual citizenship, but the United States is not one of them.

The second part of the opening paragraph, dealing with civil rights, is the one that has sent so many ripples through American society: "No State shall make or enforce any law which shall abridge the privileges or immunities of citizens of the United States ..." or deny any due process of law or equal protection of the laws.

In practical terms, the Fourteenth Amendment allowed the federal courts to extend many of the provisions of the Bill of Rights to the states, too. Free speech, fair trial, the right not to give evidence against yourself—none of those rights in the first 10 amendments applied to the states until the Supreme Court extended them, literally on a case-by-case basis, under the Incorporation Doctrine. This doctrine holds that many of the liberties in the Bill of Rights are so fundamental to our system of justice that they should be incorporated into the Fourteenth Amendment's Due Process Clause.

A prime example is the Sixth Amendment. The right to legal counsel originally covered only federal defendants, but the Supreme Court extended it to state defendants in capital cases in the Scottsboro case in 1932 (see Chapter 10) and in noncapital felonies in *Gideon* v. *Wainwright* in 1963.

Civil Rights

Due process is, in a word, fairness. It might be procedural fairness: you should get a hearing, your day in court, your chance to tell your side of the story, and for a decision to be made fairly, according to an established process and set of rules. If you lose your government job, your kid gets kicked out of college, or your property taxes go up, you might want to be sure the proper procedures have been followed. Due process might also be substantive, which covers every other aspect of fairness and protects specific rights, even if they are not mentioned specifically in the Constitution. For example, the courts have relied on substantive due process to tell the government to keep its nose out of our bedrooms.

The Equal Protection Clause is the authority behind the "one man, one vote" principle, along with many other aspects of fairness in our society. If one person or group of people is allowed to do something, we all should be allowed to do it.

However, the concept of equal protection under the Constitution is misunderstood in the sense that it does not really require that all people be treated equally, either as individuals or groups or classes. The Fourteenth Amendment requires only that the laws be applied equally to individuals and groups.

The day-to-day real-world effects of a law or regulation may turn out to be more detrimental to certain people, but it might be permissible anyway as long as there is a good reason for the law or regulation and it was not enacted for the purpose of discrimination. In other words, there can be a legal justification for lumping certain people into classifications and then prohibiting them from doing something everybody else is allowed to do.

Over time, the Fourteenth Amendment's equal protection provisions have been applied not only to racial discrimination, but also to women, gays, and other groups claiming discrimination. As with so many other aspects of constitutional law, perhaps the best way to figure out what it means today is to look at how the law evolved through the Supreme Court cases over the years.

An 1886 Supreme Court case, *Yick Wo* v. *Hopkins,* showed how a law can discriminate legally and at the same time be administered in a discriminatory fashion. During the late 1800s, San Francisco was home to many Chinese immigrants. Because of discrimination, the only work opportunities many of them could find were in laundries. San Francisco passed an ordinance requiring a permit to operate a laundry in a wooden building. Most laundries were in wooden buildings, and most laundries were owned and operated by Chinese people, so this ordinance presented an economic hardship to the Chinese community. The laundries had to either close down or get a permit.

The Supreme Court ruled that the ordinance was not unconstitutional because it had a legitimate purpose: there was a high danger of fires in laundries, and the chances of the fire spreading and causing more harm was greater if the laundry was in a wooden building. A permit allowed authorities to inspect laundries and determine if they were being run safely. The fact that Chinese suffered more than the rest of the population was an unfortunate and unintended side effect. The ordinance itself was not unconstitutional.

However, the court found that the law was being enforced unfairly, that permits were routinely approved for non-Chinese laundries and rejected for Chinese laundries. The court struck down the law not because it was discriminatory, but because it was administered in a discriminatory manner.

Incidentally, one other important point was made in that case. The court said the Chinese deserved equal protection under the Fourteenth Amendment because equal protection applies not only to citizens but to "any person" under a state's jurisdiction.

A series of cases in 1873 produced what have become known as the Supreme Court's *Slaughterhouse* decisions. The cases grew out of a New Orleans ordinance that granted a monopoly for slaughterhouses. Would-be competitors sued on Fourteenth Amendment grounds, claiming economic discrimination. They said the monopoly had been granted as patronage in return for political favors. The Supreme Court upheld the monopoly, citing the city's justifiable reasons for it: to keep slaughterhouses from dumping offal into the city's waterways.

In an 1880 decision, the Supreme Court held that a state ban on blacks serving on juries did not violate the prospective black jurors' rights, but it did violate the rights of black defendants under the Equal Protection Clause. A series of cases in 1883 known as the *Civil Rights* cases held that the Constitution does not prohibit racial discrimination by private individuals or organizations.

👉 **WHAT IT MEANS TO YOU**

In general, equal protection applies to government action only. Private individuals and organizations can discriminate. This is why country clubs, for example, can exclude women or certain racial or ethnic minorities from membership.

The 1896 Supreme Court decision in *Plessy* v. *Ferguson* overturned the Civil Rights Act of 1875, which was enacted in the hopes of bringing equality or at least legal equilibrium between blacks and whites in the former slave-owning states.

Amid a collection of Jim Crow laws that denied black people the use of various public facilities from toilets to schools, in 1890 Louisiana passed a law that required blacks and whites to ride in separate railroad cars. The "white" cars were considerably better appointed. Homer Plessy, who was one eighth black—an *octoroon* in the parlance of the day—bought a first-class ticket for the white part of a train, pointed out to a conductor that he was black, and was arrested. He was fined $25 and appealed the conviction all the way to the Supreme Court, which decided by a 7–1 vote that he was not a victim of discrimination prohibited by either the Thirteenth or Fourteenth amendments. Justice John Marshall Harlan, himself a former slave owner, filed a memorable dissent, warning about the United States developing a "caste" system. But for half a century, until *Brown* v. *Board of Education* in 1954, the "separate but equal" doctrine remained the law of the land.

From the end of the nineteenth century through the first part of the twentieth, the Supreme Court went through a long period that emphasized a business-oriented view of the Fourteenth Amendment and due process. The court, reflecting a predominant attitude at the time, took a laissez-faire stance in a number of cases. The focus of due process was not on personal, individual liberties, but rather on property. The court held a market-centric approach with echoes of social Darwinism, a theory of the era that suggested the haves in society should make the rules for the have-nots.

One of the defining cases was *Lochner* v. *New York* in 1905, when the Supreme Court overturned a law prohibiting bakers from working more than 10 hours a day or 60 hours a week. The reasoning: the bakery owner would make less profit, and that was a violation of his right to due process. The court did recognize some measure of "police power" that allowed states to set some health and safety rules—for working in mines, for instance—but other rulings came down squarely on the side of employers and owners, including one that struck down minimum wage requirements.

The courts gradually came to recognize that due process protected not only economic rights but also personal rights. They became more likely to presume there were valid reasons behind a state law and those reasons were not necessarily outweighed by business interests. "We do not sit as a superlegislature to weigh the wisdom of legislation or to decide whether the policy which it expresses offends the public welfare," the Supreme Court mused in one case.

In 1908, in *Berea College* v. *Kentucky,* the Supreme Court upheld a Kentucky law that prohibited black and white students from attending the same college. In a 1925 case, *Pierce* v. *Society of Sisters,* one of the first privacy cases extending parental rights, the court upheld a Ku Klux Klan (KKK) lawsuit allowing KKK parents to have their own private schools rather than send their kids to public schools.

During World War II, the federal government forced tens of thousands of Japanese and Americans of Japanese descent—including U.S. citizens whose families had been Americans for generations—to surrender their liberty and move to internment camps. A young Japanese American named Fred Korematsu was thrown in prison when he refused to turn himself in and live in a camp. He appealed his conviction, and in 1944 in *Korematsu* v. *United States,* the Supreme Court upheld the internment program. Yes, it was a violation of the Japanese Americans' individual rights, but the high court said it was justified because of concerns about espionage—national security, in other words.

When the Japanese Americans were finally freed, each was given $25 for train fare or $50 for a family. A commission appointed by President Jimmy Carter in 1980 subsequently found that the Japanese Americans had been subjected to "race prejudice, war hysteria, and a failure of political leadership." The government then granted $20,000 payments to each internment camp survivor still alive more than four decades later, including Fred Korematsu.

WE THE PEOPLE

In 1984, a federal judge overturned Fred Korematsu's original conviction, saying he did not get a fair trial. Korematsu remained politically active, and filed a "friend of the court" brief in the 2004 lawsuit challenging President George W. Bush's program detaining enemy combatants at Guantanamo Bay Naval Base. Korematsu died in 2005 at age 86.

Some believe the compensation to the internment camp survivors sets a precedent that could pave the way to reparations for slavery to African Americans, but others say it is unlikely there will ever be an American reparations program so long after slavery ended.

In a pair of 1948 cases, black families in Missouri and Michigan challenged racially discriminatory restrictive covenants—legal restrictions some owners put on their property to keep it from being sold to blacks. The cases were consolidated into one decision, *Shelley* v. *Kramer,* and the Supreme Court ruled that restrictive covenants that discriminate are not necessarily unlawful, at least as long as the people buying and selling voluntarily abide by them. The court held, however, that the covenants in the *Shelley* case were unconstitutional because by filing a lawsuit against their new black neighbors, the neighbors tried to get the state to enforce the discrimination.

One of the most famous Fourteenth Amendment cases was *Brown* v. *Board of Education,* handed down in 1954. Oliver Brown, a black man who worked as a welder in Topeka, Kansas, filed the suit because his daughter Linda was not allowed to go to the neighborhood schools with her white friends. Instead, she had to walk to a bus stop and take a bus to a black school. The Supreme Court consolidated the *Brown* case with several similar cases from South Carolina, Virginia, Delaware, and Washington, D.C. Thurgood Marshall, who later became the first black justice of the Supreme Court, was the lead attorney for the National Association for the Advancement of Colored People (NAACP), in charge of a legal team that included some of the top lawyers from some of the biggest—and whitest—law firms in the country.

The Supreme Court's 9–0 decision struck down the last vestiges of the "separate but equal" doctrine and sent out shock waves still being felt. Chief Justice Earl Warren wrote, "Today, education is perhaps the most important function of state and local governments …. Such an opportunity, where the state has undertaken to provide it, is a right which must be available to all on equal terms." Change was not immediate, of course, and there were many more court decisions and wrenching local controversies as schools integrated, sometimes with forced busing not only of black students to previously white schools but also white students to previously black schools.

The Fourteenth Amendment and its "one man, one vote" principle led the federal courts to get involved in reapportionment of congressional voting districts, which prevented states from redrawing or maintaining district boundaries that discriminated against black voters. These court rulings helped lead to the Civil Rights Act of 1964 and the Voting Rights Act of 1964 as well as to further advances in education and other equal opportunities for minorities.

One of the best-known—and most controversial—extensions of constitutional rights through the Fourteenth Amendment came in a series of cases beginning in the 1960s involving contraception, abortion, and homosexual acts. The cases cited due process and took steps toward recognizing a fundamental right to privacy—a right not specifically mentioned anywhere in the Constitution. The *Griswold* case in 1965 struck down Connecticut's anticontraceptive law, the *Roe* case legalized abortion in 1973, and the *Lawrence* case prohibited states from criminalizing consenting adult homosexual acts.

Miscegenation laws were not uncommon through much of U.S. history, but the last laws barring interracial marriage were struck down by the Supreme Court in a 1967 case, *Loving* v. *Virginia*. In that case, a white husband and his part-black, part–Native American wife were each sentenced to a year of prison for being married to each other. The decision overturning the law was unanimous.

In a 1968 case, *Washington* v. *Lee,* the Supreme Court struck down Alabama's laws requiring that black and white prisoners be housed separately in state prisons, and in 1970, the high court ruled in *Goldberg* v. *Kelly* that the due process provision of the Fourteenth Amendment requires that a hearing be held and evidence presented before certain benefits can be taken away by regulators or administrators, including welfare benefits, pensions, and licenses. Welfare benefits are a type of property, the high court reasoned, and property cannot be taken away without due process. In 1971, in *Reed* v. *Reed,* the court ruled that state law cannot give preference to men over women to serve as executors of estates, thereby ruling for the first time that gender-based laws can violate the Equal Protection Clause.

    🖉 **CASES**

> ***Washington v. Glucksberg* (1997):** The Supreme Court turned down a challenge to Washington's state law prohibiting physician-assisted suicide. The court said, in effect, that American law does not include the right to die.

In a 2000 "states' rights" case, *United States* v. *Morrison,* a female college student who said she had been raped by two members of the school's football team sued the men for damages under the federal Violence Against Women Act of 1994. In a 5–4 ruling, the Supreme Court held that the part of the law allowing female victims of violence to collect damages in federal court was unconstitutional because it exceeded the authority of the Fourteenth Amendment. The court noted that the law was designed to help women who did not get justice in state courts, but said under the Commerce Clause it was up to the states, not the federal government, to provide remedies for private wrongs.

The Fourteenth Amendment continues to be at the center of America's struggle to define civil rights and race relations. College admissions and affirmative action is a prime example, as seen in the recent case, *Fisher* v. *Texas,* which made its way from Texas to the Supreme Court not once but twice in recent years. Abigail Fisher challenged the University of Texas admission process, saying its affirmative action provisions unfairly gave preference to minority applicants while discriminating against her as a white applicant.

In a 7–1 ruling in 2013, the Supreme Court agreed that yes, Fisher should be allowed to challenge whether the University of Texas's admission policies were "made in good faith" and were not discriminatory. When Fisher lost her appeal in the lower courts, she appealed to the Supreme Court again, and the case was argued in late 2015. In the oral arguments, Justice Antonin Scalia's comments wondered whether affirmative action might actually hurt some black students who would be more successful at less academically rigorous universities. Court watchers said the case, argued in 2015 and scheduled to be decided in 2016, would probably go one of three ways: *Fisher* could be returned to the lower courts again, the Supreme Court could narrowly strike down the University of Texas's admission policies, or the court could declare affirmative action unconstitutional for college admissions across the country.

The Fourteenth Amendment also has been critical to one of the more sudden social transformations of American society—the expansion of gay rights in the late twentieth and early twenty-first centuries. One of the major goals of gay rights activists—the legalization of same-sex marriage—was given formal, legal recognition in two landmark Supreme Court cases in 2013 and 2015.

In *United States* v. *Windsor,* Edith Windsor and Thea Speyer were two women who had been living together as a couple for decades in New York. They were legally married in Canada, and their marriage was recognized by the State of New York. But when Speyer died in 2009, federal tax authorities denied Windsor the federal tax exemption for surviving spouses, based on the federal Defense of Marriage Act (DOMA), under which Congress required that marriage had to be between a man and a woman. Windsor appealed all the way to the Supreme Court, which ruled 5–4 in 2013 that DOMA was unconstitutional under the Fifth and Fourteenth Amendments' guarantees of equal rights and due process under the law.

Given that the *Windsor* ruling in effect legalized same-sex marriage under federal law, it was inevitable that a similar challenge under state law come before the Supreme Court. That was *Obergefell* v. *Hodges* in 2015, when the court ruled again 5–4 that all states had to allow same-sex marriage. The court opinion said, "The Fourteenth Amendment requires a state to license a marriage between two people of the same sex and to recognize a marriage between two people of the same sex when their marriage was lawfully licensed and performed out-of-state."

> **WE THE PEOPLE**
>
> "Especially against a long history of disapproval of their relationships, this denial works a grave and continuing harm, serving to disrespect and subordinate gays and lesbians," Justice Anthony Kennedy's opinion in *Obergefell* noted. "It is demeaning to lock same-sex couples out of a central institution of the nation's society, for they too may aspire to the transcendent purposes of marriage."

The Fifteenth Amendment: Voting Rights

"The right of citizens of the United States to vote shall not be denied or abridged by the United States or by any State on account of race, color, or previous condition of servitude.

"The Congress shall have the power to enforce this article by appropriate legislation."

The Fourteenth Amendment was drafted with the goal of creating no new rights. Instead, it was supposedly created to extend existing rights to the states. Specifically, the Fourteenth Amendment did not give freed slaves the right to vote. It was still up to the states to decide who would vote and who wouldn't. Congress approved the Fifteenth Amendment to counter any state laws that would deny the vote to blacks. Ratified in 1870, the third and last of the so-called Reconstruction Amendments said the states cannot use race, color, or status as a former slave as a reason for denying someone the right to vote.

As in so many other cases, the actual language of the Fifteenth Amendment was a compromise. Some people wanted no constitutional rules on voting eligibility; they wanted to let the states continue to set their own rules. Others wanted universal suffrage—or rather universal *male* suffrage because women did not generally have the right to vote and didn't get it until a half-century later. The Fifteenth Amendment as ratified staked out a middle ground: states could still set their own rules for voting eligibility, but those rules could not bar a potential voter because of race. Consequently, the Supreme Court ultimately made it clear that the amendment did not confer the right to vote on anyone.

When the newly elected President Rutherford B. Hayes withdrew federal troops from the South in 1877, the idea was to heal the nation's wounds and ease political dissent in the South, where many people felt like they were an occupied country within a country. With less federal oversight, however, a number of states brought in voter-qualification laws that seemed nondiscriminatory but had the practical effect of preventing blacks from voting. Poll taxes, for example, kept poor people from voting, and blacks were more likely to be poor. Literacy tests kept many blacks from registering, especially when administered by clerks who sometimes rejected black voters who could actually read and write more proficiently than white voters who were approved. Sometimes strict registration procedures were instituted that were not publicized in the black community and presented opportunities for clerks to reject black voters for minor technical missteps in the process.

In 1915 in *Guinn* v. *United States,* the Supreme Court overturned the "grandfather" clauses a number of states had instituted, which said that you were automatically eligible to vote if you were a descendant of someone who had voted earlier or been eligible to vote earlier—such as before blacks had the right to vote. This kept whites from having to take literary tests or meet other registration requirements, while giving clerks more opportunities to reject black voters. In a 1939 case, *Lane* v. *Wilson,* the Supreme Court struck down an Oklahoma law that said people who had voted earlier did not have to reregister, while others had a 121-day window to register— or be ineligible to ever vote. And in 1944, the high court struck down a Texas law that said you had to be a member of one of the major political parties to vote in a primary election. The parties' respective central committees decided who was a member of the party and who wasn't, and not many black people were welcomed to membership back then.

In reality, many black voters suffered discrimination for many years until the Voting Rights Act of 1965 spelled out equal voting rights for all.

WE THE PEOPLE

"Today is a triumph for freedom as huge as any victory that has ever been won on any battlefield. Yet to seize the meaning of this day, we must recall darker times."

—President Lyndon B. Johnson, during the signing ceremony for the Voting Rights Act

But the key provisions of the Voting Rights Act did not last forever, and other issues going to the heart of "one man, one vote" continue to pose constitutional issues.

In 2013, citing both the Fourteenth and Fifteenth Amendments, the Supreme Court rolled back key provisions of the Voting Rights Act of 1965 that required a number of states to get approval from the U.S. Department of Justice—*preclearance* it was called in the legislation—before changing state or local voting laws. The goal of the Voting Rights Act, of course, was to prevent states from passing laws that would make it more difficult for minorities to register and vote. The decision in the 2013 case, *Shelby County* v. *Holder,* held that the law was out of date and no longer needed because state voting laws were not discriminatory, and the states covered by preclearance had many black voters and black officeholders. The court rejected the argument that the Voting Rights Act was the reason there were so many black voters and black officeholders.

In the wake of the ruling, a number of states, both states that had been covered by preclearance and some that were not, changed their voting laws. Some of the changes made it easier for voters to register, including online, while a number of changes set new voter identification requirements.

The changes were widely viewed along partisan lines, depending on whether the party was generally predisposed to favor large voter turnouts. Supporters of voter ID laws, most of them Republicans, said those laws would prevent voter fraud. But opponents, mostly Democrats, pointed out that voter fraud was not a significant problem in any state or local jurisdiction—indeed, prosecutions for voter fraud were extremely rare—and warned that the true motive of stricter voter ID laws was to suppress voting among minorities and poor people who were less likely to have driver's licenses or other government-issued identification.

Two other cases relating to voting, *Evenwel* v. *Abbott* and *Harris* v. *Arizona Independent Redistricting Commission,* both look at aspects of redistricting—how votes are apportioned, according to the U.S. Census, among states for the purpose of determining how many congressional districts and Electoral College votes each state has. Both cases were argued before the Supreme Court in late 2015 and decisions are expected in 2016.

Some observers thought the Supreme Court would make no major changes in congressional redistricting—or in the way some critics say redistricting has amounted to gerrymandering to limit congressional districts dominated by minority voters and, thereby, presumably limiting the number of minority members of Congress. But others feared that the court, in the wake of the *Shelby County* decision weakening the Voting Rights Act, might lead to a process for redistricting that might make it even more difficult for members of minorities to be elected to Congress.

The Least You Need to Know

- The Thirteenth, Fourteenth, and Fifteenth Amendments are known as the Reconstruction Amendments.
- The Thirteenth Amendment banned slavery and involuntary servitude.
- The Fourteenth Amendment, including the Due Process Clause and the Equal Protection Clause, extended many Bill of Rights protections, including free speech and fair trial, to state as well as federal laws.
- The Fifteenth Amendment prohibited states from establishing voting laws based on race or color.

CHAPTER 14

The Sixteenth and Seventeenth Amendments: Taxes and Senators

After the Fifteenth Amendment was ratified in 1870, no amendments were added to the constitution for more than four decades. In 1913, however, two amendments were ratified: the Sixteenth, allowing Congress to enact the federal income tax system we have today, and the Seventeenth, providing for the direct election of senators.

The Sixteenth Amendment has been controversial since day 1. Critics have contended that both the amendment and the income tax are illegal. Despite losing challenge after challenge, the tax protest movement today may be stronger than ever, thanks to the internet and the willingness of some Americans to grasp any notion—and particularly any conspiracy theory—that justifies not sending Uncle Sam some of their hard-earned cash every April 15.

The Seventeenth Amendment changed the way senators are elected. Originally, the Constitution left it up to each state, and specifically up to each state's legislature, to send two senators to Washington. A number of problems in the selection system developed, however, and the public began asking: why can't we vote for our senators directly, the same way we vote for members of the House of Representatives? The Seventeenth Amendment scrapped the old system and provided for direct election of senators.

The Sixteenth Amendment

"The Congress shall have power to lay and collect taxes on incomes, from whatever sources derived, without apportionment among the several States, and without regard to any census or enumeration."

Article I of the Constitution set strict limits on how Congress could levy taxes, requiring that any "direct" tax on the people had to be proportionate to the population of each state. In other words, if Pennsylvania accounted for 15 percent of the population, the people of Pennsylvania would be required to pay no more than 15 percent of the direct taxes collected by the government. Direct taxes were generally considered taxes on property—what you owned, rather than income from your labor. Article I exempted indirect or *excise tax* from the proportional requirement.

> **DEFINITION**
>
> An **excise tax,** as it relates to the Constitution, is a tax paid not on property you own, but on some "event" in which you participate—buying or selling something, getting a license, etc. Customs, duties, tolls, and sales tax are all examples.

This system worked fine for most of the century after the Constitution was approved in 1789. The federal government paid for itself through a range of excise taxes, customs, duties, and tariffs. After all, at that time, the federal government didn't do a lot—nowhere near what it does today, anyway—and it didn't cost much to run. Things changed when the Civil War broke out. Wars are expensive, and this one cost the federal government up to $2 million a day, an astronomical sum in the 1860s.

To increase incoming funds, Congress passed the Revenue Act of 1861, which raised excise taxes and included a personal income tax: 3 percent on all incomes above $800 a year. You were doing pretty well if you made $800 a year in those days, so most Americans were not affected. Congress tweaked the new income tax in 1862, imposing a 5 percent tax rate on those with incomes over $10,000 a year, which included a relative handful of the superwealthy.

The first national income tax faded away after the Civil War, and the federal government happily subsisted on excise taxes, customs, duties, and tariffs until the late 1800s. Gradually, however, it became clear that the rapid growth of the country required government growth. In 1894, Congress passed the Wilson-Gorman Tariff, which put a 2 percent tax on incomes greater than $3,000—the equivalent of more than $70,000 today, by Consumer Price Index estimates.

Opponents challenged the new law on the grounds it violated Article I of the Constitution. Their argument was that the income tax was a direct tax and, therefore, was unconstitutional unless Congress could figure out how to ensure the people of every state contributed no more than their share, according to population. In practical terms, that was an impossible administrative task. Besides, it would have meant the tax rate would be different for every state, depending not only on population but on average income levels.

The issue came before the U.S. Supreme Court in 1895 in the case *Pollock* v. *Farmers' Loan and Trust Co.* Now, there are many good things about our system of checks and balances and the way the federal courts, and particularly the Supreme Court, can review legislation and overturn it if it violates the Constitution. But one bad thing about our system is that if the Supreme Court makes a mistake, it can be difficult to undo, and the aftereffects can ripple throughout society for a long time.

In the *Pollock* case, the Supreme Court declared the federal income tax law unconstitutional. The court, in a narrow 5–4 decision, held that the previous view was wrong. An income tax was not always indirect. Instead, the court ruled, the income tax was a direct tax if the income was generated by property—as in the case of rent collected for land, for example. In that case, the court ruled, the income tax had to be apportioned among the states. The income tax law as set up by Congress was null and void.

So the federal government went back to paying its way through excise taxes. The government sold bonds, started collecting fees for the use of land for recreational purposes, and raised a number of sales and use taxes, especially on beer and tobacco, to help pay for the Spanish American War in 1899. However, it soon became clear that a national tax was needed, a way for the government to routinely and reliably raise the money it needed to run the country. It also became clear that the apportionment provisions of Article I were not fair. If every state's contribution to the national coffers had to match its percentage of the national population, the residents of the richer, more populous states in the Northeast would have to pay less than people in the South and West.

Let's look at how it would work today if our modern income tax was subject to the apportionment provisions of Article I. New Jersey is a state with about 9 million people, or about 3 percent of the U.S. population, while Mississippi is a state with a population of about 3 million people, or about 1 percent of the U.S. population. Under the apportionment provisions of Article I, New Jersey residents would contribute 3 percent of the taxes collected by the federal government and Mississippi would contribute 1 percent. But the average household income in New Jersey is in excess of $60,000, while the typical household in Mississippi earns about half that. So taxpayers in New Jersey would have to pay only about half the percentage of taxes taxpayers in Mississippi would have to pay.

The Supreme Court apparently realized the inequities of the *Pollock* decision and began back-pedaling in subsequent decisions. At the same time, Congress wrestled with how to get around it. When the judicial branch of government interprets the law in a way that the legislative branch doesn't like, the alternative is for the legislative branch to change the law—even if it is the supreme law of the land. And that's what Congress proposed by approving an amendment to allow an income tax and sending it to the states in 1909 for ratification.

> **WE THE PEOPLE**
>
> Even some of the sponsors of the Sixteenth Amendment held their nose when it came before Congress. One of the sponsors, Sereno E. Payne, a Republican congressman from New York, said, "As to the general policy of an income tax, I am utterly opposed to it. I believe with Gladstone that it tends to make a nation of liars."

The Federal Income Tax Law

Arizona became the forty-eighth state in 1912, so 36 states needed to ratify. In February 1913, Secretary of State Philander Knox announced that 38 states had ratified the Sixteenth Amendment. If you live in one of the states that did not ratify, none of the rest of us can blame you: Virginia, Pennsylvania, Rhode Island, Connecticut, Florida, and Utah.

Eight months later, in October 1913, Congress enacted a new federal income tax law. The new tax rates began at 1 percent and went all the way up to 7 percent for those earning more than $500,000 a year—the equivalent of more than $10 million today. Because of exemptions, though, only a small percentage—less than 1 percent—of Americans were required to pay any tax at all in those early years.

It sounds simple now, and probably was, but even back then, when Congress was debating how to set up the income tax system in 1913, people were complaining about how complex it was. In 1913, during the debate on the first income tax act under the Sixteenth Amendment, Senator Elihu Root commiserated with those who said they didn't understand how the new income tax system would work: "I guess you will have to go to jail. If that is the result of not understanding the Income Tax Law I shall meet you there. We shall have a merry, merry time, for all of our friends will be there. It will be an intellectual center, for no one understands the Income Tax Law except persons who have not sufficient intelligence to understand the questions that arise under it."

March 1, incidentally, was the original tax day. The official annual filing date was changed to March 15 in 1918 and did not become the current April 15 until 1954. Form 1040, today's "U.S. Individual Income Tax Return," was used from the beginning, although of course it has changed many times and in many ways over the years.

The original law allowed Congress to tax "lawful income," but the word *lawful* was dropped in 1916 to make it clear that illegal income was not tax-exempt. The court agreed in subsequent decisions, including one in which Justice Oliver Wendell Holmes wrote, "We see no reason … why the fact that a business is unlawful should exempt it from paying the taxes that if lawful it would have to pay." This gave federal law enforcement authorities another arrow in their quiver: even if they couldn't convict crooks for their criminal acts, they could still send them up the river for failing to declare and pay taxes on their ill-gotten gains. That's how many a Prohibition-era bootlegger was sent to prison, including Al Capone.

Meanwhile, the Supreme Court continued to distance itself from the *Pollock* decision, including ruling on a series of cases that have taken a broad view of what is income, and it seemed as if the court would have reversed the decision outright if it had not become *moot* with the enactment of the Sixteenth Amendment.

DEFINITION

The courts say a question or issue is **moot** when it doesn't matter, when it is irrelevant or of academic interest only. A more relevant law or court ruling or other events can make an issue become moot.

Tax Protests

A small but busy and mostly underground industry has developed in response to the Sixteenth Amendment, the tax laws, and the court decisions interpreting the laws. Antitax entrepreneurs sell various packages, both in print and online, that challenge the legality of both the amendment and the income tax. The promoters of these schemes often end up paying not only their original tax bills, but interest and penalties, too. Sometimes they end up in jail, but the Internal Revenue Service (IRS) likes to point out that a fair number of the charlatans who sell antitax packages actually do pay their own taxes.

Let's look at some of the most frequent claims by those who say the income tax is illegal. One argument is that the Sixteenth Amendment was never approved because a number of states "amended" it before ratification. The courts agreed that the versions of the Sixteenth Amendment sent back to Congress after ratification are not identical to the wording Congress sent out to the states. However, the courts have held that these are not substantive amendments but "errors of diction, capitalization, punctuation, and spelling." The courts have noted that Philander Knox, who as secretary of state was in charge of determining whether the amendment was ratified, actually considered and rejected the argument that the amendment was invalid because of the changes by some states.

Another argument by the tax protestors is that the Sixteenth Amendment is invalid because it is in conflict with state laws prohibiting income taxes. The Supreme Court shot that one down in 1922, ruling that national income taxes are a proper federal function that cannot be taken away by the states.

Another is that the Constitution never properly defines *income,* but the courts have pointed out that the Constitution has lots of significant words and phrases that are never defined, such as *free speech* and *due process* and *fair trial.* The Supreme Court ruled in 1935 that for legal purposes, the word *income* is used in the Constitution "as used in common speech."

The protestors also claim the Sixteenth Amendment is not legal because it didn't repeal anything. But most of the amendments did not repeal anything. The Bill of Rights, for example, did not repeal anything. Some would say the only amendment that formally repealed another part of the Constitution was the Twenty-First, which explicitly wiped the Eighteenth Amendment off the books to end Prohibition.

Another argument that has gotten nowhere is that the Sixteenth Amendment violates other parts of the Constitution, including the Fourth Amendment's privacy protections, the Fifth Amendment's guarantees against giving evidence against yourself, and the Fourteenth Amendment's right to due process. T. Coleman Andrews, after serving as commissioner of the IRS from 1953 until 1955, cited these arguments when he resigned because he was unhappy over the income tax:

> "The income tax is bad because it has robbed you and me of the guarantee of privacy and the respect for our property that were given to us in Article IV of the Bill of Rights. This invasion is absolute and complete as far as the amount of tax that can be assessed is concerned. Please remember that under the Sixteenth Amendment, Congress can take 100 percent of our income anytime it wants to."

According to the courts, he was correct only about the last part of that statement.

WHAT IT MEANS TO YOU

The tax protesters have all sorts of theories and strategies for arguing that the Constitution does not allow the income tax. But the Sixteenth Amendment language specifically says Congress has the "power to lay and collect taxes on income." The bottom line: no matter how much you detest paying taxes, it is illegal not to file a return and pay the taxes you owe.

The Seventeenth Amendment

"The Senate of the United States shall be composed of two Senators from each State, elected by the people thereof, for six years; and each Senator shall have one vote. The electors in each State shall have the qualifications requisite for electors of the most numerous branch of the State legislatures.

"When vacancies happen in the representation of any State in the Senate, the executive authority of each State shall issue writs of election to fill such vacancies: Provided That the legislature of any State may empower the executive thereof to make temporary appointments until the people fill the vacancies by election as the legislature may direct.

"This amendment shall not be so construed as to affect the election or term of any Senator chosen before it becomes valid as part of the Constitution."

Article I of the Constitution specified different ways for electing members of the House and Senate. Representatives were elected directly by the people, but the two senators for each state were selected by that state's legislature. Apparently, the rule for letting the legislatures choose senators was part of an effort by the Constitutional Convention to persuade the states to support the draft Constitution. The framers reckoned that if the state legislatures had more power, they would be more likely to ratify the Constitution. In addition, the framers liked the idea that one chamber of Congress could be above the fray of street politics. Senators chosen by legislatures rather than by citizens directly would be able to do what's right in office rather than what they needed to do to get re-elected.

Problems soon developed, however. Unlike members of the House of Representatives, senators were not beholden to the public. A representative who didn't do a good job would be voted out of office; a senator could do a lousy job and then merely persuade a few friends in the state legislature to return him to office.

In addition, frequent political spats within states often resulted in stalemates, and some senate seats remained vacant for long periods. In the very first congress, New York did not have one of its senators for 3 months. Later, Indiana and Delaware each went years with a Senate vacancy.

Corruption became rampant. Senators bribed their way into office, and special interests realized that if they couldn't get their own senator into office, they could block unfriendly legislation merely by keeping someone else from getting their senator into office. The process of selecting senators was driven underground, literally, into smoke-filled rooms. A number of senators, including a wealthy Montana silver miner who paid state legislators $140,000 in bribes for his seat, ended up being kicked out of Congress and resigning in disgrace.

Naturally, the public was dissatisfied. Many of the states began having their own primary elections for the Senate, with the understanding that their legislatures would appoint the winners. Progressives such as Wisconsin Republican Governor Robert La Follette led the call for a constitutional amendment, and the movement gathered momentum as the media highlighted the corruption.

WE THE PEOPLE

An early investigative reporter, David Graham Phillips, published an article called "The Treason of the Senate" in 1906 in *Cosmopolitan* magazine that exposed the corruption over Senate seats and crystallized public opinion behind the Seventeenth Amendment.

The Seventeenth Amendment was readily approved by Congress in 1912 and sailed through the ratification process, becoming effective a year later.

The amendment has not been totally without controversy, however. Over the years, a number of conservative politicians, including former Senator Zell Miller and former House Majority Leader Tom DeLay, have called for repealing the Seventeenth Amendment on the grounds it violates the system of checks and balances. Critics say the states should still have the authority to appoint—and remove—senators. By taking power from the states, critics say, the Seventeenth Amendment led to an imbalance of power in favor of the federal government and resulted in myriad woes, including federal budget deficits.

One of the more disingenuous arguments, given that the amendment was approved because of bribery to buy Senate seats, is that repealing the Seventeenth Amendment would be a type of campaign finance reform: if there's no campaign, there can't be any campaign finance.

The Least You Need to Know

- The Sixteenth Amendment specifically authorized the federal income tax in 1913.
- Tax protesters have many theories for why the income tax is illegal. No courts have ever recognized any of those theories.
- No matter what the protestors say, if you don't pay your taxes, you could go to jail.
- Senators originally were chosen by state legislatures, but corruption led to direct election by the public.

CHAPTER 15

The Eighteenth and Twenty-First Amendments: Prohibition and Repeal

It's difficult today to imagine a United States in which drinking alcohol would be so widely criticized that the federal government would try to outlaw it entirely. But that's exactly what happened in the early part of the twentieth century—with disastrous results and a classic lesson in what happens when a government tries to go too far in regulating personal behavior in a democracy founded on individual liberty.

In This Chapter

- The Eighteenth Amendment: Prohibition
- Alcohol in America
- The Volstead Act
- The Twenty-First Amendment: repeal

The Eighteenth Amendment: Prohibition

"After one year from the ratification of this article the manufacture, sale, or transportation of intoxicating liquors within, the importation thereof into, or the exportation thereof from the United States and all territory subject to the jurisdiction thereof for beverage purposes is hereby prohibited.

"The Congress and the several States shall have concurrent power to enforce this article by appropriate legislation.

"This article shall be inoperative unless it shall have been ratified as an amendment to the Constitution by the legislatures of the several States, as provided in the Constitution, within seven years from the date of the submission thereof to the States by the Congress."

The Prohibition Amendment was unusual in that its wording portended the uncertainty and controversy over trying to impose a national ban on alcohol. For one thing, the wording recognized the challenges of implementing and enforcing the ban on alcohol: it gave a year's grace, sort of like a national "last call," before Prohibition would go into effect. For another, the amendment set a 7-year self-destruct deadline: if it proved so difficult to enact that it took 7 years, it would fail.

America and Alcohol

Perhaps there has never been a nation with so many enthusiastic drinkers and so many aggressive antidrinkers. The earliest European settlers depended on alcoholic beverages, particularly beer, because it was cleaner and healthier than water. Parents and children alike drank beer or wine with the majority of their meals—even the Puritans.

At the time the Constitution was being written and ratified, George Washington and other leaders were lamenting the way that drinking, often to excess, had become such a part of daily life. Many workers, for example, routinely took a late-morning break—"elevenses," they called it—for a stiff whiskey or two.

Temperance groups that campaigned against alcohol—some against drinking too much, some against drinking at all—began rising in influence in the early 1800s. A religious revival that disparaged alcohol use swept across the country in the 1820s and 1830s, led by prominent Methodists. In 1846, Maine became the first state to prohibit alcohol. President Abraham Lincoln, pressed for federal funding before there was an income tax, resorted to higher taxes on liquor and beer to defray the costs of the Civil War. After the war, however, the temperance movement grew through the Prohibition Party, the Woman's Christian Temperance Union (WCTU), and the Anti-Saloon League.

The WCTU reflected the growing political influence of women in American society; they could not yet vote, but they could influence public policy by marching and speaking out against the harm that alcohol abuse wreaked on marriages and families. The problems were heightened by industrialization and urbanization as more men began working in factories and drinking in nearby bars before and after their shifts. And established society came to see drinking as an immigrant problem, with the Irish and Germans devoted to their beer and the Italians to their wine. Many Protestants saw use of alcohol as a Catholic frailty. The Anti-Saloon League, formed in 1893, fought against the growing power of big-city political machines that were based on cronyism that stretched from the neighborhood tavern to city hall and beyond.

By the turn of the century, temperance education—classes in which students were taught the evils of demon rum—were standard in schools across the country. Support for a total ban on alcohol across the country grew, particularly as anti-German sentiment swelled in World War I, when there was a temporary period of Prohibition to preserve grain for food supplies. Even many drinkers favored a ban on public alcohol sales, including wealthy and upper-middle-class people who believed they would be able to continue to enjoy their decent wines in their homes while the unwashed masses would be better off without their cheap beer, gin, and whiskey. Some reasoned that less alcohol would increase productivity in the factories—and besides, the lower classes simply didn't have the self-control to handle their liquor.

As Congress was considering the constitutional amendment to impose Prohibition nationally, Republican Senator Warren Harding proposed the first time limit for ratification: if the states did not ratify within 7 years, the amendment was dead. Harding, who was elected president not long after Prohibition went into effect, was known to enjoy his whiskey, but his home state, Ohio, was a hotbed of temperance. The time limit was challenged, but the Supreme Court upheld it in *Dillon* v. *Gloss* in 1921.

WE THE PEOPLE

Republican strategists pushed Warren G. Harding to head the ticket in 1920 because he looked presidential, and he won easily. A critic said his cliché-ridden speeches were like "an army of pompous phrases moving over the landscape in search of an idea," and his brief administration, rife with scandal, ended when he died of a heart attack in San Francisco in 1923.

The Volstead Act

Congress approved the Eighteenth Amendment and sent it to the states in January 1918. Many of the state legislatures were dominated by rural lawmakers who were generally more antialcohol than city politicians, and the amendment was ratified a year later.

Scholars say the Eighteenth Amendment was one of only two amendments—the other being the Thirteenth, banning slavery—that specifically outlawed personal behavior. Subsequent challenges, all futile, argued that the amendment was illegal because it amounted to legislation, while the Constitution was supposed to offer only general guidance and principles and amendments were not supposed to break new ground but rather only clarify or rectify preexisting portions of the Constitution.

By 1919, the year the Eighteenth Amendment went into effect, 26 states had their own Prohibition laws. Congress enacted the Volstead Act, which gave enforcement teeth to the amendment. However, like the Eighteenth Amendment itself, it did not define intoxicating liquor or prohibit the purchase, possession, or consumption of alcoholic beverages. The act, named after Andrew Volstead, the Minnesota Republican congressman who introduced it, also allowed small quantities of wine for personal consumption and slightly alcoholic drinks, such as near beer, that were no more than .5 percent alcohol. The Volstead Act also allowed people to keep and enjoy alcoholic beverages they had purchased before the amendment was ratified.

The penalties for selling liquor—brandy, whiskey, rum, beer, gin, ale, porter, wine—ranged from 30 days in jail to 5 years in prison and fines of $500 to $10,000.

 WE THE PEOPLE

Andrew Volstead, a lawyer, was the mayor of Granite Falls, Minnesota, before he was elected to Congress in 1903. One of the few congressmen who favored a federal law against lynching, he was typical of the progressives who thought Prohibition would be good for the country's morals and morale. As public opinion turned against Prohibition, he was defeated in his 1922 reelection bid.

The most ardent temperance leaders exulted in Prohibition. Evangelist Billy Sunday held mock funerals for John Barleycorn and announced, "The slums will soon be only a memory. We will turn our prisons into factories and our jails into storehouses and corncribs." Indeed, absenteeism at factories declined and the welfare rolls shrank. Police received fewer calls for domestic disturbances, delinquency, disorderly conduct, vagrancy, assault, and other crimes.

The Downside of Dry

But the general public soon became disenchanted. The idea of a dry nation was more palatable than actually going without a drink. And instead of giving up booze, Americans were simply doing it more surreptitiously, and paying more for it.

California's vineyards expanded during Prohibition, and retailers legally sold "blocks" or "bricks" of dehydrated "grape juice" that carried wine names. One set of instructions read: "After dissolving the brick in a gallon of water, do not place the liquid in a jug away in the cupboard for 20 days, because then it would turn into wine." Another set of instructions reminded customers it was legal to drink wine in their own homes but not to transport it.

Illegal booze was readily available at parties where so-called gin was made in bathtubs; in the tens of thousands of speakeasies that popped up everywhere, including in private homes; and through the untold numbers of rumrunners, moonshiners, and gangsters who found a new way to make a living. Much of the money for illegal booze went to smugglers such as Al Capone, who earned tens of millions annually for several years from his Chicago headquarters. As a result, some believe Prohibition was the breeding ground for organized crime in the United States.

Enforcement was a problem as well. Both the state and federal authorities had enforcement authority, but neither seemed to want it very much. With their own laws, some states were more strict than others, but enforcement also varied from city to city, judge to judge, prosecutor to prosecutor, and even cop to cop.

Awash in money, the gangsters could bribe entire police departments. One magistrate in Philadelphia collected $88,000 in bribes in less than a year on the bench, and in South Jacksonville, Florida, virtually the entire city administration, including the mayor, chief of police, president of the city council, and even the fire chief, were indicted for corruption by a federal grand jury. One study reports that from 1921 to 1923 7,000 Prohibition-related arrests were made in New York City but only 27 convictions. In Chicago, the Untouchables, the famous crime fighters led by Eliot Ness, were celebrated as much for not taking bribes as for the arrests they made.

As the gangsters fostered violence and corruption, the bodies and the bribes both led to public disregard for government and the law. President Harding noted that Prohibition had become a divisive class issue: "Many citizens, not teetotalers in their habits, lawfully acquired stores of private stocks in anticipation of Prohibition … so there are literally American millions who resent the lawful possessions of the few, the lawless practices of a few more, and rebel against the denial to the vast majority."

Alcohol was not illegal in Canada during Prohibition, and great quantities of quality, brand-name liquor—as opposed to the often-dubious homemade stuff—were smuggled across the border. One of the most notorious smugglers was Bill McCoy, and speakeasy operators would assure customers their drinks were the "real McCoy."

It soon became clear that Prohibition was a failure—an expensive mistake. Even industrialist John D. Rockefeller, a teetotaler who had donated hundreds of thousands of dollars to the temperance movement, called for an end to Prohibition. President Herbert Hoover called it "the great social and economic experiment, noble in motive and far reaching in purpose," but agreed that it had failed. In 1932, the Democratic Party made repeal a plank in its national campaign platform, and when the Democrats swept into office, the street bands blared, "Happy Days Are Here Again."

The Twenty-First Amendment: Repeal

"The eighteenth article of amendment to the Constitution of the United States is hereby repealed.

"The transportation into any State, Territory, or possession of the United States for delivery or use therein of intoxicating liquors, in violation of the laws, thereof, is hereby prohibited.

"This article shall be inoperative unless it shall have been ratified as an amendment to the Constitution by conventions in the several States, as provided in the Constitution, within seven years from the date of the submission hereof to the States by the Congress."

After President Franklin Delano Roosevelt (FDR) took office, one of the first acts of the new Congress was to approve the Twenty-First Amendment. A few months later, Utah became the thirty-sixth and final state needed for ratification, and Prohibition ended. The Eighteenth Amendment became the only one ever repealed by another amendment, and the Twenty-First was the only one approved by state conventions rather than by legislatures; Congress had stipulated state conventions out of fear that rural-dominated legislatures would vote to keep Prohibition.

The Ontario, California, *Daily Report* newspaper noted: "A lot of factors went into the decision to do away with Prohibition. None, however, was quite as important as the nation's desire to get out from under the speakeasy and the rumrunner. They were a load too heavy to be carried any farther. We have dropped them."

The Supreme Court ruled that the Twenty-First Amendment made the Volstead Act invalid, but a number of states retained Prohibition. Mississippi was the last state to lift its complete ban on alcoholic beverages, in 1966.

WE THE PEOPLE

In his 1934 State of the Union speech, FDR said: "The adoption of the Twenty-First Amendment should give material aid to the elimination of those new forms of crime which came from the illegal traffic of liquor."

If you look at the Twenty-First Amendment, you'll note that repeal is taken care of succinctly in the 15-word opening clause. The third and final clause deals with the 7-year time limit for ratification, which was not a factor because the states voted for repeal so quickly. However, the second phrase of the amendment, prohibiting transportation or possession into any state "in violation of the laws, thereof," would appear to give broad powers to the states to regulate alcohol. That's certainly the way the Supreme Court has interpreted it.

There have been tensions and potential conflicts with other parts of the Constitution, including free speech and interstate commerce, and the Supreme Court has indicated there must be a balancing act on a case-by-case basis. But for the most part, states have wide latitude in regulating alcohol sales and distribution.

An exception was a 2005 case, *Granholm* v. *Heald,* which looked at Michigan and New York laws allowing in-state wineries to ship wine directly to in-state residents but prohibiting out-of-state wineries from shipping directly to their respective resident customers. The two states maintained that the second clause of the Twenty-First Amendment gave them unlimited authority to regulate wine sales and distribution in their states, but the Supreme Court disagreed. In a 5–4 decision, the high court said the laws were unconstitutional because they violated the Constitution's protections for interstate commerce.

A number of Supreme Court rulings relating to the Twenty-First Amendment have dealt with topless or nude dancing, pornographic movies, and sexual activities in bars and taverns. In *California* v. *LaRue* in 1972, *New York State Liquor Authority* v. *Bellanca* in 1981, and *City of Newport* v. *Iacobucci* in 1986, the Supreme Court said the states can ban or regulate nude or partly nude dancing as part of the power to regulate alcoholic beverages under the Twenty-First Amendment.

In other cases, the Supreme Court has said that performers may be enjoying their First Amendment rights of expression but made a distinction between dancing topless in a bar where drinks are served and appearing nude in a serious theater presentation. In *44 Liquormart* v. *Rhode Island* in 1996, the Supreme Court said, "Entirely apart from the Twenty-First Amendment, the state has ample power to prohibit the sale of alcoholic beverages in inappropriate locations" and "to restrict the kind of 'bacchanalian revelries' described in the *LaRue* opinion regardless of whether alcoholic beverages are involved."

> **CASES**
>
> ***Barnes v. Glen Theatre, Inc.* (1991):** Two bars, claiming that dancing nude represents freedom of expression, challenged an Indiana state law requiring dancers to wear at least a G-string and pasties. The Supreme Court turned down the appeal and held that "the enforcement of Indiana's public indecency law to prevent totally nude dancing does not violate the First Amendment's guarantee of freedom of expression."

Subsequently, however, the Supreme Court put some limits on state and local regulation of topless and nude dancing, sometimes requiring proof that the dancing would have harmful effects on the community.

The Least You Need to Know

- Prohibition was the result of a complicated combination of social, cultural, and economic factors.
- Prohibition, as enforced by the Volstead Act, lasted from 1920 until 1933.
- It was illegal to sell and transport alcoholic beverages, but it was not illegal to drink them in your own home.
- Prohibition had little impact on American alcohol consumption except to drive it underground and put it in the hands of gangsters.
- The Twenty-First Amendment repealed Prohibition and made alcohol sales legal once again.

CHAPTER 16

The Nineteenth Amendment: Women's Suffrage

"The right of the citizens of the United States to vote shall not be denied or abridged by the United States or by any State on account of sex.

"Congress shall have the power, by appropriate legislation, to enforce the provisions of this article."

American woman were first allowed to vote less than a century ago. It was a long and difficult campaign spanning decades, and many of the leaders of the movement did not live to see the Nineteenth Amendment become part of the Constitution in 1920 and give them the right to vote.

In This Chapter

- The Nineteenth Amendment
- The women's movement
- Women win the vote
- Ratifying the Nineteenth Amendment

The Birth of a Movement

Before independence, some of the colonies allowed women to vote, and some didn't. During the Revolutionary War, Abigail Adams wrote to her husband, John, insisting that the founding fathers should make room for some founding mothers, too. "If women are not represented in this new republic," she warned, "there will be another revolution." New Jersey allowed all its citizens to vote in 1776, as long as they had a certain amount of money, but the state took the vote away from women in 1807.

The attitude of the day among traditionalists who opposed women's *suffrage*—both men and women—was summed up in a nineteenth-century Supreme Court case upholding an Illinois law that banned women from becoming lawyers. A concurring opinion in that case said in part: "It is true that many women are unmarried and not affected by any of the duties, complications and incapacities arising out of the married state, but these are exceptions to the general rule. The paramount destiny and mission of woman are to fulfill the noble and benign offices of wife and mother."

Women were regarded by some as too flighty, or not smart enough, or too concerned with taking care of their homes and families. *Suffragists* were derided for abandoning their femininity, and a popular joke in the 1800s suggested that the best way to deal with demands for the women's vote was to allow it for women over age 30. The problem would disappear, the joke went, because no woman wanted to admit to being over 30.

DEFINITION

Suffrage means the right to vote. During the long campaign to win the vote, most women preferred to be called **suffragists,** a neutral term that covered both men and women and the range of the political spectrum. The term *suffragette,* used by some newspapers and by opponents of the women's vote, referred to women only and carried connotations of political and social radicalism.

Many point to the start of the women's movement as the 2-day women's rights convention held in Seneca Falls, New York, in July 1848. Organized by Lucretia Mott and Elizabeth Cady Stanton, the convention concluded with a Declaration of Sentiments that objected to the unfair treatment of women politically, culturally, and economically. It also was the first large-scale public demand for women to have the vote.

Women promoted their cause through marches, letters, pamphlets and books, lobbying, silent vigils, and hunger strikes. But they did not always agree on tactics and strategy. For example, there was a debate within the early suffragist movement over whether to fight for equal suffrage (women having the same voting rights as men) or universal suffrage (equal voting rights for everyone, including women and racial minorities). Before the Civil War, the cause lagged in the South in part because many suffragists were also abolitionists. Some suffragists feared they might hurt their cause by linking it to voting rights for blacks, but it turned out that the Fifteenth Amendment gave black men the right to vote decades before women got it.

Susan B. Anthony did not become active until she was in her 30s, in the 1850s, when she was bowled over by a speech given by suffragist leader Lucy Stone, the first woman in America to keep her own name after marriage. Anthony was swept up in the cause, and her tireless work soon made her one of the movement's national leaders. She believed the Fourteenth Amendment gave women the right to vote and felt that if the right case came up, the Supreme Court would agree.

WE THE PEOPLE

Lucy Stone attended Oberlin College in Ohio, the first college in the United States to admit women. It also was the first college in the United States to admit blacks.

In the autumn of 1872, Susan B. Anthony organized a group of women in her hometown of Rochester, New York, to register to vote in the upcoming presidential election. When election officials refused, she browbeat and intimidated them, threatening both criminal charges and lawsuits seeking damages, until they let her register. The day before the election, the local newspaper huffed, "Citizenship no more carries the right to vote than it carries the power to fly to the moon."

On November 5, shortly after the polls opened at the West End News Depot in Rochester, Susan B. Anthony voted. "Well I have been & gone & done it!" she exulted in a letter to Elizabeth Cady Stanton as soon as she got home. Incidentally, she voted a straight Republican ticket—the party of Abraham Lincoln—largely because Republicans were generally more open than the Democratic Party to at least listening to the argument for women's suffrage.

It was a Democratic poll watcher who filed the complaint that led to criminal charges against Anthony for illegal voting.

It took several days for reluctant local authorities to come to her home and arrest her, and once in custody, she refused bail. She figured that a writ of habeas corpus was the fast track to the Supreme Court. Her lawyer, however, posted her bail and tried to console the dismayed Anthony by saying he could not bear to see her behind bars.

After months of exhaustive speaking and writing, she finally came to trial in June 1873, facing up to 3 years in prison and a $500 fine. She wanted to take the stand, but the judge upheld a prosecution objection that she was not competent as a witness on her own behalf. As soon as the testimony was complete, the judge pulled a statement from his pocket that apparently had been written before the trial started. He ruled that the Fourteenth Amendment did not give women the vote and that Anthony had voted illegally. He directed the jury to return a guilty verdict and then fined her $100. Anthony refused to pay the fine. The authorities could have pursued her and taken action to collect the fine or throw her in jail, but instead, they did nothing. With the case in legal limbo, Anthony was never able to appeal.

The Supreme Court did take up women's suffrage the following year, in 1874, when a would-be voter named Virginia Minor sued a local election official in Missouri for refusing to let her register. Just as Anthony had envisioned, Minor based her appeal on the Fourteenth Amendment, on the grounds that denying women the vote abridges the privileges of citizenship. In its decision in the case, *Minor* v. *Happersett*, the Supreme Court conceded, "There is no doubt that women are citizens," and that the Fourteenth Amendment aims to protect the privileges of all citizens.

However, in a long and sometimes meandering discussion of what it means to be a citizen, the high court finally concluded that voting is not one of the rights guaranteed to citizens by the Constitution: "The Constitution does not define the privileges and immunities of citizens." Instead, the court said, it is up to the individual states to determine who can and cannot vote. If the framers had wanted women to have the right to vote, the court reasoned, they would have included that right in the original Constitution. If the right to vote was universal, the court asked, why was the Fifteenth Amendment needed to prevent the states from denying the right to vote because of race? The court held that women's suffrage was a political issue and threw it back into the laps of the women themselves. "If the law is wrong, it ought to be changed," the opinion said. "But the power for that is not with us."

Winning the Vote

Susan B. Anthony, her close ally Elizabeth Cady Stanton, and other suffragist leaders developed a two-pronged attack, state and federal, seeking both an amendment to the U.S. Constitution and state-by-state changes in voting laws.

In 1875, Anthony drafted the wording of the amendment that was eventually approved. It was first introduced in Congress in 1878 and was introduced every session after that until it was ratified. The amendment never even made it out of committee, however, until 1887, when it was slapped down in the Senate by a vote of 34–16. The amendment did not make it back to the floor of either house for 27 years.

> **WE THE PEOPLE**
>
> Although Susan B. Anthony gets more space in history books, and on dollar coins,
> her dear friend and colleague Elizabeth Cady Stanton was equally influential in the
> suffragist movement. Stanton often preferred to stay home and take care of her seven
> children, but she was the writer who composed many of Anthony's most stirring
> public utterances.

Publicly, members of Congress were concerned not only about whether women were suited to shoulder the responsibility of voting, but also about the changes women voters might bring about. For instance, women were known to be concerned—maybe overly concerned—about health, safety, education, and working conditions, especially for child labor. Newspapers fulminated about the impact an 8-hour workday for women would have on industries such as canning and millinery and bemoaned that restrictions on night work for women would backfire by putting "elevator girls" and theater ticket-takers out of work.

Privately, the men serving in Congress did not want to change the formula that got them into office and kept them there. They knew how to campaign for men's votes. If they gave women the vote, they'd risk reelection even if they changed the way they campaigned. The reaction in Congress was similar when the Seventeenth Amendment was proposed to provide for the direct election of senators. It took a national groundswell of public opinion to get the amendment through Congress, and in the late 1800s, there was no national groundswell for women's suffrage.

There were local and regional groundswells, though, and the suffragists made better progress trying to change state laws. Wyoming granted women suffrage as a territory, and in 1890, when it became a state, it was the first state where women could vote equally with men. Other Western states followed, including Colorado in 1893, Utah in 1895, and Idaho in 1896.

In 1890, two of the leading suffragist organizations merged to form the National American Woman Suffrage Association, but the movement seemed to sag around the turn of the century as its longtime leaders faded from the scene. Lucretia Mott died in 1880, Lucy Stone in 1893, Elizabeth Cady Stanton in 1902, and Susan B. Anthony in 1906. The cause was soon reinvigorated, however, in part by a surprise victory in Washington State in 1910 and another narrow victory in California the following year. By 1912, women could vote in nine Western states, and momentum was building across the country.

In 1913, one of the new generation of suffragist leaders, Alice Paul, led a march of several thousand women through Washington on President Woodrow Wilson's inauguration day. More than 250,000 spectators lined the parade route, not all of them friendly. Marchers were harassed and skirmished with taunting onlookers, and dozens of women were hospitalized with injuries.

More marches and demonstrations followed. A group of women drove—they actually drove the cars themselves, which was unusual at that time—cross-country gathering signatures and presented a petition for women's suffrage to the White House signed by half a million people. In 1916, women voted for president in 11 states, and suffragist leaders claimed women were responsible for reelecting President Wilson. The president did not disagree even though he opposed women's suffrage.

In 1917, for Wilson's second inaugural, Alice Paul led another march, this time around the White House. That same year, New York gave women the right to vote and Montana elected Jeannette Rankin the first female congresswoman. The suffragist marches, demonstrations, speeches, and lobbying intensified, and a group of women took up positions outside the White House, vowing to stand as silent sentinels until they had the right to vote. In the states, women stepped up their campaigns, working to elect prosuffragist men running against congressmen and state lawmakers who opposed women's right to vote.

WE THE PEOPLE

After losing a Senate race in 1919, largely because she had voted against the United States entering World War I, Jeannette Rankin had a long career as a social activist before again winning election to Congress in 1940. The following year, after the attack on Pearl Harbor, she was the only member of Congress to vote against declaring war on Japan. She did not run for reelection.

Ratification

Looking ahead to the 1920 elections, at least 15 states were going to allow women to vote in all races, and women would be voting for president in at least 15 other states. President Wilson changed his position and spoke ardently in favor of granting women the right to vote via the proposed Nineteenth Amendment.

The proposed amendment passed the House by the necessary two thirds by a single vote in 1918 but fell two votes short in the Senate later that year and one vote short when the Senate took it up again in early 1919. In May 1919, the amendment was approved in the House by 14 votes more than needed. It came up for a vote in the Senate for a fifth time, and the third time in less than a year, all unsuccessful. A senator from Alabama proposed that the amendment be considered by state constitutional conventions rather than the state legislatures, but that also was defeated. So was a proposal by a Louisiana senator to change the amendment so it would be enforced by the states individually rather than by the federal government.

The Senate approved the amendment by a vote of 56–25, which was 2 more than necessary to send the amendment to the states for ratification. When the vote was announced, the suffragists thronged in the galleries "broke into deafening applause," newspapers reported. "For two minutes the demonstration went on …."

Arizona became the forty-eighth state in 1912, so 36 states needed to ratify the Nineteenth Amendment for it to become part of the Constitution. Nine Southern states were vehemently opposed, so suffragists needed ratification from all but 3 of the other 39 states. Illinois, Wisconsin, and Michigan were the first to ratify, and 32 other states followed in the ensuing months.

By August 1920, only one more state was needed. The vote was coming up in Tennessee, but it appeared that the amendment was going to fall a single vote short of ratification in the state legislature. Then a lawmaker named Harry Burn, only 24 and until then an outspoken opponent of women's suffrage, changed his vote. Tennessee ratified the amendment, and the results were certified in Washington a few days later, on August 26, which is why that date is celebrated as Women's Equality Day by presidential proclamation in the United States every year. After he cast his vote, according to the story, Burn revealed a note he had been carrying in his pocket. "Don't forget to be a good boy," the note read. "Vote for suffrage." It was from his mother.

A case came before the Supreme Court in 1922, *Leser* v. *Garnett*, that challenged the Nineteenth Amendment, but the justices dismissed it quickly, briefly, and unanimously.

WE THE PEOPLE

Charlotte Woodward, only 19 when she attended the convention in Seneca Falls in 1848, was the sole surviving signer of the Declaration of Sentiments when the Nineteenth Amendment was ratified. Many historical references today assume she voted at age 91 in the 1920 election, but government archives say she stayed home ill that day and died before she ever actually cast a ballot.

The Least You Need to Know

- The Nineteenth Amendment gave women the right to vote in 1920.
- The suffragist movement had many leaders, but the two foremost were Susan B. Anthony and Elizabeth Cady Stanton.
- The unofficial beginning of the women's movement in America was the convention in Seneca Falls, New York, in 1848.

CHAPTER 17

The Twentieth, Twenty-Second, Through Twenty-Seventh Amendments

Although not as well known as other amendments that are more commonly discussed by the Supreme Court or the subject of news headlines, the most recent amendments to the Constitution are significant for a number of reasons.

Among other things, these amendments set rules for presidential succession, including the two-term limit; provide for District of Columbia residents to vote for president; allow citizens to vote at age 18; prohibit states from charging voters' fees; and prevent Congress from voting itself immediate pay raises.

In This Chapter

- The Twentieth Amendment: lame ducks
- The Twenty-Second Amendment: presidential term limits
- The Twenty-Third Amendment: voting in D.C.
- The Twenty-Fourth Amendment: no tax on voting
- The Twenty-Fifth Amendment: presidential succession
- The Twenty-Sixth Amendment: voting at 18
- The Twenty-Seventh Amendment: congressional pay

The Twentieth Amendment: Lame Ducks

"The terms of the President and the Vice President shall end at noon on the 20th day of January, and the terms of Senators and Representatives at noon on the 3d day of January, of the years in which such terms would have ended if this article had not been ratified; and the terms of their successors shall then begin.

"The Congress shall assemble at least once in every year, and such meeting shall begin at noon on the 3d day of January, unless they shall by law appoint a different day.

"If, at the time fixed for the beginning of the term of the President, the President elect shall have died, the Vice President elect shall become President. If a President shall not have been chosen before the time fixed for the beginning of his term, or if the President elect shall have failed to qualify, then the Vice President elect shall act as President until a President shall have qualified; and the Congress may by law provide for the case wherein neither a President elect nor a Vice President shall have qualified, declaring who shall then act as President, or the manner in which one who is to act shall be selected, and such person shall act accordingly until a President or Vice President shall have qualified.

"The Congress may by law provide for the case of the death of any of the persons from whom the House of Representatives may choose a President whenever the right of choice shall have devolved upon them, and for the case of the death of any of the persons from whom the Senate may choose a Vice President whenever the right of choice shall have devolved upon them.

"Sections 1 and 2 shall take effect on the 15th day of October following the ratification of this article.

"This article shall be inoperative unless it shall have been ratified as an amendment to the Constitution by the legislatures of three-fourths of the several States within seven years from the date of its submission."

Also called the Lame Duck Amendment or the Norris Amendment after its prime mover, Senator George Norris of Nebraska, the Twentieth Amendment changed the dates for the swearing in of the president, vice president, and members of Congress. The Constitution originally set March 3 as the date for swearing in members of Congress and March 4 for the inauguration of the president and vice president. But that was back in the 1700s, when the prime way of getting from one city to another was in a horse-drawn coach bouncing over rutted and often muddy roads and communication was primarily by letter. Consequently, it was presumed that newly elected officials could need weeks, perhaps months, to get their affairs in order and travel to Washington.

This sometimes left a period of 4 months when the outgoing—lame duck—administration and Congress could take action and not be answerable to voters. Even if the outgoing president and Congress did not take any action at all, the 4-month gap left a leadership void while Washington and the nation waited for their new leaders to take office.

WE THE PEOPLE

> After Abraham Lincoln was elected president in 1860, the 11 Confederate states seceded from the United States on February 4, 1861. But neither Lincoln nor the incoming Congress could do anything about it for a month, until they took office in March 1861.

Before long, of course, the telegraph and then the telephone improved communications, and railroads and then the automobile and better highways improved transportation. The incoming officials did not need months to get to Washington. But cutting down the lame duck period did not become a national issue until the Great Depression began with the stock market crash in 1929. Tired of the Hoover administration, the nation elected Franklin Delano Roosevelt (FDR), with his promises of a New Deal, in November 1932. But FDR had to wait 4 months, until the following April, to launch his eagerly anticipated programs.

In considering the proposed Twentieth Amendment, the Senate Judiciary Committee noted another potential problem with the original March swearing-in dates: if a presidential election was thrown to the House, the election would be decided by the lame ducks rather than the newly elected representatives. "It is quite apparent that such a power ought not to exist," the committee concluded, "and that the people having expressed themselves at the ballot box should through the representatives then selected, be able to select the President for the ensuing term …."

The amendment, which changed the inauguration date for president and vice president to January 20 and the swearing-in date for members of Congress to January 3, was ratified in 1933, after FDR took office. He and his first vice president, John Nance Garner, were reelected in 1936, and 2 months later became the first president and vice president to be inaugurated on January 20.

> **WE THE PEOPLE**
>
> John Nance Garner, known as Cactus Jack, was one of the real characters in twentieth-century American politics. Married to a woman he defeated for a Texas county judgeship, Garner is remembered for saying the vice presidency was "not worth a bucket of warm spit." He actually said "a bucket of warm piss," but that could not be reported in family newspapers.

The Twentieth Amendment also struck down the Constitution's original requirement for Congress to meet the month after the biennial November elections. Nobody saw much benefit in those lame duck sessions; Congress did not have time to take any meaningful action, and any legislation enacted would not only be hurried but also would be approved by a legislative body whose mandate was expiring. Finally, the amendment said that if a president-elect dies before inauguration, the vice president-elect becomes the president-elect and is inaugurated as president on January 20.

The Twenty-Second Amendment: Presidential Term Limits

"No person shall be elected to the office of the President more than twice, and no person who has held the office of President, or acted as President, for more than two years of a term to which some other person was elected President shall be elected to the office of President more than once. But this Article shall not apply to any person holding the office of President when this Article was proposed by Congress, and shall not prevent any person who may be holding the office of President, or acting as President, during the term within which this Article becomes operative from holding the office of President or acting as President during the remainder of such term.

"This article shall be inoperative unless it shall have been ratified as an amendment to the Constitution by the legislatures of three-fourths of the several States within seven years from the date of its submission to the States by the Congress."

The Constitution originally set no term limits despite the framers' concerns about a monarchy style of leadership. George Washington probably would have been easily reelected to a third term, and possibly more, but he did not think it was seemly to serve more than two terms. And it wasn't good for the country, he reasoned. If he served longer than 8 years, Americans might start thinking of him as a king who served for life. And a long-serving president could upset the delicate balance of power among the three branches of government.

> ### WE THE PEOPLE
>
> National politics has always been a rich man's game in America. George Washington, considered one of if not the wealthiest man in the country at the time, refused to take his presidential salary of $25,000 a year—the equivalent of more than half a million in today's dollars.

None of the early presidents who succeeded Washington considered a third term, either, and a maximum of two terms became a tradition. President Ulysses Grant, elected in 1869 and reelected in 1873, went on a 3-year world tour after his successor, Rutherford B. Hayes, took office. Grant, who had been a much better Civil War general than postwar president, returned from his travels renewed, thinking he had learned much that would make him a better president. Hayes kept his word to serve only one term, so Grant threw his hat in the ring in 1880—insisting that he had honored the tradition against serving three consecutive terms but there was no tradition against him serving a third term after a break. Whether because he was seeking a third term or because he had not been a sparkling president the first time around, the Republicans refused to nominate Grant. James Garfield, a dark horse, was nominated and subsequently elected.

Vice President Theodore Roosevelt became president in 1901 after William McKinley was assassinated only a few months into his second term. Roosevelt was elected to his own full term in 1904 and had served 7½ years by the time he left office in 1909. After a series of lusty pursuits such as going on safari in Africa, Roosevelt formed the Progressive Party and ran for president again in 1912. His third-party bid failed, but he drew enough votes away from the Republicans, his former party, that the Democrat Woodrow Wilson was elected.

Franklin Delano Roosevelt had served two terms in 1940, but the two-term tradition went by the wayside because of his popularity for leading the country out of the Great Depression and because of concerns about a new president coming into office while World War II was heating up in Europe. Roosevelt became the first president elected to a third term. Despite concerns about FDR's "imperial" presidency and that he might set a new tradition allowing president to feel entitled to serve for life, Roosevelt was elected to a fourth term in 1944, when it became clear that U.S. involvement had tipped the war in the Allies' favor.

When FDR died and then the war ended in 1945, Congress turned its attention to constitutional term limits for president. Congress approved the Twenty-Second Amendment in 1947, and the states ratified it in 1951. The amendment said no one could be elected president more than twice, even if the terms were not consecutive. In addition, a vice president who moved up to president because of a vacancy could not be elected more than once if the partial term was more than 2 years. The practical effect was that no one could serve more than 10 years as president—up to 2 years of an unexpired term, and then two full terms.

Lyndon Johnson could have become the only president other than FDR to serve more than two full terms. He took office in 1963, with less than 2 years remaining in John F. Kennedy's first term, and was elected to his own full term in 1964. If he had been reelected in 1968 and served his full term, he would have been president for more than 9 years. He decided against running for reelection amid the turmoil over the Vietnam War.

WE THE PEOPLE

When the Twenty-Fifth Amendment was approved in 1951, it specifically excluded the sitting president, Harry Truman, who had succeeded FDR only weeks into Roosevelt's fourth term. Truman actually planned to take advantage of the exception and run for another full term, but he scrapped his reelection bid after a disappointing showing in the New Hampshire primary.

Proposals to repeal the Twenty-Second Amendment are introduced regularly in Congress, usually by representatives or senators who think the sitting president is doing a wonderful job. One rationale is that every second-term president becomes a lame duck, and the possibility of a third term would preserve some of the president's authority and accountability. On the other hand, some observers say that second lame-duck term is when presidents can reach their crowning achievements, doing things they might not do if they had to worry about political popularity and being reelected.

Presidents themselves have had mixed thoughts on the Twenty-Second Amendment. In the 1950s, Dwight Eisenhower opposed it, arguing that Americans should be able to elect whomever they want. Bill Clinton, who was only 54 when he left office in 2001, liked the idea of changing the amendment so a former president could serve consecutive terms; leave office; and then return for a third, nonconsecutive term. Incidentally, two other former presidents, Jimmy Carter and George H. W. Bush, could have been elected again because they each lost their reelection bids and served only one term.

The Twenty-Second Amendment does not mention the vice president, but constitutional scholars presume that because the qualifications are the same for both president and vice president, a former president cannot run for vice president and then become president again if a vacancy occurs. Under that reasoning, comedian Al Franken's tongue-in-cheek idea would not work:

Franken suggested that he would run as president with Bill Clinton as his running mate, and as soon as they were sworn in, Franken would resign so Clinton could once again be president.

The Twenty-Third Amendment: D.C. Voting

"The District constituting the seat of Government of the United States shall appoint in such manner as Congress may direct:

"A number of electors of President and Vice President equal to the whole number of Senators and Representatives in Congress to which the District would be entitled if it were a State, but in no event more than the least populous State; they shall be in addition to those appointed by the States, but they shall be considered, for the purposes of the election of President and Vice President, to be electors appointed by a State; and they shall meet in the District and perform such duties as provided by the twelfth article of amendment.

"The Congress shall have power to enforce this article by appropriate legislation."

The Twenty-Third Amendment gives the District of Columbia electors in the Electoral College, which allows D.C. residents to vote for president and vice president.

George Washington, who started his career as a land surveyor, apparently never envisioned the District of Columbia as a major city when he chose the site to become the seat of the new government. And neither did any of the other founding fathers. They saw it as a place where government workers would serve, rather than where hundreds of thousands would live and work.

The original Constitution said that only the residents of states could vote for president, and the District of Columbia was not a state. This amendment recognized that people really do live and work in the District—and that they were American citizens who were not allowed to vote for president, even though they had all the obligations of citizenship, such as paying taxes and serving in the military. The amendment was approved by Congress in 1960 and ratified by the states in 1961, when the District had a population larger than 13 other states. Today the District's population is larger than only two states, barely: Wyoming and Vermont.

The amendment put a ceiling on the number of electors the District could have—no more than the state with the smallest population. Because Wyoming and Vermont each has three electors, that's what D.C. has, too.

George Washington chose the specific site of the District of Columbia, but the decision to move the nation's capital from New York was the result of an infamous closed-door dinner meeting attended by Alexander Hamilton, Thomas Jefferson, and James Madison. The meeting has become much better known because of the "The Room Where It Happens" scene in the hit musical *Hamilton* by Lin-Manuel Miranda. The Compromise of 1790, as it came to be called, let Hamilton, then Secretary of the Treasury, come away with the capability to pay war debts and promote big-city commercial expansion. Jefferson and Madison, both Virginians, came away with much shorter commutes to work.

A proposed constitutional amendment sent to the states in 1978 would have given the District representation in Congress just like a state—a representative and two senators—but that proposed amendment expired, unratified, after 7 years in 1985.

The Twenty-Fourth Amendment: No Tax on Voting

"The right of citizens of the United States to vote in any primary or other election for President or Vice President, for electors for President or Vice President, or for Senator or Representative in Congress, shall not be denied or abridged by the United States or any State by reason of failure to pay poll tax or other tax.

"The Congress shall have power to enforce this article by appropriate legislation."

This amendment outlaws the poll tax in federal elections. The poll tax, a fee citizens had to pay to vote or to register to vote, dates to colonial times. The idea was that people who contribute to society, people who were making their way economically and socially, were the ones who should be able to have a say in how the government operates through the vote. Later, it became a way of keeping poor people, especially blacks, from voting.

After Reconstruction, following the Civil War, 11 states in the South enacted poll taxes, largely as a way of keeping black people from voting. By the time the Twenty-Fourth Amendment was approved by Congress in mid-1962, only five states still had poll taxes: Alabama, Arkansas, Mississippi, Texas, and Virginia. The states ratified the amendment outlawing poll taxes in federal elections in early 1964, and the following year, Congress outlawed them again as part of the Voting Rights Act of 1965.

That same year the Supreme Court, in a decision in a Virginia case, *Harman* v. *Forssenius*, threw out the state's attempt to get around the poll tax prohibition. Virginia had a law requiring voters to either pay a poll tax or file a "certificate of residence" 6 months in advance of an election. The high court was unanimous in overturning the law.

The following year, in 1966, in *Harper* v. *Virginia State Board of Elections*, the Supreme Court relied on the Equal Protection Clause of the Fourteenth Amendment to extend the ban on poll taxes from federal elections only to state elections, too.

The Twenty-Fifth Amendment: Presidential Succession

"In case of the removal of the President from office or of his death or resignation, the Vice President shall become President.

"Whenever there is a vacancy in the office of the Vice President, the President shall nominate a Vice President who shall take office upon confirmation by a majority vote of both Houses of Congress.

"Whenever the President transmits to the President pro tempore of the Senate and the Speaker of the House of Representatives his written declaration that he is unable to discharge the powers and duties of his office, and until he transmits to them a written declaration to the contrary, such powers and duties shall be discharged by the Vice President as Acting President.

"Whenever the Vice President and a majority of either the principal officers of the executive departments or of such other body as Congress may by law provide, transmit to the President pro tempore of the Senate and the Speaker of the House of Representatives their written declaration that the President is unable to discharge the powers and duties of his office, the Vice President shall immediately assume the powers and duties of the office as Acting President.

"Thereafter, when the President transmits to the President pro tempore of the Senate and the Speaker of the House of Representatives his written declaration that no inability exists, he shall resume the powers and duties of his office unless the Vice President and a majority of either the principal officers of the executive department or of such other body as Congress may by law provide, transmit within four days to the President pro tempore of the Senate and the Speaker of the House of Representatives their written declaration that the President is unable to discharge the powers and duties of his office. Thereupon Congress shall decide the issue, assembling within forty-eight hours for that purpose if not in session. If the Congress, within twenty-one days after receipt of the latter written declaration, or, if Congress is not in session, within twenty-one days after Congress is required to assemble, determines by two-thirds vote of both Houses that the President is unable to discharge the powers and duties of his office, the Vice President shall continue to discharge the same as Acting President; otherwise, the President shall resume the powers and duties of his office."

In the original language of the Constitution, Article II says that if the president is unable to carry out his duties, the office "shall devolve upon the Vice President." But it did not clarify whether the vice president actually becomes president or acting president or remains vice president but does the president's job. The Twenty-Fifth Amendment, approved by Congress in 1965 and ratified by the states in 1967, clarifies that the vice president becomes the full-fledged president. It also provides for appointing a replacement if the vice presidency becomes vacant and sets out procedures in the event that a president is still alive but is unable to carry out the responsibilities of the office.

A precedent was set the first time a president died in office, when President William Henry Harrison was succeeded by his vice president, who became President John Tyler. Questions remained about procedures in the event of presidential vacancy, disability, or inability to serve, but Congress did not address them until after the assassination of President John F. Kennedy in 1963. But that question was raised: what if Kennedy had survived, incapacitated?

WE THE PEOPLE

President Kennedy's vice president, Lyndon Johnson, was sworn in aboard *Air Force One* at Love Field in Dallas, the eighth time a vice president had succeeded a president who died in office. Jacquelyn Kennedy, the widowed First Lady, stood at Johnson's side on the plane as he took the oath of office.

James Garfield, shot by an assassin, had been in a coma for 80 days before he died in 1881, and Woodrow Wilson was an invalid for the last 18 months of his presidency before leaving office in 1921. In either case, the country would have been better served if the vice president had been able to take over, if only temporarily, until it became clear whether the president could recover and resume office. Who would decide if and when a president had recovered sufficiently to resume the office?

While considering presidential succession, Congress also decided to address vacancies in the vice presidency. Besides the eight times a vice president had stepped up to the presidency and left the office vacant, there were seven other occasions when a vice president had died in office and not been replaced. The Twenty-Fifth Amendment gave the president the authority to appoint a vice president, with the confirmation of Congress, if and when the office became vacant.

It did not take long for the Twenty-Fifth Amendment to come into play. Vice President Spiro Agnew resigned amid a scandal in October 1973 and President Richard Nixon, following the procedure laid out in the second section of the amendment, nominated longtime Congressman Gerald Ford, who was promptly confirmed by the House and Senate. When Nixon resigned in disgrace because of the Watergate scandal in August 1974, Ford succeeded him as president. Ford then named former New York Governor Nelson Rockefeller as his vice president.

WE THE PEOPLE

Longtime Michigan Republican Congressman Gerald Ford was the first person to serve as vice president, and then the first person to serve as president, without running for either office. When he did run, in 1976, he was defeated by Democrat Jimmy Carter.

If a president cannot fulfill the duties of the office, the president can send a letter to Congress asking to be relieved. The vice president then becomes acting president until the president sends another letter notifying Congress that he is reassuming the duties. If there is no objection from the vice president, the president is back on the job. However, if there is an objection within 4 days from the vice president and a majority of the Cabinet—the heads of the administration's executive agencies, all appointed by the president—it is up to Congress to decide, by a two-thirds vote of both houses, whether the president is fit enough to be returned to office.

The Twenty-Fifth Amendment lays out a comparable process for removing a president who is unable or unwilling to ask Congress to be relieved of the office. If a president is in a coma, for example, or a president goes crazy—which some wags would say has already happened more than once in U.S. history—the vice president and a majority of the Cabinet can invoke the Twenty-Fifth Amendment and notify Congress that the president is "unable to discharge the powers and duties of his office." Congress does not need to do anything right away. Instead, the vice president "shall immediately assume the powers and duties of the office as Acting President." The vice president continues as acting president unless the president objects. Again, Congress then decides by a two-thirds vote whether the vice president should continue to serve as acting president.

When President Ronald Reagan was shot in 1981, he probably should have invoked the Twenty-Fifth Amendment and allowed Vice President George H. W. Bush to serve as acting president, at least while he was in surgery and perhaps in the early stages of his recovery. Bush argued against it, saying he did not want to be seen as usurping the president's authority. Constitutional scholars, however, say that was exactly the sort of circumstances for which the Twenty-Fifth Amendment had been designed.

The amendment has been invoked at least twice in recent history, and there may be other instances that were never made public. When Reagan had a colonoscopy in 1985, he temporarily transferred power to Bush as acting president. Similarly, in 2002, Vice President Dick Cheney was briefly acting president when President George W. Bush underwent a colonoscopy.

WE THE PEOPLE

The government's top officials—the president, vice president, Cabinet members, and Congressional leaders—all the top people in the line of succession to the presidency—typically all attend the State of the Union Address in January. But one Cabinet member does not attend. Instead, this "designated survivor" or "designated successor" typically spends the evening far away with a large Secret Service contingent and "the football," the black case with the nation's nuclear weapon codes. One Cabinet member said he spent the evening in New York, attending the theater and enjoying dinner with family. As soon as the State of the Union was over and the other government leaders dispersed, the Secret Service disappeared and took the football with them back to Washington and the president.

The Constitution does not list the order of succession after the vice president, but the Twenty-Fifth Amendment supplements the Presidential Succession Act of 1947, listing Cabinet offices in the order in which they were created, which sets out the following order of succession:

- Vice President
- Speaker of the House
- President Pro Tempore of the Senate
- Secretary of State
- Secretary of the Treasury
- Secretary of Defense
- Attorney General
- Secretary of the Interior
- Secretary of Agriculture
- Secretary of Commerce
- Secretary of Labor

- Secretary of Health and Human Services

- Secretary of Housing and Urban Development

- Secretary of Transportation

- Secretary of Energy

- Secretary of Education

- Secretary of Veterans Affairs

- Secretary of Homeland Security

The Twenty-Sixth Amendment: Voting at Age 18

"The right of citizens of the United States, who are eighteen years of age or older, to vote shall not be denied or abridged by the United States or by any State on account of age.

"The Congress shall have power to enforce this article by appropriate legislation."

Historically, 21 was the age of majority, the age of official adulthood, and the age for voting. But in the 1960s, during the Vietnam War, the age for young men to register for the military draft—and to be drafted, and to go serve, often in Vietnam—was 18. It was not fair, people said, for young men who were giving their lives for their country not to be able to vote for the leaders of that country.

President Lyndon Johnson called for lowering the voting age to 18 in 1968, and Congress did so in 1970, as an extension of the Voting Rights Act of 1965. Oregon appealed, and the Supreme Court upheld the appeal, ruling that Congress had the authority to set the age for federal elections only and not state or local elections.

This presented a dilemma—another issue of basic fairness. It meant that although everyone 18 and older could vote for president, in some states, voters still had to be 21 before they could cast ballots for governor, mayor, or dogcatcher.

Besides the fairness issue, there were logistical problems: with two different sets of voting rolls, state and federal, election officials would have to maintain two sets of records. That would be cumbersome and expensive, and it raised the possibility that we might have two sets of elections, state and federal.

The Twenty-Sixth Amendment was approved by Congress in 1971 and ratified later that year—the fastest approval ever for a constitutional amendment. Most but not all states fell in line by lowering not only the voting age to 18 but also the minimum age for signing contracts and other privileges of legal adulthood.

Along with lowering the voting age, many states also lowered their minimum drinking age to 18. But an increase in drunk driving and traffic deaths among teenagers led to a backlash campaign by Mothers Against Drunk Driving and other groups. In 1984, Congress passed the National Minimum Drinking Age Act of 1984, which threatened states with losing a chunk of their federal highway funding unless they raised the drinking age back to 21.

The Twenty-Seventh Amendment: Congressional Pay

"No law, varying the compensation for the services of the Senators and Representatives, shall take effect, until an election of representatives shall have intervened."

This amendment prevents members of Congress from voting themselves pay raises and then starting to collect them immediately. Instead, they have to wait until the next session of Congress, after the next even-year election. The amendment was originally presented to the states for ratification back in the 1700s with the amendments that became the Bill of Rights, but it was ratified by only 6 of the 11 states needed.

That was long before the 7-year time limit for ratification became standard, so in theory, the amendment remained pending, even though most constitutional scholars considered it dead in the water, a historical footnote.

In 1982, a University of Texas sophomore named Gregory Watson was working on a paper for a government course on the Equal Rights Amendment (ERA) when he stumbled onto the still-pending amendment. Intrigued, Watson dropped the ERA and wrote his paper about the amendment, arguing that it was still on the table and that if enough states ratified it, it would become part of the Constitution.

He got a C on the paper. The professor said she didn't think he had made the case that the amendment was still alive. Undeterred, Watson undertook a one-man campaign, writing to state legislatures and persuading them to take up the amendment and ratify it. Ten years later, in 1992, the amendment was ratified.

The Twenty-Seventh Amendment has largely been ignored by Congress, and it has not kept members of Congress from taking regular cost-of-living increases. But the fact remains: one man, an everyday citizen, amended the U.S. Constitution. Gregory Watson went on to become a researcher in the Texas legislature. When the professor who gave him the C learned that the paper had led to actually amending the Constitution, she apologized to Watson. But it was too late to change his grade.

The Least You Need to Know

- Inauguration Day is January 20.
- A president who has been elected twice cannot run for a third term.
- It is unconstitutional to charge poll taxes or other fees to vote.
- If the president is unable to carry out the duties of the office, the vice president can become acting president.
- Gregory Watson was just exercising his citizenship when he worked to amend the U.S. Constitution; you should, too.

Modifying the Government

The Constitution is sometimes characterized as a living document that can be refashioned for the needs of an evolving society. Part 4 looks at attempted amendments that failed—notably the Equal Rights Amendment—along with other modern proposals for amending the Constitution.

Finally, we scan the horizon of current political, economic, and social questions that present contemporary Constitutional issues and the possible implications in the years ahead. We look at not only discussions about amending the Constitution, including calls for the first Constitutional Convention since 1789, but also at controversies such as the constitutional crisis raised by the death of Justice Antonin Scalia in February 2016, which led members of the Republican majority in the Senate to vow not to consider a replacement appointment until after a new president is sworn in to succeed President Barack Obama in January 2017.

CHAPTER 18

The ERA and
Other Failed Amendments

We know the Constitution has been successfully amended 27 times since 1789, including 10 amendments—the Bill of Rights—that came out of the first Congress. Besides the 27 amendments that have become part of the Constitution, 6 other proposed amendments have gone before the states and not been ratified. Two of those are apparently dead beyond revival, but four others are still pending and, at least in theory, could be approved someday, although that seems impossible because they are outdated, irrelevant, and unnecessary today.

Let's review, briefly, from Article V: two thirds of each chamber of Congress, the House and the Senate, must approve a proposed constitutional amendment for it to be presented to the states for ratification. Three quarters of the states must ratify the proposed amendment for it to become part of the Constitution. Since Alaska and Hawaii joined the Union, that means 38 states must ratify.

So it's rare for the Constitution to be amended. The framers of the Constitution wanted it to be difficult back in 1789, and since then, Americans generally have been reluctant to tinker with the supreme law of the land.

In This Chapter

- Proposed, yet still pending, amendments
- The Equal Rights Amendment
- The D.C. Representation Amendment
- Amendments that failed to pass Congress

But attempts to amend the Constitution are far from rare. Besides those 33 proposed amendments that have gone before the states, more than 10,000 other proposed constitutional amendments have been introduced in Congress over the years.

Early Amendments Still Pending

Twelve possible amendments came before the first Congress after the Constitution was approved in 1789. Amendments Three through Twelve were approved by two thirds of both the House and Senate and then ratified by three quarters of the states—10 of the 13 states at the time—and incorporated into the Constitution as the Bill of Rights.

What about those first two proposed amendments? The second one said that if senators and representatives vote themselves pay raises, they cannot start collecting them until the next session of Congress. That's the proposed amendment that languished for more than 200 years before being revived and becoming the Twenty-Seventh Amendment in 1992.

The Congressional Representation Amendment

The initial proposed amendment to come before that first Congress—it would have become the First Amendment had it been approved, rather than the free speech/press/religion First Amendment so familiar to us today—is still languishing and is unlikely to ever be revived. No doubt that proposed amendment seemed really important at the time: it was designed to ensure that the House of Representatives reflected the one-man, one-vote principle. It specified that as the country grew, there eventually would never be fewer than 200 members of the House.

Here's the text of that proposed amendment:

"After the first enumeration required by the first article of the Constitution, there shall be one Representative for every thirty thousand, until the number shall amount to one hundred, after which the proportion shall be so regulated by Congress, that there shall be not less than one hundred Representatives, nor less than one Representative for every forty thousand persons, until the number of Representatives shall amount to two hundred; after which the proportion shall be so regulated by Congress, that there shall not be less than two hundred Representatives, nor more than one Representative for every fifty thousand persons."

Of course, the House now has 435 members, so there would be little point in trying to revive the proposed amendment aimed at guaranteeing there would be at least 200 representatives. However, there was no time limit for ratification for those initial amendments—that's why the Congressional pay raise amendment could be brought back and approved two centuries later—so in theory, the amendment requiring the House to have at least 200 representatives could be revived someday, too. But don't hold your breath.

The Noble Title Amendment

Another amendment that is technically still before the states for ratification came out of Congress in 1810 and was aimed at keeping U.S. citizens from taking positions or titles in foreign governments and from taking gifts from foreign leaders. Under this proposed amendment, an American who accepted a British knighthood, for example, could be stripped of his U.S. citizenship:

> "If any Citizen of the United States shall accept, claim, receive or retain any Title of Nobility or Honour, or shall, without the Consent of Congress, accept and retain any present, Pension, Office or Emolument of any kind whatever, from any Emperor, King, Prince or foreign Power, such Person shall cease to be a Citizen of the United States, and shall be incapable of holding any Office of Trust or Profit under them, or either of them."

Twelve states had approved this amendment by 1812, not enough for ratification. At least in theory, however, the proposed amendment is still on the table and could be revived in much the same way that the Twenty-Seventh Amendment languished for a couple hundred years before being approved.

There's an arcane, perhaps spurious—and some might say wacky—argument connected to that 1810 amendment. Some claim the amendment actually was ratified and has been in effect for all those years. Furthermore, the argument goes, since American lawyers sometimes use the *Esquire* honorific, as in "John Lawyer, Esq.," that is a title that could be regarded as illegal under the amendment. Therefore, according to the theory, all lawyers should be stripped of their citizenship. And because so many lawyers served in Congress over the years—illegally, under this theory—all or most of the actions taken by Congress since 1812 have been illegal.

Don't count on using this argument to say the income tax law is unconstitutional, though.

The Slavery Amendment

In 1861, as war clouds were gathering, Congress approved a joint resolution that would have allowed individual states to retain slavery and taken away the federal government's power to outlaw it. The amendment is widely viewed as a last-ditch effort by the Union to keep the South from seceding. The thinking, even among those who hated slavery, was that it was better to keep the Union together and outlaw slavery later, when it was politically more expedient. Besides, it did not appear that the amendment would ever get the necessary approval of three quarters of the states. President Lincoln signed the resolution—it is the only proposed amendment to carry a presidential signature—in hopes that voting on the amendment would head off war.

The proposed Corwin amendment, named after the congressman who introduced it, read:

> "No amendment shall be made to the Constitution which will authorize or give to Congress the power to abolish or interfere, within any State, with the domestic institutions thereof, including that of persons held to labor or service by the laws of said State."

Only two states approved the amendment before the Civil War broke out later in 1861. Eventually slavery was abolished by the Thirteenth Amendment, and the proposed Corwin amendment became a historical footnote.

The Child Labor Amendment

Besides the three proposed amendments from the nineteenth century that were never ratified—congressional representation, noble titles, and allowing slavery—there is one other proposed amendment, this one from the twentieth century, which is still on the table, at least in theory. In 1926, Congress sent the states a proposed amendment to pave the way for federal child labor laws and counter the exploitation of children in the workforce:

> "Section 1. The Congress shall have power to limit, regulate, and prohibit the labor of persons under eighteen years of age.

> "Section 2. The power of the several States is unimpaired by this article except that the operation of State laws shall be suspended to the extent necessary to give effect to legislation enacted by the Congress."

So far, 28 states have ratified that proposed amendment, but none since 1937. Ten more states would have to ratify it to write the proposed child labor amendment into the Constitution, but that seems unlikely considering that a great many state and federal rules and regulations are in place, along with court decisions that seem to be adequately protecting child labor.

The first proposed amendment to carry a time limit for ratification was the Eighteenth, otherwise known as Prohibition. Congress said the states had 7 years to ratify it or else the proposed amendment would expire and the country would be able to drink to that. The amendment was ratified within the time limit, of course, and nobody drank to that—at least not legally. The 7-year time limit has become standard for ratification, but Congress could change that at any time—and did, for one recent proposed amendment.

The Equal Rights Amendment

Most people think the Equal Rights Amendment (ERA) was initiated by the feminist movement of the 1960s. In fact, a version of the ERA was first offered in Congress in 1923, when the American women's movement was flush with its biggest victory: ratification of the Nineteenth Amendment, which gave women the vote in 1920.

That original ERA might have had a better chance of passage if it wasn't opposed by so many of the same women who had worked so hard to get themselves the vote. The big fear among the women's movement was that the proposed amendment's "equality" provisions would overrule existing laws that provided extra protection—protection men didn't get—for women working in factories and shops.

Five decades later, when the feminist movement captured the imagination and the commitment of so many women—especially baby boomers—Congress approved the ERA in this form:

"Section 1. Equality of rights under the law shall not be denied or abridged by the United States or by any State on account of sex.

"Section 2. The Congress shall have the power to enforce, by appropriate legislation, the provisions of this article.

"Section 3. This amendment shall take effect two years after the date of ratification."

When the proposed ERA went to the states in 1972, it seemed inevitable to many observers that it would be ratified. To many, it seemed like the next logical step in the civil rights movement. Indeed, 22 of the required 38 states ratified the ERA in the first year.

But times were changing, and opposition to the ERA grew as the country became more conservative and an economic downturn led to more competition between men and women for jobs. The practical realities of feminism had many people thinking about the changing roles of men and women, and many people decided they didn't like the changes. A Midwestern housewife and political activist named Phyllis Schlafly led a grassroots backlash. Only 13 more states, for a total of 35, had passed the ERA by 1977, and the 7-year time limit meant it would expire in 1979.

WE THE PEOPLE

Phyllis Schlafly struck a chord with her newsletter, articles, speeches, and grassroots movement that appealed to many other women—and many men—who made it clear they did not want the ERA. "I like being a woman, and the protections the law now allows," Schlafly said. She has continued to work for conservative causes, including a constitutional amendment banning same-sex marriage, into the twenty-first century.

In a controversial and much-debated move—was it constitutional?—Congress added 3 years to the 7-year deadline. But it didn't do the ERA's supporters any good. One of the battleground states was Utah, which had long been at the forefront among states in guaranteeing rights for women—the state had given women the right to vote in 1896. But Mormon church leaders declared that the ERA was a moral issue that would "strike at the family," and many nonreligious leaders in Utah joined the opposition. Amid ardent campaigning by both sides—busloads of women pro and con flooded into the state—Utah considered the ERA twice and defeated it both times.

Schlafly's home state, Illinois, had been considered sure to ratify but instead rejected it eight times. The Republican Party, which had been on record as favoring equal rights for women for decades, removed that plank from its national platform as Ronald Reagan, an outspoken ERA opponent, defeated incumbent Democratic President Jimmy Carter, whose wife, Rosalynn, was one of the leading campaigners for the amendment. A number of states that had ratified the ERA earlier tried to rescind ratification.

The ERA officially died on June 30, 1982, after its 10-year limit had expired. If it had somehow garnered 38 states, no doubt there would have been a huge legal battle over whether it was legal for Congress to extend the original deadline and whether states could rescind ratification.

It is doubtful that a new ERA will be presented, at least in the foreseeable political landscape, for a couple reasons: there's no guarantee it would pass, and many of the feminists who would be the strongest supporters of another ERA now shrug and say it's not needed. Court rulings under the Equal Protection Clause of the Fourteenth Amendment, along with the Civil Rights Act of 1964, have accomplished many of the goals of the ERA. Perhaps even more significantly, changes in society, including advances by women in so many aspects of the economic marketplace, have made a constitutional amendment for women seem less urgent.

The D.C. Representation Amendment

The most recent proposed amendment to the Constitution would have treated the District of Columbia as if it were a state in terms of representation in Congress: two senators and a proportionate number of representatives, depending on its population:

"Section 1. For purposes of representation in the Congress, election of the President and Vice President, and article V of this Constitution, the District constituting the seat of government of the United States shall be treated as though it were a State.

"Section 2. The exercise of the rights and powers conferred under this article shall be by the people of the District constituting the seat of government, and as shall be provided by the Congress.

"Section 3. The twenty-third article of amendment to the Constitution of the United States is hereby repealed.

"Section 4. This article shall be inoperative, unless it shall have been ratified as an amendment to the Constitution by the legislatures of three-fourths of the several States within seven years from the date of its submission."

There was never a great deal of support for the proposed amendment anywhere except in Washington, D.C., and it died in 1985, when its 7-year time limit ran out.

Amendments That Never Got Out of Congress

It is unusual for Congress to send a proposed amendment to the states, and even more unusual for an amendment to be ratified. But it is not at all unusual for members of Congress to run their ideas for amendments up the flagpole and see if anyone salutes.

Several dozen amendments are proposed to Congress in a typical year—more than 800 in the 1990s alone, for example. Some are good old standbys that seem to pop up reliably every session of Congress. Others come and go, depending on the times. When Reagan was elected president in 1980 at age 69—he served until age 77, the oldest president ever—there was some talk about amending the Constitution to set a maximum age limit, but it never got very far.

Here are some proposed amendments that have failed to get out of Congress in the twenty-first century:

- Guaranteeing women the right to abortion

- Restricting abortion

- Allowing the president line-item veto power

- Allowing the president to serve more than two terms

- Restricting the president to one 6-year term

- Allowing foreign-born citizens (Arnold Schwarzenegger, for example) to become president

- Abolishing the Electoral College in favor of direct voting for president and vice president

- Permitting school prayer

- Restricting eminent domain

- Requiring a balanced budget

The Balanced Budget Amendment

One old reliable, to require the government to balance the federal budget, has had a checkered history and shows just how political the whole process of amending the Constitution can be.

For decades, the Democrats were viewed as the free-spending party, and whenever they were in control of Congress, the Republicans agitated for a balanced budget.

When the George W. Bush administration expanded the federal budget deficit, with the support of Republicans in Congress, some congressional Democrats began making noise about an amendment requiring a balanced budget. And when the budget deficit expanded further under President Barack Obama, some congressional Republicans began making noise about an amendment requiring a balanced budget. (More on this in Chapter 19.)

The Flag Desecration Amendment

Another suggested amendment that always seems to be around but has yet to get the necessary two-thirds approval of Congress is the so-called flag-burning amendment. In its latest incarnation, in 2006, the text was short and simple:

> "The Congress shall have the power to prohibit the physical desecration of the flag of the United States."

The House has approved a flag-burning amendment on a number of occasions, and in June 2006, it fell a mere 1 vote short in the Senate, getting 66 votes in favor and 34 against.

Supporters say the amendment is necessary in the face of Supreme Court decisions that in 1989 overturned a Texas flag-burning law and in 1990 overturned a federal law approved by Congress. In both instances, the high court said the laws violated the First Amendment's guarantees of free speech.

The flag-burning issue is a classic illustration of the attitude many Americans have toward the Constitution. Polls show people are against desecration of the flag and are in favor of laws against it, but they're not in favor of a constitutional amendment.

WE THE PEOPLE

Hawaiian senator Daniel Inouye, who lost an arm in World War II, called desecrating the flag obscene. "But I believe Americans gave their lives in the many wars to make certain that all Americans have a right to express themselves—even those who harbor hateful thoughts," he said in opposition to a flag-burning amendment.

The Least You Need to Know

- Even when Americans feel strongly about an issue, they are reluctant to amend the Constitution.
- Thousands of amendments have been proposed to Congress.
- The states have ratified 27 amendments.
- Six amendments have been approved by Congress but not ratified by the states.

CHAPTER 19

Future Constitutional Issues

Cases related to the controversial issues of the day—many of them growing out of cases that have already been decided, or partially decided—are sure to be heard by the Supreme Court in the near or not-too-distant future. And some of those issues are already, or are likely to be, the subject of proposed amendments to the Constitution.

In This Chapter

- Anticipated Supreme Court cases
- Possible proposed amendments
- Concern over a "political" Supreme Court

Expected Supreme Court Cases

If an issue is in the headlines, if it leads the newscast, or if it's trending, there's a very good chance it is going to end up in the courts. If it poses constitutional issues, it'll go before the Supreme Court.

Issues of race, especially related to voting rights and affirmative action, are far from settled. Criminal investigations, police conduct, the judicial process, and terms of incarceration always have been and will continue to be evolving legal issues. Climate change and the response to it have already raised constitutional issues, and no doubt will raise more, along with other environmental and public health and safety concerns.

It seems the court will sooner or later decide questions relating to immigration, class action lawsuits, union organizing, insider trading, and product liability for drug companies. Other issues that are not going away include presidential power, citizen surveillance, and religion in public life. You can probably name a half-dozen other issues you think will be before the Supreme Court—or that you'd like to see before the Supreme Court.

Here is a quick look at some issues that are likely to be taken up by the Supreme Court in coming terms.

Abortion

Like gun control, abortion is an issue that elicits passionate responses. People on either side have difficulty finding any middle ground, and so do the courts. A constitutional amendment banning abortion seems unlikely in the foreseeable future, considering it never has gotten any appreciable traction in Congress since *Roe* v. *Wade* in 1973. But the kind of sharp swing to the right across the country, and the sort of "moral renewal" envisioned by some Republican presidential candidates, could lead to proposals for an abortion amendment.

That's not to say the abortion laws won't continue to change, however, particularly as states pass laws that limit abortion availability and tighten requirements for both doctors and patients—and as appeals of those new state laws come before the Supreme Court.

On one hand, *Roe* v. *Wade* has been upheld by the Supreme Court on a number of occasions, and precedent counts for a lot in constitutional law. On the other hand, the courts have approved a number of laws and policies that restrict or limit abortion, and future court rulings could make it harder for women to obtain abortions even if *Roe* v. *Wade* is not explicitly overturned.

Crime and Punishment

The death penalty is sure to continue to come under attack as cruel and unusual punishment under the Eighth Amendment. A growing number of individual states and foreign governments outlaw the practice, and the frequency of executions has declined in the states that still have the death penalty.

One factor in the decline of the death penalty has been the growing evidence that it is imposed unevenly and unfairly—more often against blacks than whites. Recent dissents by Justices Breyer and Ginsburg indicate that at least two members of the Supreme Court may be ready to declare the death penalty unconstitutional in all cases. Others among the court's liberal wing could be satisfied with continuing to restrict how and whether the death penalty may be applied. For example, it was a narrow 5–4 ruling in 2015 that upheld the use of a specific drug that had been blamed for botching lethal-injection executions.

WE THE PEOPLE

"I believe it is highly likely that the death penalty violates the Eighth Amendment," Justice Breyer wrote in *Glossip* v. *Gross,* the lethal-injection case. "At the very least, the court should call for a full briefing on the question."

The ultimate goal of death penalty opponents is to find the "perfect" case for that full briefing for the court to consider. They thought they may have found that perfect appellant in Shonda Walter, 36, a black woman on Pennsylvania's death row for a murder conviction when she was in her early 20s. Her case was particularly attractive, supporters said, in part because her lawyers had done such a poor job of defending her. Why should she pay with her life simply because her lawyers made mistakes?

The Pennsylvania Supreme Court acknowledged the poor defense work but refused to allow her a new trial—another reason for the U.S. Supreme Court to grant the appeal. Instead, however, the high court turned down Walter's appeal in January 2016, and death penalty opponents were left hoping for the next "perfect" case to present to the court.

In other sentencing issues, the growing national sentiment toward less incarceration could present more cases to the court that could extend its recent rulings limiting sentences for minors and the intellectually challenged. It also could further restrict no-parole sentences and use of solitary confinement in prisoners.

In terms of law enforcement, a number of legal scholars have said the Supreme Court may be moving toward overturning the exclusionary rule entirely, pointing out that only the guilty benefit directly from it and that people who are wronged still have the option of suing for monetary damages.

The Right to Petition

When asked to name the rights protected by the First Amendment, most people can come up with freedom of speech, freedom of religion, and freedom of the press. Some will come up with the freedom of assembly. Not many remember the fifth freedom—the freedom to petition the government. And no wonder.

In the scope of American history, the right to petition was a real issue only in Revolutionary times, when the colonists felt they had no way of getting the king and Parliament to listen to their complaints. The right "to petition the Government for a redress of grievances" was important when the Constitution was drafted in Philadelphia in 1787 and has been largely ignored since.

But the internet has breathed new life into the right to petition. It's suddenly become much easier to gather signatures and fire off a petition to the White House or Congress. The White House website (whitehouse.gov) has a "We the People" section specifically for receiving petitions, with rules set up for how to submit and instructions for how to search the database of previously submitted petitions and sign one or more petitions yourself. When the site was launched in 2011, it required a petition to have 5,000 signatures to merit a response from a government official, but that was quickly raised to 10,000, and then to 100,000 signatures in 2013. Many of the petitions are serious, dealing with the major issues of the day, but many are less serious, such as the popular petition asking the government to build a *Death Star* like the one in *Star Wars* or the one filed by comedian Bill Maher demanding that President Barack Obama appear on his television show.

Despite the requirements for responses, some petitioners say they have been kept waiting months for a reply, or that the replies they received were little more than an acknowledgment that the petition was received. It is very possible that the Supreme Court may be asked to decide if the Constitution's right to petition includes the right to a meaningful response from the government.

Free Speech and National Security

From Revolutionary days through the world wars—"Loose lips sink ships!"—through the Pentagon Papers to the Patriot Act, the American democracy historically has tried to balance national security against free speech and the public's right to know.

New threats and new technology have added troubling dimensions to the age-old tensions in the twenty-first century. The advances of the internet and the digital world have made it easier for people around the world to communicate and share information—and to glorify, recruit, train, and manage terrorists who can stage sudden and deadly attacks.

The new technology and the new threats have led to calls for reconsidering the First Amendment and the long line of twentieth-century court cases, through *Schenk* and *Brandenburg* (see Chapter 6), which protect speech unless it specifically and directly incites violence—unless it presents "imminent danger," in other words. Merely calling for revolution or overthrow—or jihad—or other acts of violence is protected by that long line of court cases.

But some politicians, legal scholars, and security specialists say the twentieth century standards do not apply to the twenty-first century. They call for certain internet sites and digital means of communication to be closed or restricted. In return, defenders of the First Amendment, many of them prominent lawyers and legal scholars, warn that limiting civil rights means giving in to terrorists who condemn American values such as the right to free speech and the freedom of religion.

"Never before in our history have enemies outside the United States been able to propagate genuinely dangerous ideas on American territory in such an effective way," warned Eric Posner, a University of Chicago law professor who says current U.S. free speech protections need to be revamped.

> **WE THE PEOPLE**
>
> Garry Wills, professor emeritus of history at Northwestern University, noted in 2007, "The wartime discipline imposed in 1941 has never been lifted .... World War II melded into the cold war, with greater secrecy than ever—more classified information, tougher security clearances. And now the cold war has modulated into the war on terrorism."

Presidential Power

A looming issue, with implications for many political, social, and economic implications, is presidential power. The issue—is the president usurping his constitutional authority—came to the fore as a result of a number of actions by President Obama. Frustrated by an inability to get legislation through the Republican-dominated Congress, he sometimes resorted—on immigration, gun control, climate change, and other issues—to executive orders and regulations meant to put his policies in place without going through Congress.

Republican leaders in Congress and a number of states objected, of course, and turned to legal action that challenged him for exceeding his executive powers and violating the constitutional separation of checks and balances. Sometimes the court agreed with the Republicans. One notable example with potentially far-ranging impact, both in terms of the environment and in the way the U.S. government operates, came in a Republican-led challenge to Obama's Clean Power Plan, an executive order growing out of the 2015 international climate agreement in Paris. Part of that agreement called for the United States to curb coal emissions, and Obama's plan set rules for the coal industry to restrict emissions.

The legal challenge, brought by coal and utility companies along with more than two dozen states, included a request that President Obama's plan be delayed until the federal courts could rule on its validity. A U.S. appeals court rejected the request for a delay, but the plaintiffs appealed to the Supreme Court and—to the surprise of many legal observers—the court not only accepted the case but ruled that the coal industry and states did not have to start implementing the plan and meeting its deadlines until the appeal had been decided by the courts.

It was a rare decision, some say unprecedented, in which the Supreme Court stepped in before the case had been decided by the lower courts. Even lawyers representing the coal industry said they were surprised. Environmentalists, sent reeling by the decision, feared that the Court's decision to block President Obama's plan meant that the conservative justices (the vote was the usual 5–4) were indicating that the case would indeed end up before them and they would indeed strike it down.

The Political Court

Election-year complaints that the U.S. Supreme Court has become more "political" raged through 2015 and into the election year 2016 on the heels of the court's controversial 2015 decisions upholding the Affordable Care Act and legalizing gay marriage. Those decisions increased criticism that the court had become in general too political and—despite widespread understanding that five of the nine justices more often voted on the conservative side of issues—specifically too liberal. Nine "unelected lawyers"—or five, if you consider the 5–4 majority in the marriage equality decision—should not be deciding the fate of 320 million Americans, the critics said.

The controversy led to calls on the Republican primary campaign trail for changes to the Constitution to do away with lifetime tenure for Supreme Court justices. One proposal would have set "term limits" so justices had to step down after a certain number of years on the bench. Another called for having justices run for election—an idea that struck many as an odd approach to taking politics out of the judicial branch.

The makeup of the Supreme Court was a hot-button campaign issue in the early stages of the 2016 presidential campaign for both major parties. With four of the sitting justices 77 or older at the start of 2016, many Americans told pollsters they would cast their votes, both in the primary elections and in November, at least in part out of consideration that the next president could appoint several justices. The candidates themselves—again, oddly, for critics of politics on the Supreme Court—were quick to promise they would appoint only justices who would vote a certain way on issues such as abortion and campaign spending, even if that meant overturning precedent.

The politics of the court became even more of a national issue with the death of Justice Antonin Scalia in February 2016. Scalia, who was 79, had been on the Supreme Court nearly 30 years and was known for advancing "originalist" and "textual" views that often led him, as perhaps the most forceful and influential conservative voice in decades, to cite the exact wording of the Constitution and what he regarded as the intent of the framers in 1787. He relied on originalist arguments to reject many modern interpretations of the Constitution when the court was asked to consider changes in society in its decisions.

With 11 months left on his final term in office when Scalia died, President Obama vowed to move quickly to appoint a successor. And besides, it was his duty under the Constitution to nominate a new Supreme Court justice and submit the nomination to the Senate for confirmation. Leaders of the Republican-dominated Senate, however, urged Obama to wait and let the next president pick Scalia's successor after the January 2017 inauguration. The threat was clear—if Obama submitted a nominee—any nominee—there was a real risk the Senate would reject the nominee. Republican leaders said the American people should have a say in who picks the next justice; Democratic leaders said the American people *did* have a say when they elected Obama.

Obama himself said the Supreme Court should not be hampered any longer than necessary by not being at full strength. Besides, the president added, Article II, Section 2, of the Constitution says the president "shall nominate" Supreme Court justices; it is the president's duty, not an option. A number of Supreme Court observers suggested that Scalia, the originalist dedicated to the exact text of the Constitution, would have agreed with Obama—and would have pointed out there is nothing in the Constitution prohibiting lame duck presidents from nominating Supreme Court justices.

WE THE PEOPLE

"To the extent that we know their views, the founders disagreed about most important matters, and generally understood the need to adapt to changing circumstances. Given that we are today a postindustrial society governed by a preindustrial document, thank heavens that the Constitution itself is often naggingly vague; it could not have otherwise survived ... those who swear fealty to originalism play a legal fool's game by pretending that most profound society changes somehow cannot or should not factor into present decisions."

—Professor Robert J. Spitzer, SUNY Cortland, author of *Saving the Constitution from Lawyers*, in a letter to *The New York Times*

Future Changes to the Constitution

Frustration over what the Constitution says—or, more often, over what the Supreme Court decides it says—has led to calls for a small raft of constitutional amendments, via bills introduced in Congress and what would be the first constitutional convention since 1787.

Suggested Amendments

Retired Supreme Court Justice John Paul Stevens, in his book *Six Amendments: How and Why We Should Change the Constitution*, suggested amendments that would abolish the death penalty, impose tighter campaign finance regulations, soften the Second Amendment and impose strict gun control, block gerrymandering, give federal officials more authority over state officials, and give citizens the right to sue state governments. Other proposed amendments that have gathered high-profile support in recent years would establish a right to a good education and require Congress to balance the federal budget.

Campaign finance is another area of elections where we are likely to see more court rulings that call upon constitutional principles. We've already had a number of court rulings, of course, including decisions that uphold limits on how much a donor can give to a candidate's campaign, but it is fair to expect more court challenges and more court rulings that set the rules on who can give what and how it can be given, along with when and how—and how much—money can be spent.

The following sections offer a quick overview of other suggested amendments you're likely to be hearing about.

A Balanced Budget

Late in the eighteenth century, even before he became president, Thomas Jefferson called for an amendment requiring the United States to operate under a balanced budget and prohibiting the country from deficit spending that ran up a national debt. He warned that deficit spending would allow presidents to wage undeclared wars and would economically cripple the country in the future. "Loading up the nation with debt and leaving it for the following generations to pay is morally irresponsible. No nation has a right to contract debt for periods longer than the majority contracting it can expect to live," Jefferson wrote.

An amendment requiring a balanced budget first came before Congress in 1936 and has been revived periodically, particularly in times when the nation is running large budget deficits. Congressional hearings on balancing the budget were held around the country in 1979, and in 1982, a balanced budget amendment got the necessary two-thirds approval in the Senate but did not come before the House.

The one time the amendment came close to being put before the states for ratification was in 1996, when the economy was booming, we had a budget surplus, and the national debt was declining. The House approved a proposed balanced budget amendment, but it fell three votes short of the necessary two-thirds approval in the Senate.

New attention was focused on a requirement to balance the budget during the George W. Bush administration, when tax cuts and the war in Iraq combined to create record budget deficits.

Opponents of a balanced budget amendment say deficit spending causes no real long-term harm to an ever-growing economy and point out that instead of proposing a Constitutional amendment, Congress could simply stop appropriating excess funding for government programs and approve a balanced budget each year.

WE THE PEOPLE

By 2016, the U.S. national debt was approaching $20 trillion—nearly $60,000 for every U.S. citizen. The interest on that debt is paid out of our tax dollars—and the tax dollars our kids will pay in the future.

One Man, One Woman

Perhaps the recent Supreme Court decisions most likely to be the target of a proposed constitutional amendment are rejection of the federal Defense of Marriage Act in the *Windsor* decision in 2013 and then the recognition of same-sex marriage in the *Obergefell* decision in 2015 (see Chapter 13).

Opponents of same-sex marriage have vowed to continue their fight to legally define marriage as between one man and one woman throughout the United States—and the only way that can happen, short of the Supreme Court suddenly reversing itself, is a constitutional amendment. Typical wording, lifted from a failed proposed amendment offered in Congress before *Obergefell*, might read like this:

"Marriage in the United States of America shall consist only of the union of a man and a woman.

"Neither this constitution or the constitution of any state, nor state or federal law, shall be construed to require that marital status or the legal incidents thereof be conferred upon unmarried couples or groups."

Elections

As the 2016 election campaigns played out, the success of Texas Senator Ted Cruz as an early Republican frontrunner increased the chances that the federal courts would be asked to rule on his eligibility to serve as president—and the eligibility of any candidate not born with the borders of the United States. Cruz, born in Canada, insists he is eligible because his mother was American. Some legal scholars back him up, but others are not so sure.

The Constitution requires that "No person except a natural born citizen … shall be eligible to the Office of President." The issue is the definition of *natural born*. Cruz supporters said he was "naturalized" because his mother was a citizen, but skeptics cited centuries of British common law holding that only people born within the boundaries of a country are "natural born" citizens.

Meanwhile, many other election issues were on the horizon, some inspired by new technology and some lingering concerns over the old technology and old voting system. If and when the basics of national elections are changed, it will have to be through an amendment to the Constitution. Some view the Electoral College as antiquated and outdated, arguing that we should be able to vote directly for president and vice president, and that they should be elected not by state-by-state electors but rather by a simple nationwide popular vote to avoid results such as the 2000 election, when Al Gore won the popular vote but George W. Bush became president by winning more states and more electoral votes (and one crucial 5–4 vote in the Supreme Court giving him Florida).

That key Supreme Court decision in the 2000 elections, which rejected Florida recounts before a winner could be declared, came in the case *Bush* v. *Palm Beach County Canvassing Board* in December 2000. In that decision, the court reminded us there is no constitutional right to vote for president; it remains up to the states to determine how their voters choose the members of the Electoral College.

Even if the Supreme Court had not cleared the way for Bush to win the election, a decision that came after a month of America not knowing who won the election or who would be the next president, the court indicated that the Florida legislature could have simply decided to throw all the state's electoral votes behind Bush to give him the election.

Critics point out that the Electoral College was created in a time when the United States seemed too large and communications too slow and difficult for everyday citizens to become adequately informed about a presidential race. On the other hand, many others say our system of electing a president has worked pretty well for more than two centuries, so if it ain't broke, don't fix it.

Guns and Gun Control

Second Amendment absolutists have been buoyed by recent Supreme Court recognition of the right of everyday citizens to bear arms, but they remain unhappy with any attempts, at any level of government, to restrict gun ownership. And gun control advocates, citing the increase in mass shootings, want more restrictions by any means possible. A few of the more flexible thinkers on both sides have called for a new Second Amendment that would, at least in theory, make both sides happier.

The key language of the amendment would say, "The right of the people to keep arms reasonable for hunting, sport, collecting, and personal defense shall not be infringed," and at least one version of the proposed amendment would require approval by two thirds of Congress in two consecutive sessions.

It remains to be seen, if and when a new Second Amendment is given serious consideration, how specifically it will outline what kind of restrictions federal, state, and local laws may impose on gun ownership and use.

Eminent Domain

Since the Supreme Court expanded the reach of eminent domain in 2005 in *Kelo* v. *New London*, making it easier for governments to take property from private owners, legislators and governors of a number of states have called for amendments to their state constitutions to limit the reach of eminent domain. Some members of Congress think a federal constitutional amendment is needed, too, to shore up the part of the Fifth Amendment that says "private properties shall not be taken for public use without just compensation."

The *New London* decision expanded the definition of "public use" beyond the traditional park or highway the public would use directly, and said New London, Connecticut, could condemn and take away property to turn over to a private developer for a shopping mall.

A proposed constitutional amendment would limit the use of eminent domain for private purposes, such as a new shopping mall, that may offer indirect economic benefits.

WE THE PEOPLE

To the surprise of many, eminent domain became a minor campaign issue during the 2016 Republican primary race. Libertarians and conservatives generally speak with one voice in opposing eminent domain, but Donald Trump, in one of several ways he bucked the traditional conservative wisdom, embraced the concept. In one Republican primary debate, Trump, who had used or tried to use eminent domain a number of times to acquire property for his developments, declared, "Eminent domain is an absolute necessity."

A Constitutional Convention

So far, all the amendments that have been approved to the Constitution have been initiated by and preapproved by Congress. But what if Congress is the problem?

Critics who believe Congress has become the big problem in American government—and there are many who believe that—say a convention is the only answer because Congress will never fix itself. Under the Constitution, if 34 states demand a convention, Congress has to stage one. Historically, there's never been much popular sentiment for a convention; the common thinking, under the "opening a can of worms" theory, is that a convention could consider anything and everything in the Constitution. Perhaps the most-cited fear is that a "runaway" convention might do away with the First Amendment. Those who think a convention is a good idea argue it would still take 38 states to ratify any changes or additions to the Constitution; it would take rejection by just one house in 13 state legislatures to kill any proposed amendment.

During the 2015–2016 election campaigns, Texas Governor Greg Abbott called for a new constitutional convention and quickly won the support of several other governors and Republican presidential candidates. Abbott proposed nine specific amendments, including several to limit the power of Congress and federal regulators over the states and others requiring a balanced federal budget, giving the states the power to overrule Supreme Court decisions with a two-thirds majority, and demanding a 7–2 "super majority" on the Supreme Court for any decisions striking down laws made by Congress or a state legislature. Abbott and other supporters were hoping that the results of the 2016 elections, both national and in the states, would yield more support for a constitutional convention.

The Constitution: Our Continuing National Conversation

This has been an admittedly cursory overview of the U.S. Constitution. But if you've gotten this far, you probably know quite a bit more about the Constitution than you did. And more importantly, you probably recognize how it has evolved and continues to evolve.

The Constitution represents a remarkable dialogue between a people and a process—between the American people and the U.S. government. Our experiment in democracy continues to work, sometimes better than others, as long as we continue to buy into the notion that we will participate as citizens to make it work.

Indeed, there is one significant benefit frequently overlooked in the often-heated national debates over constitutional issues: we become better citizens. When we think about fair trials for enemy combatants versus the war on terror, for instance, or the freedoms of speech and religion versus school prayer or national security, your right to marry the person you love versus my right not to help stage a gay wedding, we are participating in the ongoing American experiment in democracy under the rule of law. In learning, considering, and debating the issues, we are practicing exactly the sort of citizenship that the Constitution was designed to accommodate—and that the Constitution needs to survive and thrive.

The Least You Need to Know

- Many of today's most pressing social, political, and economic issues are raising constitutional questions the Supreme Court may ultimately be asked to decide.

- Concern over the makeup of the Supreme Court, and that the court is "too political," has itself become a political issue.

- A number of amendments may be proposed in the next few years—to ban abortion, define gun control, and balance the federal budget, among others—but enacting a constitutional amendment is a long and arduous process.

- A number of states are pushing to hold the first constitutional convention since 1787 in Philadelphia.

Glossary

act   A bill that has passed the legislature and become law.

adjourn   To end a session or meeting.

alien   A resident who is not a citizen.

amendment   A change to existing law.

antifederalists   A group of early American leaders who opposed the Constitution, including Patrick Henry, George Mason, and George Clinton.

appellate   Pertaining to appeals from lower courts.

apportioned   Distributed proportionately, by percentage.

appropriation   Funds authorized by the legislature for spending.

autonomy   Independence, or self-rule.

bail   A bond or payment to get out of jail, repaid upon appearance for trial.

balanced budget   Government planning so expenditures will not exceed revenues.

bicameral   Two legislative chambers or branches.

bill   Proposed legislation that has been formally introduced to a legislature.

bill of attainder   An act that singles out an individual or specific group of people for punishment without trial.

Bill of Rights   The first 10 amendments to the Constitution, aimed at guaranteeing individual rights.

census   An official count of the population.

chamber   A large room; often refers to the legislative body that meets there. In Congress, the House is the lower chamber and the Senate is the upper chamber.

checks and balances   The Constitution's system for the executive, legislative, and judicial branches of government to limit each other's authority.

citizen   A member of a nation who enjoys the rights and protection of that nation.

clear and present danger   A Supreme Court doctrine giving the government the authority to take action for security purposes that might otherwise violate the First Amendment.

commerce   Trade, business, the sale of goods or services, and/or financial dealings.

common law   The body of law, largely unwritten, that evolved in England through prevailing customs, widely accepted principles, and decisions by courts rather than through administrative rule or legislative action.

compensation   Payment.

concur   To agree.

concurrent powers   Authority shared by the federal government and the states.

confederation   A formal governing alliance.

confirmation   Verification or approval, as in Senate votes required to confirm a presidential appointee before taking office.

construed   Explained; clarified.

counsel   An adviser, usually referring to a lawyer.

deficit spending   Government expenditures that exceed revenues.

delegate   As a noun, a representative; as a verb, to assign.

delegated power   Authority specifically enumerated for the federal government in Article I of the Constitution.

democracy   A government based on equality for all, with the people choosing their leaders.

discrimination   Attitudes or actions denying equal treatment to groups of people.

domestic   Pertaining to home or internal national issues.

domestic tranquility   Peace at home, referring to a family or a nation.

due process   The principle that proper legal rules and procedures must be followed before depriving a person of freedom or property.

duty   A tariff or tax.

Electoral College   The process (rather than a physical entity) for the indirect election of the president by electors from each state.

eminent domain   The doctrine that allows governments to take over ownership of private property for the benefit of the public.

enumerated   Listed or specified.

equal representation   The doctrine providing that all the states have equal influence in the federal system.

ex post facto   Determined after the fact, retroactively. An ex post facto law, for example, makes an action illegal after it has happened.

excise taxes   Taxes on some sort of transaction or event rather than on property.

exclusionary rule   The Fourth Amendment doctrine that makes unlawfully obtained evidence inadmissible at trial.

executive agreement   An agreement between the president of the United States and another country that does not need Senate approval.

executive branch   The presidency and the administrative arm of the government charged with executing and enforcing the law.

exempt   Not covered by a requirement.

express powers   Powers enumerated in Article I of the Constitution.

federal   Pertaining to the national government.

federal mandate   An order or requirement demanded by the national government.

federal supremacy clause   The stipulation in Article VI of the Constitution that holds federal law to be superior to state law.

federalism   Regional or state governments arranged under a central or national government.

Federalists   Influential supporters who campaigned for the Constitution to be ratified, including Alexander Hamilton, James Madison, and John Jay.

filibuster   A Senate procedure for blocking a vote with long-winded speeches. Under the rules, a senator who has the floor cannot be interrupted—even to take a vote. As long as the senator keeps speechifying, no action can be taken.

full faith and credit   The clause in Article IV of the Constitution that requires the states to respect each other's laws, judgments, licenses, and public documents.

gerrymandering   The manipulation of voting districts by political parties to gain advantages in elections.

grand jury   A group of citizens sworn in to consider evidence and determine whether evidence is adequate to issue an indictment that forces a defendant to go on trial.

habeas corpus   A writ or document demanding that authorities show there is good reason for holding a person in custody.

hearing   A public session held to gather information.

immigrant   A resident who has come from another country.

impartial   Fair, unbiased.

impeachment   A formal legislative accusation against an elected official that could lead to removal from office.

implied power   Authority not specifically stated but understood or assumed.

inalienable rights   Natural rights all humans claim and deserve that cannot be taken away by laws or governments.

incumbent   An official currently in office.

indictment   A formal accusation listing specific charges, usually returned by a grand jury, allowing a prosecutor to take a defendant to trial.

infringe   To encroach, violate, or disturb.

inherent powers   National authority assumed by the federal government, particularly in foreign affairs, that are not listed in the Constitution.

interest group   An organization trying to influence public issues and policies.

judicial branch   The branch of the government that interprets laws through courts, judges, and juries.

judicial review   The authority of courts to determine whether laws are constitutional and to void unconstitutional laws.

jurisdiction   The right of a court to hear a case or interpret certain laws in certain places.

lame duck   An official whose term is expiring but who was not reelected.

legislative branch   The elected officials who propose, debate, and enact laws.

lobbyist   A person who works for a special interest.

majority   More than half.

militia   A military or paramilitary group, typically citizens rather than professional soldiers, that serves temporarily in times of need or emergency.

misdemeanor   A minor or lesser crime usually characterized by punishments of fines only or no more than a year in jail.

naturalized citizen   Someone who was not born a citizen but has acquired the full rights of citizenship.

necessary and proper clause   The section of Article I of the Constitution the courts have said gives Congress the authority to pass laws that are not enumerated but are required for the good of the nation.

nominate   To propose, name, or give preliminary approval to a candidate.

oath   A statement swearing to keep a promise, as in to testify truthfully.

override   To overrule, as when Congress musters the necessary two-thirds vote to enact legislation despite a presidential veto.

pardon   An executive order to free or dismiss the charges against an accused person.

petition   To ask or request, sometimes but not always with a list of required signatures.

pocket veto   A presidential rejection of legislation not by outright veto, but rather by failing to sign it before the legislature adjourns.

poll tax   A fee paid to vote.

prescribe   To set out a course of action with authority, usually in legislation or a court decision.

preside   To oversee or direct a meeting, session, or hearing.

president pro temporare   The vice president or, if the vice president is absent, a senator who serves as presiding officer.

primary   A preliminary election during which parties choose their candidates.

prior restraint   A court order restricting freedom of speech, such as an order blocking the publication of a book or the showing of a movie.

probable cause   The required finding that there is legitimate reason for a certain legal action, such as the search of a home or business.

proportional representation   A system for providing different levels of influence or participation to political entities, such as states, based on their population.

prosecutor   A government official who conducts criminal proceedings against defendants.

public domain   Government-owned property.

quarter   To provide room and board for, as in quartering troops.

quorum   The minimum number of members required to take legal action.

ratification   Formal approval, as when the Senate approves a treaty or the states approve an amendment to the Constitution.

reapportionment   Recalculating according to population shifts, such as the number of representatives each state is determined to have after a national census.

redistricting   Redrawing districts to maintain proportional representation, such as in House districts after census results show population shifts.

redress   To correct or rectify.

referendum   A direct vote by the public on an issue, instead of the usual indirect voting by their elected representatives.

regulatory   Pertaining to government oversight functions, usually of business or industry or professions, carried out by the executive branch.

representative government   A system in which the public elects officials to make and enforce the laws. Also called indirect democracy or a republic form of government.

reserved powers   Authority specified in the Tenth Amendment that remained with the states rather than being taken over by the federal government.

resident   A person who lives in a certain state or other area.

revenue   Income from all sources.

rule of law   The principle holding that everyone in society, including top officials, are equally subject to the law.

security   Safety; freedom from danger. Also a financial instrument, a bond, issued by a government or private enterprise.

sedition   An attempted overthrow or interruption of a government.

separation of powers   The principle delineating three branches of government and giving them a series of checks and balances to limit each other's authority.

sovereign   Superior, as in a monarch or a national government.

Speaker of the House   The presiding officer of the House of Representatives, chosen by the majority party.

special interest   An organization seeking to influence policy.

states' rights   The philosophy that holds that the states have their own sovereignty and at least as much authority as the federal government if not more.

strict interpretation   A philosophy that takes a conservative view of the Constitution and limits federal authority to powers specifically enumerated in Article I.

subpoena   A document issued by a court ordering a person to appear to testify or surrender documents.

suffrage   The right to vote.

territory   Land controlled by a nation that is not part of that nation.

title of nobility   Aristocratic or honorific names banned by the Constitution, such as *queen, prince, countess, duke, baroness,* etc.

treason   Betrayal, usually of a nation.

treaty   An agreement between two or among more than two countries.

tyranny   An unjust and often cruel form of rule.

unconstitutional   A law, rule, or administrative action ruled invalid by the courts for violating the principles of the Constitution.

unicameral   Pertaining to a single-chamber legislature.

veto   An executive's rejection of legislation.

warrant   A document empowering law enforcement authorities, usually to search or seize someone or something for evidence in a possible prosecution.

welfare   As used in the Constitution, the well-being, happiness, and prosperity of the public.

writ   A formal written order, usually issued by a court.

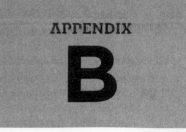

Resources

In this appendix, I've collected some books and websites you might find interesting for further reading and research. But don't feel limited by this list, or any list. For example, see the musical *Hamilton,* if you can. It has brought the people and issues of 1789 to life—and song—for many Americans.

Further Reading

Academic Solutions, Inc. *The United States Constitution Study Guide*. Academic Solutions, Inc., 2003.

Amar, Akhil Reed. *America's Constitution: A Biography*. Random House, 2006.

Baker, Thomas E. *Constitutional Analysis: In a Nutshell*. West Group, 2003.

Berkin, Carol. *A Brilliant Solution: Inventing the American Constitution*. Harvest Books, 2003.

Bordewich, Fergus M. *The First Congress: How James Madison, George Washington, and a Group of Extraordinary Men Invented the Government*. Simon & Schuster, 2016.

Currie, David P. *The Constitution of the United States: A Primer for the People*. University of Chicago Press, 2000.

Fink, Sam. *The Constitution of the United States of America*. Welcome Books, 2006.

Jordan, Terry L. *The U.S. Constitution: And Fascinating Facts About It*. Oak Hill Publishing, 1999.

JusticeLearning.org. *The United States Constitution: What It Says, What It Means: A Hip Pocket Guide*. University of Oxford Press, 2005.

Lutz, Donald S. *The Origins of American Constitutionalism*. LSU Press, 1988.

Maier, Pauline. *Ratification: The People Debate the Constitution*. Simon & Schuster, 2011.

Monk, Linda R. *The Bill of Rights: A User's Guide*. Close Up, 2004.

Paulsen, Michael Stokes, and Paulsen, Luke. *The Constitution: An Introduction*. Basic Books, 2015.

———. *The Words We Live By: Your Annotated Guide to the Constitution*. Hyperion, 2004.

Roberts, Cokie. *Founding Mothers: The Women Who Raised Our Nation*. HarperPerennial, 2005.

Vile, John R. *A Companion to the United States Constitution and Its Amendments, Fourth Edition*. Praeger Publishers, 2006.

Websites

American Library Association: The First Amendment
ala.org/advocacy/intfreedom/censorshipfirstamendmentissues/firstamendment

American Memory: Historical Documents from the Library of Congress
memory.loc.gov/ammem/help/constRedir.html

Bill of Rights Institute
billofrightsinstitute.org

ConSource: The Constitutional Sources Project
consource.org

The Constitution: Government Printing Office
caselaw.lp.findlaw.com/data/constitution/articles.html

Legal Information Institution
law.cornell.edu/constitution/constitution.overview.html

The National Archives
archives.gov/national-archives-experience/charters/constitution.html

National Constitution Center
constitutioncenter.org

Optimus Law Library Online
lawlibraryonline.com

This Nation: American Government and Politics Online
thisnation.com/constitution.html

The U.S. Constitution: About.com
americanhistory.about.com/od/usconstitution/United_States_Constitution.htm

The U.S. Constitution Online
usconstitution.net/const.html

U.S. House of Representatives, Educational Resources
house.gov/content/learn

U.S. Senate References: The Constitution
senate.gov/civics/constitution_item/constitution.htm

Wikipedia: The U.S. Constitution
en.wikipedia.org/wiki/United_States_Constitution

Yale University: The Avalon Project
avalon.law.yale.edu/18th_century/usconst.asp

Petitioning the Government

In this appendix, I share a step-by-step guide on how to petition the U.S. government. It's pulled directly from petitions.whitehouse.gov/how-why/step-step-guide.

You Create a Petition

Before you start a petition, take some time to think about your goal. What do you want [the president] or the White House to do? Why others should support your cause? This will help you clearly articulate your position and make your petition more effective. You should also check to be sure there isn't already a petition with the same goal on the site.

Here's how to create a new petition:

Enter Basic Information   Start by entering a short (120 characters or less) headline for the petition by completing the sentence "We believe the current administration should…." Your headline should be clear and compelling and describe the goal of your petition. Next you'll select up to three issue categories. If you want to add additional information about the topic of your petition, you can do that later by adding tags.

Look for Similar Petitions   Once you submit your petition headline and categories, [you'll] search the system to see if there are any existing petitions that are similar. If there is already an existing petition that addresses the concerns you have, you may want to sign that petition instead rather than creating a new one. You will increase the likelihood of getting a response by signing onto an existing petition rather than creating a duplicate petition on the same issue.

Provide Additional Details   If you don't find an existing petition that is similar, next you'll enter additional details about the petition. This is where you have a chance to make your case. Use this space to clearly articulate your goals and what you would like the [current administration] to do. Include additional information or research to support your request. Keep the petition description brief, you only have 800 characters including spaces. You'll also have a chance to add additional tags to help further define the topic of your petition. Please note that petitions on the We the People site will be moderated. Some petitions may be removed from the site consistent with the Terms of Participation and Moderation Policy.

Preview, Publish and Promote.   Next you'll have a chance to preview the petition and make changes. Be sure to double-check for spelling, punctuation and grammar because once you publish a petition it cannot be edited. Once you've published a petition, the real work begins: it's time to start promoting it with your friends, family and others who care about the issue.

Others Sign

After you publish the petition, it's up to you to promote it and get others to sign. You'll get an automatic email once your petition is published that you can forward to get started. Remember you have just 30 days to get 100,000 signatures in order to get a response from the White House. And it's up to you to get to 150 signatures in order for your petition to be publicly searchable on the We the People tool on WhiteHouse.gov.

The White House Reviews and Responds

Once the petition reaches the required threshold, it will be put in a queue to be reviewed by the White House. Others can still sign the petition while it is awaiting a response from the White House. When the White House responds, everyone who has signed the petition will get email from the White House to let you know that we've reviewed and responded to the petition.

The U.S. Constitution

Now that you've read all about what the Constitution means, here it is, from its famous opening line, "We the People of the United States, in Order to form a more perfect Union ..." to the Twenty-Seventh Amendment.

Preamble

We the People of the United States, in Order to form a more perfect Union, establish Justice, insure domestic Tranquility, provide for the common defence, promote the general Welfare, and secure the Blessings of Liberty to ourselves and our Posterity, do ordain and establish this Constitution for the United States of America.

Article I

Section 1

All legislative Powers herein granted shall be vested in a Congress of the United States, which shall consist of a Senate and House of Representatives.

Section 2

The House of Representatives shall be composed of Members chosen every second Year by the People of the several States, and the Electors in each State shall have the Qualifications requisite for Electors of the most numerous Branch of the State Legislature.

No Person shall be a Representative who shall not have attained to the Age of twenty five Years, and been seven Years a Citizen of the United States, and who shall not, when elected, be an Inhabitant of that State in which he shall be chosen.

Representatives and direct Taxes shall be apportioned among the several States which may be included within this Union, according to their respective Numbers, which shall be determined by adding to the whole Number of free Persons, including those bound to Service for a Term of Years, and excluding Indians not taxed, three fifths of all other Persons. The actual Enumeration shall be made within three Years after the first Meeting of the Congress of the United States, and within every subsequent Term of ten Years, in such Manner as they shall by Law direct. The Number of Representatives shall not exceed one for every thirty Thousand, but each State shall have at Least one Representative; and until such enumeration shall be made, the State of New Hampshire shall be entitled to chuse three, Massachusetts eight, Rhode-Island and Providence Plantations one, Connecticut five, New-York six, New Jersey four, Pennsylvania eight, Delaware one, Maryland six, Virginia ten, North Carolina five, South Carolina five, and Georgia three.

When vacancies happen in the Representation from any State, the Executive Authority thereof shall issue Writs of Election to fill such Vacancies.

The House of Representatives shall chuse their Speaker and other Officers; and shall have the sole Power of Impeachment.

Section 3

The Senate of the United States shall be composed of two Senators from each State, chosen by the Legislature thereof, for six Years; and each Senator shall have one Vote.

Immediately after they shall be assembled in Consequence of the first Election, they shall be divided as equally as may be into three Classes. The Seats of the Senators of the first Class shall be vacated at the Expiration of the second Year, of the second Class at the Expiration of the fourth Year, and of the third Class at the Expiration of the sixth Year, so that one third may be chosen every second Year; and if Vacancies happen by Resignation, or otherwise, during the Recess of the Legislature of any State, the Executive thereof may make temporary Appointments until the next Meeting of the Legislature, which shall then fill such Vacancies.

No Person shall be a Senator who shall not have attained to the Age of thirty Years, and been nine Years a Citizen of the United States, and who shall not, when elected, be an Inhabitant of that State for which he shall be chosen.

The Vice President of the United States shall be President of the Senate, but shall have no Vote, unless they be equally divided.

The Senate shall chuse their other Officers, and also a President pro tempore, in the Absence of the Vice President, or when he shall exercise the Office of President of the United States.

The Senate shall have the sole Power to try all Impeachments. When sitting for that Purpose, they shall be on Oath or Affirmation. When the President of the United States is tried, the Chief Justice shall preside: And no Person shall be convicted without the Concurrence of two thirds of the Members present.

Judgment in Cases of Impeachment shall not extend further than to removal from Office, and disqualification to hold and enjoy any Office of honor, Trust or Profit under the United States: but the Party convicted shall nevertheless be liable and subject to Indictment, Trial, Judgment and Punishment, according to Law.

Section 4

The Times, Places and Manner of holding Elections for Senators and Representatives, shall be prescribed in each State by the Legislature thereof; but the Congress may at any time by Law make or alter such Regulations, except as to the Places of chusing Senators.

The Congress shall assemble at least once in every Year, and such Meeting shall be on the first Monday in December, unless they shall by Law appoint a different Day.

Section 5

Each House shall be the Judge of the Elections, Returns and Qualifications of its own Members, and a Majority of each shall constitute a Quorum to do Business; but a smaller Number may adjourn from day to day, and may be authorized to compel the Attendance of absent Members, in such Manner, and under such Penalties as each House may provide.

Each House may determine the Rules of its Proceedings, punish its Members for disorderly Behaviour, and, with the Concurrence of two thirds, expel a Member.

Each House shall keep a Journal of its Proceedings, and from time to time publish the same, excepting such Parts as may in their Judgment require Secrecy; and the Yeas and Nays of the Members of either House on any question shall, at the Desire of one fifth of those Present, be entered on the Journal.

Neither House, during the Session of Congress, shall, without the Consent of the other, adjourn for more than three days, nor to any other Place than that in which the two Houses shall be sitting.

Section 6

The Senators and Representatives shall receive a Compensation for their Services, to be ascertained by Law, and paid out of the Treasury of the United States. They shall in all Cases, except Treason, Felony and Breach of the Peace, be privileged from Arrest during their Attendance at the Session of their respective Houses, and in going to and returning from the same; and for any Speech or Debate in either House, they shall not be questioned in any other Place.

No Senator or Representative shall, during the Time for which he was elected, be appointed to any civil Office under the Authority of the United States, which shall have been created, or the Emoluments whereof shall have been encreased during such time; and no Person holding any Office under the United States, shall be a Member of either House during his Continuance in Office.

Section 7

All Bills for raising Revenue shall originate in the House of Representatives; but the Senate may propose or concur with Amendments as on other Bills.

Every Bill which shall have passed the House of Representatives and the Senate, shall, before it become a Law, be presented to the President of the United States; If he approve he shall sign it, but if not he shall return it, with his Objections to that House in which it shall have originated, who shall enter the Objections at large on their Journal, and proceed to reconsider it. If after such Reconsideration two thirds of that House shall agree to pass the Bill, it shall be sent, together with the Objections, to the other House, by which it shall likewise be reconsidered, and if approved by two thirds of that House, it shall become a Law. But in all such Cases the Votes of both Houses shall be determined by yeas and Nays, and the Names of the Persons voting for and against the Bill shall be entered on the Journal of each House respectively. If any Bill shall not be returned by the President within ten Days (Sundays excepted) after it shall have been presented to him, the Same shall be a Law, in like Manner as if he had signed it, unless the Congress by their Adjournment prevent its Return, in which Case it shall not be a Law.

Every Order, Resolution, or Vote to which the Concurrence of the Senate and House of Representatives may be necessary (except on a question of Adjournment) shall be presented to the President of the United States; and before the Same shall take Effect, shall be approved by him, or being disapproved by him, shall be repassed by two thirds of the Senate and House of Representatives, according to the Rules and Limitations prescribed in the Case of a Bill.

Section 8

The Congress shall have Power To lay and collect Taxes, Duties, Imposts and Excises, to pay the Debts and provide for the common Defence and general Welfare of the United States; but all Duties, Imposts and Excises shall be uniform throughout the United States;

To borrow Money on the credit of the United States;

To regulate Commerce with foreign Nations, and among the several States, and with the Indian Tribes;

To establish an uniform Rule of Naturalization, and uniform Laws on the subject of Bankruptcies throughout the United States;

To coin Money, regulate the Value thereof, and of foreign Coin, and fix the Standard of Weights and Measures;

To provide for the Punishment of counterfeiting the Securities and current Coin of the United States;

To establish Post Offices and post Roads;

To promote the Progress of Science and useful Arts, by securing for limited Times to Authors and Inventors the exclusive Right to their respective Writings and Discoveries;

To constitute Tribunals inferior to the supreme Court;

To define and punish Piracies and Felonies committed on the high Seas, and Offences against the Law of Nations;

To declare War, grant Letters of Marque and Reprisal, and make Rules concerning Captures on Land and Water;

To raise and support Armies, but no Appropriation of Money to that Use shall be for a longer Term than two Years;

To provide and maintain a Navy;

To make Rules for the Government and Regulation of the land and naval Forces;

To provide for calling forth the Militia to execute the Laws of the Union, suppress Insurrections and repel Invasions;

To provide for organizing, arming, and disciplining, the Militia, and for governing such Part of them as may be employed in the Service of the United States, reserving to the States respectively, the Appointment of the Officers, and the Authority of training the Militia according to the discipline prescribed by Congress;

To exercise exclusive Legislation in all Cases whatsoever, over such District (not exceeding ten Miles square) as may, by Cession of particular States, and the Acceptance of Congress, become the Seat of the Government of the United States, and to exercise like Authority over all Places purchased by the Consent of the Legislature of the State in which the Same shall be, for the Erection of Forts, Magazines, Arsenals, dock-Yards, and other needful Buildings;—And

To make all Laws which shall be necessary and proper for carrying into Execution the foregoing Powers, and all other Powers vested by this Constitution in the Government of the United States, or in any Department or Officer thereof.

Section 9

The Migration or Importation of such Persons as any of the States now existing shall think proper to admit, shall not be prohibited by the Congress prior to the Year one thousand eight hundred and eight, but a Tax or duty may be imposed on such Importation, not exceeding ten dollars for each Person.

The Privilege of the Writ of Habeas Corpus shall not be suspended, unless when in Cases of Rebellion or Invasion the public Safety may require it.

No Bill of Attainder or ex post facto Law shall be passed.

No Capitation, or other direct, Tax shall be laid, unless in Proportion to the Census or enumeration herein before directed to be taken.

No Tax or Duty shall be laid on Articles exported from any State.

No Preference shall be given by any Regulation of Commerce or Revenue to the Ports of one State over those of another: nor shall Vessels bound to, or from, one State, be obliged to enter, clear, or pay Duties in another.

No Money shall be drawn from the Treasury, but in Consequence of Appropriations made by Law; and a regular Statement and Account of the Receipts and Expenditures of all public Money shall be published from time to time.

No Title of Nobility shall be granted by the United States: And no Person holding any Office of Profit or Trust under them, shall, without the Consent of the Congress, accept of any present, Emolument, Office, or Title, of any kind whatever, from any King, Prince, or foreign State.

Section 10

No State shall enter into any Treaty, Alliance, or Confederation; grant Letters of Marque and Reprisal; coin Money; emit Bills of Credit; make any Thing but gold and silver Coin a Tender in Payment of Debts; pass any Bill of Attainder, ex post facto Law, or Law impairing the Obligation of Contracts, or grant any Title of Nobility.

No State shall, without the Consent of the Congress, lay any Imposts or Duties on Imports or Exports, except what may be absolutely necessary for executing it's inspection Laws: and the net Produce of all Duties and Imposts, laid by any State on Imports or Exports, shall be for the Use of the Treasury of the United States; and all such Laws shall be subject to the Revision and Controul of the Congress.

No State shall, without the Consent of Congress, lay any Duty of Tonnage, keep Troops, or Ships of War in time of Peace, enter into any Agreement or Compact with another State, or with a foreign Power, or engage in War, unless actually invaded, or in such imminent Danger as will not admit of delay.

Article II

Section 1

The executive Power shall be vested in a President of the United States of America. He shall hold his Office during the Term of four Years, and, together with the Vice President, chosen for the same Term, be elected, as follows

Each State shall appoint, in such Manner as the Legislature thereof may direct, a Number of Electors, equal to the whole Number of Senators and Representatives to which the State may be entitled in the Congress: but no Senator or Representative, or Person holding an Office of Trust or Profit under the United States, shall be appointed an Elector.

The Electors shall meet in their respective States, and vote by Ballot for two Persons, of whom one at least shall not be an Inhabitant of the same State with themselves. And they shall make a List of all the Persons voted for, and of the Number of Votes for each; which List they shall sign and certify, and transmit sealed to the Seat of the Government of the United States, directed to the President of the Senate. The President of the Senate shall, in the Presence of the Senate and House of Representatives, open all the Certificates, and the Votes shall then be counted. The Person having the greatest Number of Votes shall be the President, if such Number be a Majority of the whole Number of Electors appointed; and if there be more than one who have such Majority, and have an equal Number of Votes, then the House of Representatives shall immediately chuse by Ballot one of them for President; and if no Person have a Majority, then from the five highest on the List the said House shall in like Manner chuse the President. But in chusing the President, the Votes shall be taken by States, the Representation from each State having one Vote; A quorum for this Purpose shall consist of a Member or Members from two thirds of the States, and a Majority of all the States shall be necessary to a Choice. In every Case, after the Choice of the President, the Person having the greatest Number of Votes of the Electors shall be the Vice President. But if there should remain two or more who have equal Votes, the Senate shall chuse from them by Ballot the Vice President.

The Congress may determine the Time of chusing the Electors, and the Day on which they shall give their Votes; which Day shall be the same throughout the United States.

No Person except a natural born Citizen, or a Citizen of the United States, at the time of the Adoption of this Constitution, shall be eligible to the Office of President; neither shall any Person be eligible to that Office who shall not have attained to the Age of thirty five Years, and been fourteen Years a Resident within the United States.

In Case of the Removal of the President from Office, or of his Death, Resignation, or Inability to discharge the Powers and Duties of the said Office, the Same shall devolve on the Vice President, and the Congress may by Law provide for the Case of Removal, Death, Resignation or Inability, both of the President and Vice President, declaring what Officer shall then act as President, and such Officer shall act accordingly, until the Disability be removed, or a President shall be elected.

The President shall, at stated Times, receive for his Services, a Compensation, which shall neither be increased nor diminished during the Period for which he shall have been elected, and he shall not receive within that Period any other Emolument from the United States, or any of them.

Before he enter on the Execution of his Office, he shall take the following Oath or Affirmation:—"I do solemnly swear (or affirm) that I will faithfully execute the Office of President of the United States, and will to the best of my Ability, preserve, protect and defend the Constitution of the United States."

Section 2

The President shall be Commander in Chief of the Army and Navy of the United States, and of the Militia of the several States, when called into the actual Service of the United States; he may require the Opinion, in writing, of the principal Officer in each of the executive Departments, upon any Subject relating to the Duties of their respective Offices, and he shall have Power to grant Reprieves and Pardons for Offences against the United States, except in Cases of Impeachment.

He shall have Power, by and with the Advice and Consent of the Senate, to make Treaties, provided two thirds of the Senators present concur; and he shall nominate, and by and with the Advice and Consent of the Senate, shall appoint Ambassadors, other public Ministers and Consuls, Judges of the supreme Court, and all other Officers of the United States, whose Appointments are not herein otherwise provided for, and which shall be established by Law: but the Congress may by Law vest the Appointment of such inferior Officers, as they think proper, in the President alone, in the Courts of Law, or in the Heads of Departments.

The President shall have Power to fill up all Vacancies that may happen during the Recess of the Senate, by granting Commissions which shall expire at the End of their next Session.

Section 3

He shall from time to time give to the Congress Information of the State of the Union, and recommend to their Consideration such Measures as he shall judge necessary and expedient; he may, on extraordinary Occasions, convene both Houses, or either of them, and in Case of Disagreement between them, with Respect to the Time of Adjournment, he may adjourn them to such Time as he shall think proper; he shall receive Ambassadors and other public Ministers; he shall take Care that the Laws be faithfully executed, and shall Commission all the Officers of the United States.

Section 4

The President, Vice President and all civil Officers of the United States, shall be removed from Office on Impeachment for, and Conviction of, Treason, Bribery, or other high Crimes and Misdemeanors.

Article III

Section 1

The judicial Power of the United States, shall be vested in one supreme Court, and in such inferior Courts as the Congress may from time to time ordain and establish. The Judges, both of the supreme and inferior Courts, shall hold their Offices during good Behaviour, and shall, at stated Times, receive for their Services, a Compensation, which shall not be diminished during their Continuance in Office.

Section 2

The judicial Power shall extend to all Cases, in Law and Equity, arising under this Constitution, the Laws of the United States, and Treaties made, or which shall be made, under their Authority;—to all Cases affecting Ambassadors, other public Ministers and Consuls;—to all Cases of admiralty and maritime Jurisdiction;—to Controversies to which the United States shall be a Party;—to Controversies between two or more States;—between a State and Citizens of another State,—between Citizens of different States,—between Citizens of the same State claiming Lands under Grants of different States, and between a State, or the Citizens thereof, and foreign States, Citizens or Subjects.

In all Cases affecting Ambassadors, other public Ministers and Consuls, and those in which a State shall be Party, the supreme Court shall have original Jurisdiction. In all the other Cases before mentioned, the supreme Court shall have appellate Jurisdiction, both as to Law and Fact, with such Exceptions, and under such Regulations as the Congress shall make.

The Trial of all Crimes, except in Cases of Impeachment, shall be by Jury; and such Trial shall be held in the State where the said Crimes shall have been committed; but when not committed within any State, the Trial shall be at such Place or Places as the Congress may by Law have directed.

Section 3

Treason against the United States, shall consist only in levying War against them, or in adhering to their Enemies, giving them Aid and Comfort. No Person shall be convicted of Treason unless on the Testimony of two Witnesses to the same overt Act, or on Confession in open Court.

The Congress shall have Power to declare the Punishment of Treason, but no Attainder of Treason shall work Corruption of Blood, or Forfeiture except during the Life of the Person attainted.

Article IV

Section 1

Full Faith and Credit shall be given in each State to the public Acts, Records, and judicial Proceedings of every other State. And the Congress may by general Laws prescribe the Manner in which such Acts, Records and Proceedings shall be proved, and the Effect thereof.

Section 2

The Citizens of each State shall be entitled to all Privileges and Immunities of Citizens in the several States.

A Person charged in any State with Treason, Felony, or other Crime, who shall flee from Justice, and be found in another State, shall on Demand of the executive Authority of the State from which he fled, be delivered up, to be removed to the State having Jurisdiction of the Crime.

No Person held to Service or Labour in one State, under the Laws thereof, escaping into another, shall, in Consequence of any Law or Regulation therein, be discharged from such Service or Labour, but shall be delivered up on Claim of the Party to whom such Service or Labour may be due.

Section 3

New States may be admitted by the Congress into this Union; but no new State shall be formed or erected within the Jurisdiction of any other State; nor any State be formed by the Junction of two or more States, or Parts of States, without the Consent of the Legislatures of the States concerned as well as of the Congress.

The Congress shall have Power to dispose of and make all needful Rules and Regulations respecting the Territory or other Property belonging to the United States; and nothing in this Constitution shall be so construed as to Prejudice any Claims of the United States, or of any particular State.

Section 4

The United States shall guarantee to every State in this Union a Republican Form of Government, and shall protect each of them against Invasion; and on Application of the Legislature, or of the Executive (when the Legislature cannot be convened), against domestic Violence.

Article V

The Congress, whenever two thirds of both Houses shall deem it necessary, shall propose Amendments to this Constitution, or, on the Application of the Legislatures of two thirds of the several States, shall call a Convention for proposing Amendments, which, in either Case, shall be valid to all Intents and Purposes, as Part of this Constitution, when ratified by the Legislatures of three fourths of the several States, or by Conventions in three fourths thereof, as the one or the other Mode of Ratification may be proposed by the Congress; Provided that no Amendment which may be made prior to the Year One thousand eight hundred and eight shall in any Manner affect the first and fourth Clauses in the Ninth Section of the first Article; and that no State, without its Consent, shall be deprived of its equal Suffrage in the Senate.

Article VI

All Debts contracted and Engagements entered into, before the Adoption of this Constitution, shall be as valid against the United States under this Constitution, as under the Confederation.

This Constitution, and the Laws of the United States which shall be made in Pursuance thereof; and all Treaties made, or which shall be made, under the Authority of the United States, shall be the supreme Law of the Land; and the Judges in every State shall be bound thereby, any Thing in the Constitution or Laws of any State to the Contrary notwithstanding.

The Senators and Representatives before mentioned, and the Members of the several State Legislatures, and all executive and judicial Officers, both of the United States and of the several States, shall be bound by Oath or Affirmation, to support this Constitution; but no religious Test shall ever be required as a Qualification to any Office or public Trust under the United States.

Article VII

The Ratification of the Conventions of nine States, shall be sufficient for the Establishment of this Constitution between the States so ratifying the Same.

Done in Convention by the Unanimous Consent of the States present the Seventeenth Day of September in the Year of our Lord one thousand seven hundred and Eighty seven and of the Independance of the United States of America the Twelfth In witness whereof We have hereunto subscribed our Names,

George Washington—President and deputy from Virginia

New Hampshire—John Langdon, Nicholas Gilman

Massachusetts—Nathaniel Gorham, Rufus King

Connecticut—William Samuel Johnson, Roger Sherman

New York—Alexander Hamilton

New Jersey—William Livingston, David Brearley, William Paterson, Jonathan Dayton

Pennsylvania—Benjamin Franklin, Thomas Mifflin, Robert Morris, George Clymer, Thomas Fitzsimons, Jared Ingersoll, James Wilson, Gouvernour Morris

Delaware—George Read, Gunning Bedford Jr., John Dickinson, Richard Bassett, Jacob Broom

Maryland—James McHenry, Daniel of St Thomas Jenifer, Daniel Carroll

Virginia—John Blair, James Madison Jr.

North Carolina—William Blount, Richard Dobbs Spaight, Hugh Williamson

South Carolina—John Rutledge, Charles Cotesworth Pinckney, Charles Pinckney, Pierce Butler

Georgia—William Few, Abraham Baldwin

Attest: William Jackson, Secretary

Amendment I

Congress shall make no law respecting an establishment of religion, or prohibiting the free exercise thereof; or abridging the freedom of speech, or of the press; or the right of the people peaceably to assemble, and to petition the Government for a redress of grievances.

Amendment II

A well regulated Militia, being necessary to the security of a free State, the right of the people to keep and bear Arms, shall not be infringed.

Amendment III

No Soldier shall, in time of peace be quartered in any house, without the consent of the Owner, nor in time of war, but in a manner to be prescribed by law.

Amendment IV

The right of the people to be secure in their persons, houses, papers, and effects, against unreasonable searches and seizures, shall not be violated, and no Warrants shall issue, but upon probable cause, supported by Oath or affirmation, and particularly describing the place to be searched, and the persons or things to be seized.

Amendment V

No person shall be held to answer for a capital, or otherwise infamous crime, unless on a presentment or indictment of a Grand Jury, except in cases arising in the land or naval forces, or in the Militia, when in actual service in time of War or public danger; nor shall any person be subject for the same offence to be twice put in jeopardy of life or limb; nor shall be compelled in any criminal case to be a witness against himself, nor be deprived of life, liberty, or property, without due process of law; nor shall private property be taken for public use, without just compensation.

Amendment VI

In all criminal prosecutions, the accused shall enjoy the right to a speedy and public trial, by an impartial jury of the State and district wherein the crime shall have been committed, which district shall have been previously ascertained by law, and to be informed of the nature and cause of the accusation; to be confronted with the witnesses against him; to have compulsory process for obtaining witnesses in his favor, and to have the Assistance of Counsel for his defence.

Amendment VII

In Suits at common law, where the value in controversy shall exceed twenty dollars, the right of trial by jury shall be preserved, and no fact tried by a jury, shall be otherwise re-examined in any Court of the United States, than according to the rules of the common law.

Amendment VIII

Excessive bail shall not be required, nor excessive fines imposed, nor cruel and unusual punishments inflicted.

Amendment IX

The enumeration in the Constitution, of certain rights, shall not be construed to deny or disparage others retained by the people.

Amendment X

The powers not delegated to the United States by the Constitution, nor prohibited by it to the States, are reserved to the States respectively, or to the people.

Amendment XI

The Judicial power of the United States shall not be construed to extend to any suit in law or equity, commenced or prosecuted against one of the United States by Citizens of another State, or by Citizens or Subjects of any Foreign State.

Amendment XII

The Electors shall meet in their respective states and vote by ballot for President and Vice-President, one of whom, at least, shall not be an inhabitant of the same state with themselves; they shall name in their ballots the person voted for as President, and in distinct ballots the person voted for as Vice-President, and they shall make distinct lists of all persons voted for as President, and of all persons voted for as Vice-President, and of the number of votes for each, which lists they shall sign and certify, and transmit sealed to the seat of the government of the United States, directed to the President of the Senate; — the President of the Senate shall, in the presence of the Senate and House of Representatives, open all the certificates and the votes shall then be counted; — The person having the greatest number of votes for President, shall be the President, if such number be a majority of the whole number of Electors appointed; and if no person have such majority, then from the persons having the highest numbers not exceeding three on the list of those voted for as President, the House of Representatives shall choose immediately, by ballot, the President. But in choosing the President, the votes shall be taken by states, the representation from each state having one vote; a quorum for this purpose shall consist of a member or members from two-thirds of the states, and a majority of all the states shall be necessary to a choice. [And if the House of Representatives shall not choose a President whenever the right of choice shall devolve upon them, before the fourth day of March next following, then the Vice-President shall act as President, as in case of the death or other constitutional disability of the President.—]* The person having the greatest number of votes as Vice-President, shall be the Vice-President, if such number be a majority of the whole number of Electors appointed, and if no person have a majority, then from the two highest numbers on the list, the Senate shall choose the Vice-President; a quorum for the purpose shall consist of two-thirds of the whole number of Senators, and a majority of the whole number shall be necessary to a choice. But no person constitutionally ineligible to the office of President shall be eligible to that of Vice-President of the United States.

Amendment XIII

Section 1

Neither slavery nor involuntary servitude, except as a punishment for crime whereof the party shall have been duly convicted, shall exist within the United States, or any place subject to their jurisdiction.

Section 2

Congress shall have power to enforce this article by appropriate legislation.

Amendment XIV

Section 1

All persons born or naturalized in the United States, and subject to the jurisdiction thereof, are citizens of the United States and of the State wherein they reside. No State shall make or enforce any law which shall abridge the privileges or immunities of citizens of the United States; nor shall any State deprive any person of life, liberty, or property, without due process of law; nor deny to any person within its jurisdiction the equal protection of the laws.

Section 2

Representatives shall be apportioned among the several States according to their respective numbers, counting the whole number of persons in each State, excluding Indians not taxed. But when the right to vote at any election for the choice of electors for President and Vice-President of the United States, Representatives in Congress, the Executive and Judicial officers of a State, or the members of the Legislature thereof, is denied to any of the male inhabitants of such State, being twenty-one years of age,* and citizens of the United States, or in any way abridged, except for participation in rebellion, or other crime, the basis of representation therein shall be reduced in the proportion which the number of such male citizens shall bear to the whole number of male citizens twenty-one years of age in such State.

Section 3

No person shall be a Senator or Representative in Congress, or elector of President and Vice-President, or hold any office, civil or military, under the United States, or under any State, who, having previously taken an oath, as a member of Congress, or as an officer of the United States, or as a member of any State legislature, or as an executive or judicial officer of any State, to support the Constitution of the United States, shall have engaged in insurrection or rebellion against the same, or given aid or comfort to the enemies thereof. But Congress may by a vote of two-thirds of each House, remove such disability.

Section 4

The validity of the public debt of the United States, authorized by law, including debts incurred for payment of pensions and bounties for services in suppressing insurrection or rebellion, shall not be questioned. But neither the United States nor any State shall assume or pay any debt or obligation incurred in aid of insurrection or rebellion against the United States, or any claim for the loss or emancipation of any slave; but all such debts, obligations and claims shall be held illegal and void.

Section 5

The Congress shall have the power to enforce, by appropriate legislation, the provisions of this article.

Amendment XV

Section 1

The right of citizens of the United States to vote shall not be denied or abridged by the United States or by any State on account of race, color, or previous condition of servitude.

Section 2

The Congress shall have the power to enforce this article by appropriate legislation.

Amendment XVI

The Congress shall have power to lay and collect taxes on incomes, from whatever source derived, without apportionment among the several States, and without regard to any census or enumeration.

Amendment XVII

The Senate of the United States shall be composed of two Senators from each State, elected by the people thereof, for six years; and each Senator shall have one vote. The electors in each State shall have the qualifications requisite for electors of the most numerous branch of the State legislatures.

When vacancies happen in the representation of any State in the Senate, the executive authority of such State shall issue writs of election to fill such vacancies: Provided, That the legislature of any State may empower the executive thereof to make temporary appointments until the people fill the vacancies by election as the legislature may direct.

This amendment shall not be so construed as to affect the election or term of any Senator chosen before it becomes valid as part of the Constitution.

Amendment XVIII

Section 1

After one year from the ratification of this article the manufacture, sale, or transportation of intoxicating liquors within, the importation thereof into, or the exportation thereof from the United States and all territory subject to the jurisdiction thereof for beverage purposes is hereby prohibited.

Section 2

The Congress and the several States shall have concurrent power to enforce this article by appropriate legislation.

Section 3

This article shall be inoperative unless it shall have been ratified as an amendment to the Constitution by the legislatures of the several States, as provided in the Constitution, within seven years from the date of the submission hereof to the States by the Congress.

Amendment XIX

The right of citizens of the United States to vote shall not be denied or abridged by the United States or by any State on account of sex.

Congress shall have power to enforce this article by appropriate legislation.

Amendment XX

Section 1

The terms of the President and the Vice President shall end at noon on the 20th day of January, and the terms of Senators and Representatives at noon on the 3d day of January, of the years in which such terms would have ended if this article had not been ratified; and the terms of their successors shall then begin.

Section 2

The Congress shall assemble at least once in every year, and such meeting shall begin at noon on the 3d day of January, unless they shall by law appoint a different day.

Section 3

If, at the time fixed for the beginning of the term of the President, the President elect shall have died, the Vice President elect shall become President. If a President shall not have been chosen before the time fixed for the beginning of his term, or if the President elect shall have failed to qualify, then the Vice President elect shall act as President until a President shall have qualified; and the Congress may by law provide for the case wherein neither a President elect nor a Vice President elect shall have qualified, declaring who shall then act as President, or the manner in which one who is to act shall be selected, and such person shall act accordingly until a President or Vice President shall have qualified.

Section 4

The Congress may by law provide for the case of the death of any of the persons from whom the House of Representatives may choose a President whenever the right of choice shall have devolved upon them, and for the case of the death of any of the persons from whom the Senate may choose a Vice President whenever the right of choice shall have devolved upon them.

Section 5

Sections 1 and 2 shall take effect on the 15th day of October following the ratification of this article.

Section 6

This article shall be inoperative unless it shall have been ratified as an amendment to the Constitution by the legislatures of three-fourths of the several States within seven years from the date of its submission.

Amendment XXI

Section 1

The eighteenth article of amendment to the Constitution of the United States is hereby repealed.

Section 2

The transportation or importation into any State, Territory, or possession of the United States for delivery or use therein of intoxicating liquors, in violation of the laws thereof, is hereby prohibited.

Section 3

This article shall be inoperative unless it shall have been ratified as an amendment to the Constitution by conventions in the several States, as provided in the Constitution, within seven years from the date of the submission hereof to the States by the Congress.

Amendment XXII

Section 1

No person shall be elected to the office of the President more than twice, and no person who has held the office of President, or acted as President, for more than two years of a term to which some other person was elected President shall be elected to the office of the President more than once. But this Article shall not apply to any person holding the office of President when this Article was proposed by the Congress, and shall not prevent any person who may be holding the office of President, or acting as President, during the term within which this Article becomes operative from holding the office of President or acting as President during the remainder of such term.

Section 2

This article shall be inoperative unless it shall have been ratified as an amendment to the Constitution by the legislatures of three-fourths of the several States within seven years from the date of its submission to the States by the Congress.

Amendment XXIII

Section 1

The District constituting the seat of Government of the United States shall appoint in such manner as the Congress may direct:

A number of electors of President and Vice President equal to the whole number of Senators and Representatives in Congress to which the District would be entitled if it were a State, but in no event more than the least populous State; they shall be in addition to those appointed by the States, but they shall be considered, for the purposes of the election of President and Vice President, to be electors appointed by a State; and they shall meet in the District and perform such duties as provided by the twelfth article of amendment.

Section 2

The Congress shall have power to enforce this article by appropriate legislation.

Amendment XXIV

Section 1

The right of citizens of the United States to vote in any primary or other election for President or Vice President, for electors for President or Vice President, or for Senator or Representative in Congress, shall not be denied or abridged by the United States or any State by reason of failure to pay any poll tax or other tax.

Section 2

The Congress shall have power to enforce this article by appropriate legislation.

Amendment XXV

Section 1

In case of the removal of the President from office or of his death or resignation, the Vice President shall become President.

Section 2

Whenever there is a vacancy in the office of the Vice President, the President shall nominate a Vice President who shall take office upon confirmation by a majority vote of both Houses of Congress.

Section 3

Whenever the President transmits to the President pro tempore of the Senate and the Speaker of the House of Representatives his written declaration that he is unable to discharge the powers and duties of his office, and until he transmits to them a written declaration to the contrary, such powers and duties shall be discharged by the Vice President as Acting President.

Section 4

Whenever the Vice President and a majority of either the principal officers of the executive departments or of such other body as Congress may by law provide, transmit to the President pro tempore of the Senate and the Speaker of the House of Representatives their written declaration that the President is unable to discharge the powers and duties of his office, the Vice President shall immediately assume the powers and duties of the office as Acting President.

Thereafter, when the President transmits to the President pro tempore of the Senate and the Speaker of the House of Representatives his written declaration that no inability exists, he shall resume the powers and duties of his office unless the Vice President and a majority of either the principal officers of the executive department or of such other body as Congress may by law provide, transmit within four days to the President pro tempore of the Senate and the Speaker of the House of Representatives their written declaration that the President is unable to discharge the powers and duties of his office. Thereupon Congress shall decide the issue, assembling within forty-eight hours for that purpose if not in session. If the Congress, within twenty-one days after receipt of the latter written declaration, or, if Congress is not in session, within twenty-one days after Congress is required to assemble, determines by two-thirds vote of both Houses that the President is unable to discharge the powers and duties of his office, the Vice President shall continue to discharge the same as Acting President; otherwise, the President shall resume the powers and duties of his office.

Amendment XXVI

Section 1

The right of citizens of the United States, who are eighteen years of age or older, to vote shall not be denied or abridged by the United States or by any State on account of age.

Section 2

The Congress shall have power to enforce this article by appropriate legislation.

Amendment XXVII

No law, varying the compensation for the services of the Senators and Representatives, shall take effect, until an election of Representatives shall have intervened.

Index

W–X

Y–Z